# The Art of Shooting

GUN BOOKS BY CHARLES EDWARD CHAPEL

*The Art of Shooting*

*Field, Skeet and Trap Shooting*

*Forensic Ballistics*

*Gun Care and Repair—A Manual of Gunsmithing*

*Gun Collecting*

*The Gun Collector's Handbook of Values*

*Guns of the Old West*

# The Art of Shooting

by Charles Edward Chapel

*Drawings by Sanford Strother*

New York: A. S. Barnes and Company, Inc.
London: Thomas Yoseloff Ltd.

*Dedicated to*
*My Wife*
*Dorothy M. Chapel*

# Preface

Shooting is both an art and a science. As an art, shooting consists of skill, dexterity, knack, and ability to perform the actions necessary for hitting a target, whether the target is human, animal or made of paper. Such art is acquired by study, observation, and experience. As a science, shooting is systematized knowledge based upon study, observation, and classified facts. These definitions overlap to some extent. They can be summarized best by saying that the science of shooting teaches us to know how to achieve success in marksmanship, whereas the art is the application of scientific knowledge.

This book covers rifle, pistol, and revolver shooting. The historical development of shoulder arms roughly parallels the long process of improving hand guns. The principles of gun safety are similar for short and long weapons. Holding the weapons and assuming the various shooting positions are obviously different. Aiming, squeezing the trigger, and calling the shot are fundamentally the same for shoulder and hand arms. The care and cleaning of firearms, the construction and operation of target ranges, rifling and ballistics, and technical details about cartridges all overlap in many respects, and there are other marksmanship subjects which apply in many major respects to both shoulder and hand guns. Nevertheless, in this text rifle shooting is treated in one major section and pistol and revolver marksmanship in another.

The right to own firearms and acquire skill in their use is a basic part of the democratic way of life. In Europe it was the gun in the hands of ordinary men on foot which unseated the armored knights, destroyed feudalism and serfdom, and eventually led to the representative form of government which prevails in many nations today. In America the gun contributed to the building and preservation of the nation. Skill with rifles, pistols, and revolvers has helped to maintain American and British freedom and leadership among nations throughout history.

7

The development of artillery, the airplane, rockets, missiles, and atomic bombs has not eliminated the importance of the foot soldier who must occupy and hold with hand and shoulder arms the land shelled by the larger and more impressive weapons. Infantry is still the "Queen of Battles."

Regardless of the importance of rifles, pistols, and revolvers as weapons for personal protection and military purposes, marksmanship is an excellent sport in its own right. Fortunately, it is a year-round sport that can be conducted on both indoor and outdoor ranges. Furthermore, neither sex nor age are limitations. Many of the champion shots of America, for example, are young men and women who can be seen competing at regional and national tournaments against people in their sixties and seventies.

In selecting the first firearm for a young boy or girl, it is customary to choose a .22 caliber rifle which is adapted to the size, weight, and particular physique of the youngster who will fire it. Nevertheless, thousands of boys and girls have received their first instruction with pistols and revolvers.

Marksmanship, because of the traditions behind it, and because it has never been cursed by professionalism and commercialism, encourages true sportsmanship. Since hand and shoulder guns are mechanical instruments of precision, and the rules permit a wide choice in equipment, the shooter unavoidably becomes interested in the elementary phases of chemistry, physics, and the mechanical arts. Metalworking and woodworking hobbies are frequently acquired in an effort to improve the appearance or functioning of a shooter's weapons.

Some shooters develop an interest in collecting antique firearms, primarily for fun, but often for profit, too. This is a hobby which has clubs all over the United States and Great Britain and has done much to revive an interest in history.

Finally, whether you learn to shoot for self-protection, military service, hunting, sport, or any other reason, you will find that the greatest reward comes from the splendid men and women of all ages and occupations whom you will meet if you engage in marksmanship competition. More than any other sport, marksmanship attracts to its ranks people who are warm, helpful friends.

C. E. C.

# Acknowledgments

The author expresses his gratitude for the assistance given him in the writing of all his gun books by the staff of the *American Rifleman*, the official publication of the National Rifle Association of America, and especially for their help in preparing this book. It would be impossible to list all of the staff of the National Rifle Association of America who have read manuscripts and checked galley and page proofs through the years, but the author is especially indebted to Walter J. Howe, Editor; Julian S. Hatcher, Major General, U.S. Army, Retired, who is Technical Editor; and M. D. Waite, Associate Technical Editor.

In addition, the author would not have been able to prepare this book without the help of the manufacturers of rifles, pistols, and revolvers mentioned and illustrated in this text.

Although a few of the line drawings were made by the author, the majority of illustrations not credited to others were drawn by Mr. Sanford Strother.

C. E. C.

# Contents

## PART II: Pistol and Revolver Shooting

# Part I

# RIFLE SHOOTING

# Foreword

That a knowledge of shooting on the part of its citizens is an asset to the nation can be accepted without question. That a familiarity with firearms based on proper instruction in their use removes much of the danger usually associated with guns is equally true. The use of guns by persons who have been made safety conscious by proper instruction is relatively safe, but that is certainly not true if instruction has been omitted and knowledge is lacking.

It is therefore an advantage to all concerned to have available material on guns and shooting that is sound and easily understood. Such material is provided in this book, and it is presented interestingly and in simple terms. The material is concise and to the point, yet it adequately covers the essentials of rifle marksmanship, and no necessary information has been omitted.

The author is a retired officer of the United States Marine Corps and a writer of note. He knows his guns and has a happy facility with the pen. That combination has resulted in several excellent and highly useful books on firearms, and this latest effort by Lieutenant Chapel is no exception.

JULIAN S. HATCHER
Major General U. S. A., Retired,
Technical Editor, *The American
Rifleman*

Washington, D. C.

# Chapter 1

## THE DEVELOPMENT
## OF THE RIFLE

### The Importance of the Rifle
### in American History

The United States was made a nation and its existence has been maintained by the rifle. Regardless of the development of the airplane, the atom bomb, and other tools of war, the rifle will always be the principal weapon of the infantry, upon which all other arms and branches of our military and naval forces depend for final victory.

In the early days of our history, the rifle was used to provide food, drive back the wild animals that menaced the little settlements along the Atlantic Coast, and defeat the Indians who resisted the onward sweep of civilization. Today, the rifle provides healthy outdoor sport for thousands of men and boys who fire in competition at targets or emulate their ancestors in the hunting field.

### Gunpowder

The development of the rifle has been a slow process. It started with the discovery of gunpowder. The first gunpowder made was black powder, which was simply a mixture of charcoal, sulphur, and saltpeter. In this crude form it was used from its discovery until long after 1900, and it is still widely used for several purposes, but modern rifle cartridges are loaded with smokeless powder, a far different compound from the black powder of our ancestors.

No one knows when or where gunpowder was first discovered.

15

The ancient people of China, India, Arabia, and Greece had many fiery mixtures, some of which were explosive. Greek fire, a composition that burned under water, was extensively used, but it was not an explosive.

Gunpowder was probably known in Europe as early as the year 846. Roger Bacon, an English monk, mentioned it in his writings in 1267 and inferred that it had been known long before his time. In 1820, Bishop Albertus Magnus said that gunpowder was employed during the siege of Seville, Spain, in 1247.

For centuries, gunpowder was used in battle principally to frighten enemy soldiers who thought that it had some relation to thunder and lightning and was produced by the devil. Its flash and noise frightened the horses ridden by knights, caused them to throw their riders, and run to the rear. In this manner, it gradually led to the overthrow of knighthood and increased the importance of the foot soldier, thus paving the way for the downfall of kingdoms and the rise of republics.

The earliest gunpowder was a coarse meal-like mixture called serpentine powder, but in the fifteenth century men learned to form the powder into grains. Probably by accident, they learned that if they varied the size of the powder grains they could control its strength.

Fine-grain powder, which burns faster than coarse-grain powder, was referred to as Fg. When a finer grade was made, it was called FFg., and when a much finer grade was developed, it was designated FFFg. These terms are still used by men who handle black powder.

Black powder always has had three important disadvantages. First, it is difficult to control its rate of burning. Second, it is useless if it is damp. Third, when it is fired, there is a great cloud of white smoke and a loud bang. The noise and smoke reveal the position of the shooter, and the smoke makes it difficult for him to see his target.

In an effort to produce a powder that would lack these faults, Major Schultz of the Prussian Artillery developed a smokeless powder in 1865, and later in the nineteenth century employees of the Explosive Company of Great Britain accomplished the same thing by a different method. Unfortunately, both powders burned too fast to be used successfully in rifles, although they could be employed in shotgun cartridges and for other purposes.

In 1884, French chemists produced a smokeless powder that burned slowly enough for use in rifles, but it was left to Americans to carry the work to its present form. Cotton is now used as a base, nitrated, coated with various chemicals, and made in grains of various diameters and lengths so that it can be used in any firearm from a .22-caliber pistol to a coast defense cannon.

Semismokeless powders and Lesmok powders were developed as a cross or compromise between the original black powder and the latest form of smokeless powder. These were used to a limited extent in loading some cartridges until 1947, but today Lesmok powders are obsolete and semismokeless powders are used to a very limited extent by ammunition manufacturers.

## Early Shoulder Weapons

The first firearms were probably rockets fired from bamboo tubes used to give direction and elevation. The next step was the construction of crude cannon. Some were made of wood wound with

Fig. 1. A semiportable cannon.

Fig. 2. A hand cannon being fired
by a soldier of the fifteenth century.

iron hoops and others were cast in iron and bronze by pouring
molten metal into molds. Stones were the earliest projectiles for
cannon, followed by lead, brass, and iron balls.

Gradually, men overcame their fear of gunpowder and experimented with semiportable cannon such as the one shown in Figure
1. At first they were fired by holding a red hot iron, a torch, or a
burning rope at the muzzle, but eventually someone drilled a hole
near the rear, called a *touchhole*. This enabled the shooter to make
his powder burn from the rear toward the front, and it also increased
his safety. Figure 2 shows a soldier of the fifteenth century firing a
*hand cannon*.

Soldiers and hunters were familiar with the crossbow. Although
it was used to shoot arrows, its wooden stock fitted comfortably

Fig. 3. A matchlock.

against the shoulder and provided the inspiration for the design of the stock of later weapons.

The *matchlock*, illustrated in Figure 3, was developed in Europe about 1450. A burning wick, called a match, was carried to the hole at the rear of the barrel (touchhole) by means of a curved and pivoted piece of metal on the side of the barrel. Figure 4 shows the details of an early matchlock. The lighted match is marked A, the clamp in which the match is carried is marked C, and the trigger is marked B. When the trigger is pulled to the rear, the burning match is lowered into the pan marked D, where powder is lighted and starts a fire, which goes through the touchhole, marked E, to the powder in the rear of the barrel. The main charge of powder then explodes and forces the bullet out of the barrel.

The S-shaped piece of metal suggested a snake and was called a serpentine. Since the match was the source of fire, the gun was called

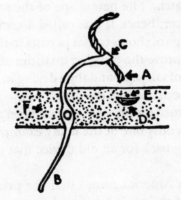

Fig. 4. The details of an early matchlock. *National Rifle Association of America.*

a matchlock. The first colonists who came to America brought weapons of this type.

The powder and ball were loaded from the muzzle of the smooth-bore barrel. A small quantity of fine powder was placed in the pan. When the trigger was pulled, the burning match was lowered into the pan, setting fire to the powder in the pan. The flame from the pan then passed through the touchhole and set fire to the main charge of powder in the barrel.

Our ancestors found that the matchlock was slow to load, inaccurate, and usually useless in damp weather. The gunner had to blow on the match before firing so that the end would glow, he had to keep the hot ashes knocked off the end of the match to keep them from falling into the pan and causing a premature discharge, and he had to lower the match very carefully or it would either miss the pan entirely or hit it so hard that it knocked out the powder. Furthermore, he had to lift not only the burning end of the match when he pulled the trigger, but part of the slack portion as well.

All of these troubles led to the invention of the snapping matchlock. It had a spring and lever arranged so that the trigger would be held back by a spring until it was pulled. The clamp to hold the burning end of the match was replaced by a tube which held only a short piece of match. The new shape of the serpentine suggested the head of a rooster, hence it was called a cock, thus admitting a word to the language of shooters that persists to this day. Meanwhile, men learned to improve the burning qualities of the match by soaking it in a solution of saltpeter and then drying it.

The snapping mechanism of the matchlock was actually borrowed from the ancient crossbow on which it had been used for firing darts and arrows. This is only one of the many examples in the history of warfare of reaching back for an old device that can be adapted to a new purpose.

The colonists in America found that the principal value of the matchlock was in fighting Indians with its roar and flash. Matchlocks became almost obsolete in America during the latter part of the seventeenth century, but they were used in Europe long after

Fig. 5. A soldier firing an arquebus.

more efficient weapons were developed, simply because they were cheap and easy to make.

## The Arquebus

Stories of early colonial days in America often mention the arquebus. Figure 5 shows a soldier resting an arquebus on a forked stick to steady his aim and absorb some of the recoil. This gun was merely a variation of the matchlock, except that the butt of the stock was lower than the barrel so that the shooter could sight along the barrel better. In addition, the cock (serpentine) fell to the rear into the pan, instead of falling forward.

## The Wheellock

The first important improvement in firearms after the development of the matchlock was the wheellock, illustrated in Figure 6.

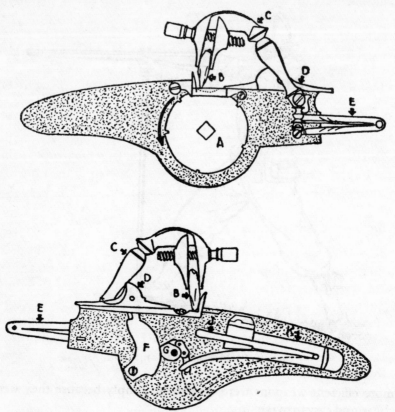

Fig. 6. Details of the wheellock.    *National Rifle Association of America.*

It was invented in Germany about 1515. Mechanically, its action resembled a modern cigarette lighter. A notched wheel with a spring was wound with a key. When the trigger was pulled, the wheel was released and revolved rapidly against a piece of flint or pyrites held in the jaws of a cock. This produced sparks that lighted the powder in the pan and set fire to the main charge of powder in the barrel. The wheellock was more expensive and difficult to make than the matchlock, hence most men continued to use either the ancient cross-bow or the inefficient matchlock for war or hunting until about 1700. Only wealthy men owned wheellocks in Europe. Comparatively few were brought to America for the simple reason that most of the early settlers were poor.

In Figure 6, the notched wheel is marked A. It rotates in a counter-clockwise direction. It strikes sparks from a piece of flint, marked B, which is held against the wheel by a clamp, marked C, and the spring, marked E. When the lock is cocked, the cam, marked G, presses against the arm, marked F. This holds the cover, marked D, away from the pan holding the priming powder. Pulling the trigger releases the catch, marked J, which holds the wheel in the locked position, and also the spring, marked K, which rotates the wheel when it returns to the normal position shown in the drawing by a dotted line.

## The Introduction of Rifling

The arms we have been discussing were usually smoothbores. Rifling is the system of spiral grooves cut into the bore of a rifle, pistol, or revolver to give the bullet a spin that will insure its steady flight, nose forward, to the target. Between the grooves cut into the bore are "lands." These are the raised surfaces of the bore that remain after the grooves have been cut. These lands cut into the bullet as it moves through the barrel and spin it about its long axis.

Rifled arms were probably introduced in Germany sometime between 1515 and 1550, hence rifling was known during the wheel-lock period, although it did not come into general use for many years after its discovery.

A musket is a shoulder arm with a long barrel having a smooth bore, that is, the inside of the barrel has no rifling. A musketoon is a musket with a short barrel. A rifle is a shoulder arm having grooves cut in the bore. If the rifle has a short barrel it is known as a carbine.

## The Flintlock

The flintlock was probably invented sometime before 1630, it reached its final form about 1675, and it almost entirely displaced the wheellock by 1700. Figure 7 shows the lock of a typical flintlock. When the trigger is pulled, the hammer, marked B, springs forward and strikes the flint, marked A, against the anvil, marked C. The

anvil flies forward, and the sparks drop into the powder pan, marked
D, where they set fire to the priming powder. The fire in the pan
passes through the touchhole in the side of the barrel and fires the
main charge of powder.

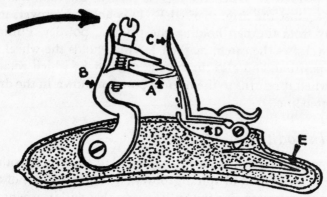

Fig. 7. The lock of a typical flintlock.     *National Rifle
Association of America.*

The object set in motion by the trigger to fire the gun was originally called a serpentine, then a cock, and finally it became known
as a hammer when it became a part of a flintlock.

The flintlock was simpler and cheaper to make than the wheel-
lock, and it was much more reliable. This form of shoulder weapon
was used for more than three and one-half centuries. Americans
carried it under the British flag in the French and Indian Wars
and against the British in the Revolution and the War of 1812. A
few soldiers were armed with flintlocks as late as the Civil War. Even
in this advanced age, the flintlock is used in remote regions where
modern ammunition is scarce and expensive.

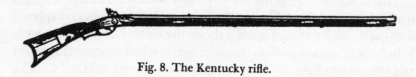

Fig. 8. The Kentucky rifle.

## The Kentucky Rifle

The flintlock found its greatest development in the Kentucky Rifle, illustrated in Figure 8. It was so typical of American arms in the beginning of our national life that it was known in Europe as the "American rifle." Actually, it was developed in what is now the state of Pennsylvania and should be called the Pennsylvania rifle.

Washington's men carried the Kentucky rifle when they saved the forces of General Braddock in the French and Indian War. When the British General Wolfe defeated the French and captured Quebec, the victory was made possible by Pennsylvania Provincials carrying the Kentucky rifle.

Many of our history books say that King George III hired Hessians because Englishmen refused to fight Americans in our Revolution. This is false. The Hessians were hired because they were experienced riflemen who were expected to be able to counteract the deadly fire of Americans armed with the Kentucky rifle. Much of the credit for our independence from England belongs to the backwoodsmen who went into battle with the Kentucky rifle.

In the War of 1812 at the Battle of New Orleans, Americans armed with the Kentucky rifle defeated the British General Pakenham, who had 10,084 regulars opposing 3,918 Americans, most of whom had little or no military training. The American fire was so accurate that the British lost 3,336 dead and wounded while the Americans lost only 8 killed and 13 wounded. It was this battle that gave Andrew Jackson the fame that carried him to the White House.

## The Percussion or Cap-and-Ball Gun

In 1807, the Reverend Alexander Forsyth, a Scotch Presbyterian minister, received a patent for a lock in which a steel hammer exploded a small quantity of detonating powder placed in the flashpan of a gun. He found that a sensitive compound, such as fulminate of mercury, could be exploded by a blow and that it would ignite the main charge of powder in the bore. Although the exact method of making and using the sensitive compound has varied, the basic principle has remained the same to this day and is followed in all hand and shoulder arms.

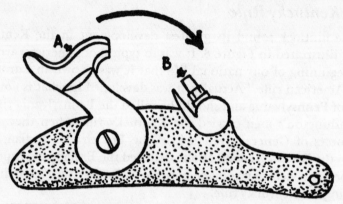

Fig. 9. The lock of a percussion (cap-and-ball) rifle.
*National Rifle Association of America.*

The early percussion arms were known as cap-and-ball weapons.
They were usually single-shot muzzle loaders and most of them
were muskets, although the best scores were obtained with rifles.
Figure 9 shows the lock. When the trigger is pulled, the hammer,
marked A, springs forward and strikes the anvil, marked B, with
enough force to set off a percussion cap containing the primer
charge.

## Breechloaders

Breechloading existed centuries ago. King Henry VIII of England
owned a breechloading matchlock arquebus which is still on exhibition in the Tower of London. However, in spite of its ancient
origin, breechloading was regarded with suspicion by most gun-
makers. Lieutenant Colonel Patrick Ferguson of the British Army
commanded men armed with breechloading flintlock rifles at the
Battle of Brandywine during the American Revolution, but he was
killed in that battle and with his death went any possibility of the
British Army's adopting this method of loading until forced to do
so by foreign competition.

The first breechloading weapon officially adopted by the United
States was the U. S. rifle model 1819, made at the U. S. National
Armory, at Harpers Ferry, Virginia, from 1824 to 1844. This was a

breechloading flintlock rifle invented by J. H. Hall. Unfortunately, it was in advance of its time and breechloading rifles were not widely used in the armed forces of the United States until the close of the Civil War.

## Modern Progress

The first truly modern rifle issued to the armed forces of the United States was the U. S. rifle, model 1903 caliber .30, commonly known as the Springfield, illustrated in Figure 10. This is a bolt-action rifle developed from the German Mauser action. It was carried by our forces in World War I and to some extent in World War II. President Theodore Roosevelt carried it on his African hunting expedition and encouraged American sportsmen to use it in hunting deer and other large game. It is still the most popular rifle for either hunting or large-caliber marksmanship.

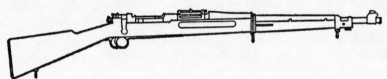

Fig. 10. The U. S. rifle, caliber .30, model 1903 (Springfield).

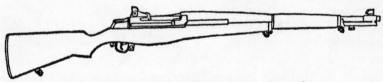

Fig. 11. The U. S. rifle, caliber .30, M1 (Garand).

The semiautomatic rifle invented by John M. Garand, an American employee of the Frankfort Arsenal, known officially as U.S. rifle, caliber .30, M1, is illustrated in Figure 11. This rifle was adopted in 1936 and used by the armed forces of the United States as the principal shoulder weapon of World War II. It is strictly a military weapon and will never be popular with hunters. Three views of the Garand and one view of its clip of cartridges are shown in Figure 12.

With this brief summary of the development of the rifle, we can
turn to actual instruction in marksmanship, confident that behind
us is a long and glorious history of men and boys who made and
preserved a nation by the aimed fire of the rifle.

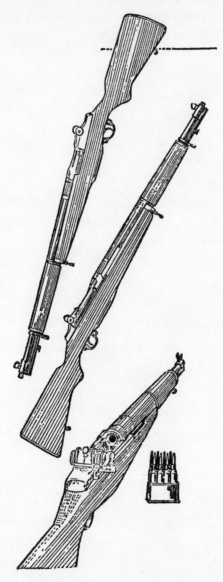

Fig. 12. Three views of the Garand and
one view of its clip of cartridges.

# Chapter 2

## RIFLE NOMENCLATURE

*Types of Rifles*

Rifles may vary in appearance and construction, but the opening of the breech, the extraction and ejection of the fired cartridge, the loading of a fresh cartridge, and the method of cocking are similar for all types.

Figure 1 shows a lever-action rifle. The lever is merely an extension of the trigger guard. When the lever is pulled down, the breech block slides back, exposing the breech and at the same time extracting and ejecting the fired cartridge. When the lever is pushed back up, the rifle is loaded and cocked, and the breech is sealed. It helps to understand the operation if it is remembered that the breech block is essentially a solid, movable block of metal against which the cartridge rests in firing.

A lever-action rifle may be a single shot, or it may be a repeater with a tubular magazine for extra cartridges, which are automatically fed into the breech when the breech block is closed. This type of rifle is not used in marksmanship competitions.

Figure 2 shows a falling-block type of rifle. It resembles the lever-action rifle but the breech block drops vertically instead of moving horizontally when the lever is pulled down. All falling-block rifles are single shots and are used in certain kinds of marksmanship contests. Figure 3 is a close-up view of the action, and it also shows a rear sight mounted on the tang of the rifle.

Figure 4 shows a slide, pump, or trombone-action rifle. It is operated by a sliding fore end. The shooter pulls the fore end to the rear

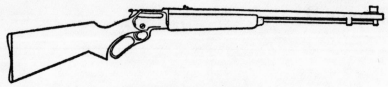

Fig. 1. A lever-action rifle.

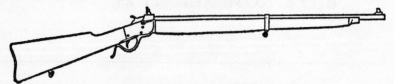

Fig. 2. A falling-block type of rifle.

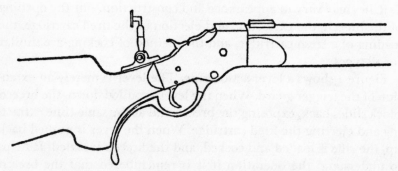

Fig. 3. A close-up view of the action of a falling-block rifle.

with his left hand to eject the empty cartridge. When he pushes the fore end forward, a fresh cartridge is loaded into the chamber. Rifles of this type are usually fed by a tubular magazine and are not used in target competitions.

Figure 5 shows a bolt-action rifle. It is actuated by the movement of a breech bolt. The shooter pulls the bolt handle upward and to the rear to extract and eject the fired cartridge. He pushes the bolt handle forward and downward to insert a fresh cartridge, close the breech, and cock the rifle.

Figure 6 shows a semiautomatic or autoloading rifle. Rifles of this type use some of the force from the cartridge previously fired to operate the loading and cocking devices. High-powered semiautomatic rifles, especially military arms, are usually gas operated,

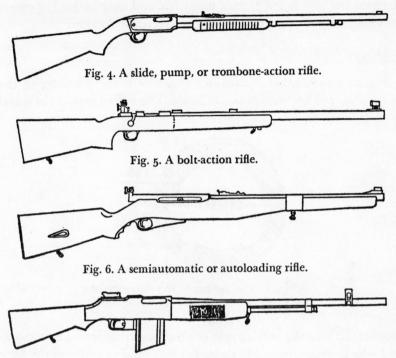

Fig. 4. A slide, pump, or trombone-action rifle.

Fig. 5. A bolt-action rifle.

Fig. 6. A semiautomatic or autoloading rifle.

Fig. 7. An automatic rifle.

while .22-caliber rifles are usually operated by the recoil from the fired cartridge of what is known as the blow-back principle. The shooter loads the first cartridge by hand and thereafter squeezes the trigger for each shot. These rifles are sometimes mistakenly referred to as automatic, even by the manufacturers, but they are not fully automatic.

Figure 7 shows an automatic rifle. A rifle that is fully automatic uses some of the force from the discharge of the previous cartridge to unlock the rifle, extract the fired cartridge, eject the fired cartridge, reload, lock the arm, and fire continuously as long as the supply of ammunition in a magazine lasts and as long as the shooter maintains pressure on the trigger.

It is obvious that any rifle is either a single-shot rifle or a repeater. A single-shot rifle must be reloaded by hand for each cartridge fired.

A repeating rifle is fed from a magazine and may be loaded either automatically or manually, according to its construction.

## Caliber

Figure 8 shows that the caliber of a rifle is the diameter of the bore measured between opposite lands. The rifling consists of spiral

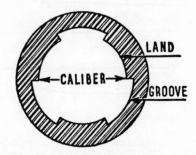

Fig. 8. The caliber is the diameter of the bore measured between opposite lands.

grooves cut into the bore to spin the bullet so that it will fly steadily and nose forward toward the target. The raised portions of the bore between the grooves are called lands.

The number of grooves that constitute the rifling may vary from two to eight for rifled firearms in general, but the number of grooves in rifles (as distinguished from pistols and revolvers) varies from four to eight. Figure 8 was drawn with three grooves for the sake of simplicity. Figure 9 is a cut-away view of a rifle barrel which shows lands and grooves.

The caliber may be expressed in decimal fractions of an inch or in millimeters. Caliber does not indicate speed or power. For example, the .220 Swift cartridge is only a .22-caliber cartridge but it is more powerful than the much larger .30-30.

At one time, a small-bore rifle was any rifle of comparatively small caliber, but today it refers only to a .22 rimfire rifle. A large-bore rifle is any rifle of a large caliber, such as a .30-caliber rifle.

A high-power cartridge is theoretically one having a muzzle velocity of more than 2,000 feet per second and a low-power cartridge is

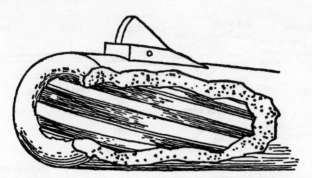

Fig. 9. A cut-away view of a rifle barrel which shows lands and grooves.

supposed to be one having a velocity of 2,000 feet per second or less. Actually, these terms overlap in practice and have little or no precise meaning. From these expressions have come high-power rifle and low-power rifle, referring to the power of the cartridge used.

In the United States and in most English-speaking nations, caliber is designated in hundredths of an inch or thousandths of an inch. Thus, the .22-caliber cartridge has a bullet having a diameter of approximately .22 inch. Further information about cartridge designation is given in the next chapter.

## The Principal Parts of a Rifle

Figure 10 is a simplified drawing of a typical .22-caliber, bolt-action rifle. Fundamentally, its principal parts perform the same functions as those of any other type or model. Since the bolt-action rifle is the safest and most practical rifle for training, target competition, and hunting, it is used as the basis for most of the instruction in this book.

The four principal parts of this, or of any other rifle, are the stock, the barrel, the action, and the receiver.

The stock is the wooden frame that holds the metal parts. The butt is that portion of the stock which is held against the shoulder. The butt plate is made of steel, protects the butt from injury, and keeps the butt from sliding off the shoulder. The small of the stock is that portion of the stock directly to the rear of the trigger guard

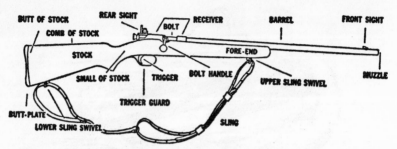

Fig. 10. A simplified drawing of a typical .22-caliber, bolt-action rifle.
*National Rifle Association of America.*

and receiver. The hand that operates the trigger is placed around
the small of the stock. The hand that supports the rifle grips the
fore end, sometimes referred to as the forearm. The shooter's cheek
is placed against the comb, which is the forward upper edge of the
butt of the stock. The upper sling swivel and the lower sling swivel
are used for attaching the sling to the stock.

The barrel is the metal tube through which the bullet passes when
the rifle is fired. The bore is the hole through the barrel. The muzzle is the mouth or front end of the barrel from which the bullet
leaves. The breech is the rear opening of the barrel into which the
cartridge is loaded. The chamber is the enlarged rear portion of
the bore into which the cartridge is placed for firing. The front
sight and the rear sight are the devices used for guiding the eye in
aiming.

The action is the mechanism that fires the cartridge. It consists of
several moving parts. The trigger is a curved metal lever which is
part of the action. When it is squeezed by the shooter's finger, it
disengages the sear and discharges the rifle. The sear is essentially
a small lever connected with the trigger for the purpose of releasing
the firing pin at the moment of firing. The firing pin is a sharp-
pointed steel rod which strikes the primer in the base of the cartridge
to fire it. The mainspring drives the firing pin forward when the
trigger is squeezed. The mainspring and the firing pin are housed
in the bolt, which is the sliding part moving within the receiver and
closing the breech. The bolt handle is simply the handle grasped by
the shooter when he operates the bolt.

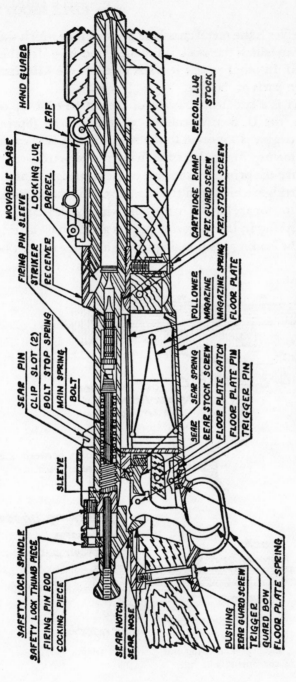

Fig. 11. A cut-away drawing of the action of the U. S. rifle, caliber, .30, model 1903 (Springfield).

The receiver is the metal chassis or housing into which the barrel is screwed, to which the stock is fastened, and in which the action is contained. In other words, it holds together the principal metal and wooden parts of the rifle.

Figure 11 is a cut-away drawing of the action of a typical bolt-action rifle, the U. S. rifle, caliber .30, model 1903 (Springfield). When the trigger is squeezed to the rear, the sear is released. This allows the mainspring to drive the firing pin forward with enough force to strike the primer in the base of the cartridge, thus discharging the cartridge, which is in the chamber. The mainspring, firing pin, and extractor are housed in the bolt, which slides in the receiver. The large spring in the magazine pushes additional cartridges upward into the loading position. Figure 12 shows the contact between

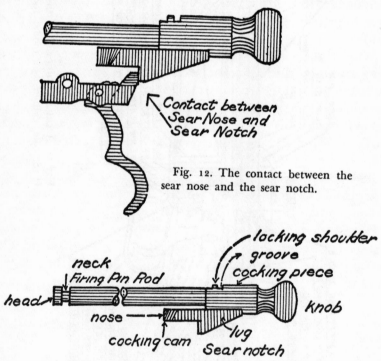

Contact between Sear Nose and Sear Notch

Fig. 12. The contact between the sear nose and the sear notch.

locking shoulder
groove
cocking piece
neck
Firing Pin Rod
head
Knob
nose
lug
cocking cam
Sear notch

Fig. 13. The firing pin, sear, and trigger details of the Springfield rifle.

the sear nose and the sear notch. Fig. 13 shows firing pin, sear, and trigger details.

## Loading and Firing

In operating a bolt-action rifle, the shooter lifts the bolt handle. This unlocks the bolt and permits it to be pulled to the rear by the shooter's right hand. Since the bolt is to the rear, the action is open. If the rifle is a single shot or if the shooter wants to fire a repeater as a single shot, a cartridge is placed by hand in the chamber.

The shooter then pushes forward the bolt handle to close the action and feed the cartridge all the way into the chamber. This movement of the bolt handle also·compresses the mainspring.

Having pushed the bolt handle all the way forward, the shooter pushes it down to the right. This rotates little projections called locking lugs so that the face of the bolt is now firmly against the breech where it seals the cartridge in the chamber. The rifle is ready to fire.

When the shooter squeezes the trigger, the pressure on the trigger causes the cartridge to be fired. When the bolt is lifted and pulled to the rear, clawlike extractors on the face of the bolt seize the rim of the empty cartridge case and withdraw it from the chamber as the bolt moves to the rear. When the rim of the cartridge case strikes a projection called the ejector, the case is knocked out of the rifle.

The operation of the rifle has been described as though it were a single-shot weapon. Actually, most bolt-action rifles are repeaters. When the bolt is pulled to the rear after firing a shot, a spring in the magazine pushes a fresh cartridge upward into place and then the forward movement of the bolt feeds it into the chamber. This makes it unnecessary to feed cartridges manually into the rifle, one at a time.

# Chapter 3

## CARTRIDGES

### *The Cartridge and Its Parts*

A cartridge consists of the cartridge case, the primer, the powder, and the bullet. One cartridge is sometimes referred to as a round, two cartridges are described as two rounds, etc. Small-arms ammunition includes cartridges fired in rifles, semiautomatic rifles, automatic rifles, pistols, machine guns, and shotguns.

Figure 1 shows a large centerfire cartridge on the left and a small rimfire cartridge on the right. Figure 2 shows the component parts of a cartridge. All cartridges are not constructed alike. The one in Figure 2 is typical of caliber .30 cartridges for a bolt-action military rifle.

The cartridge case is a brass (or copper) case inside which the primer, powder, and bullet are assembled. It is sometimes called a shell, especially after the cartridge has been fired.

The primer is the compound in the base of the cartridge case which explodes when crushed by the firing pin and sends a hot flame into the powder charge. In rimfire cartridges, such as the ordinary .22-caliber cartridges, the primer composition is placed in a tiny gutter around the rim of the case and inserted from the inside. The case must be crushed easily by the firing pin in order to explode the primer, hence the case is made of a soft metal that will not withstand high pressures.

The primer for a centerfire cartridge is a separate unit, contained in a soft brass cup, and inserted into a primer pocket in the base of the cartridge case from the outside. Since the firing pin is not re-

41

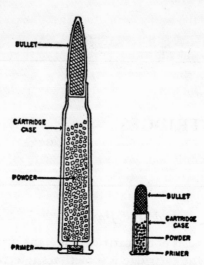

Fig. 1. A large centerfire cartridge
and a small rimfire cartridge.    *National Rifle Association of America.*

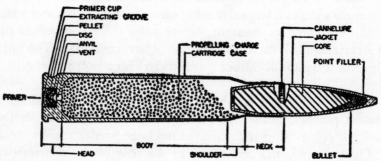

Fig. 2. Component parts of a cartridge.    *National Rifle Association
of America.*

quired to crush the case in order to crush the primer, the case may
be made of stronger metal than that used in rimfire cases. High-
power cartridges are always of the centerfire type because they develop high pressures that the soft case of the rimfire type could not
withstand.

The powder is the compound in the body of the cartridge which,
when set afire by the primer, burns and produces rapidly expanding

gases which force the bullet from the rifle. The powder in a modern cartridge is called smokeless powder, but it is not entirely smokeless and it is by no means a powder. It is made in the form of cylindrical grains, flakes, strips, or pellets, depending upon the size and type of cartridge and the purpose for which it is intended.

Smokeless powder is not a high explosive. It is not sensitive to shock and must be ignited by a spark or flame. When the flash from the primer sets it afire, it burns and generates gas so rapidly that in a fraction of a second it produces a pressure of several thousand pounds per square inch.

The bullet is the projectile fired from the rifle. It is a lead or alloy or metal-jacketed missile seated securely at the front of the cartridge case. Since the face of the bolt is held behind the base of the cartridge case and the bore of the rifle surrounds the sides of the case, the expanding gases generated by the burning powder cannot escape unless they drive the bullet through the bore and out the muzzle.

## Cartridge Designation

Years ago, centerfire cartridges of .45 caliber, having a 70-grain powder charge, and a bullet weighing 500 grains, were described as .45-70-500. This made it possible for anyone to tell by the cartridge designation its caliber, powder weight, and bullet weight, in that order. Gradually, the use of the three hyphenated numbers was dropped and only two facts were given. For example, the cartridge mentioned here became known as a .45-70. Figure 3 shows a Winchester centerfire cartridge known as the 45-70 government. It has a 405-grain bullet hence its complete designation is .45-70-405 government.

Fig. 3. Winchester .45-70 government cartridge.     *Winchester Repeating Arms Co.*

Later, the name of either the manufacturer or the inventor was used to designate cartridges. Examples are the .30 Newton, the .22 W.R.F. (Winchester Rim Fire), and the .257 Roberts Super Speed, the latter being illustrated in Figure 4.

Fig. 4. .257 Roberts Super Speed cartridge made by Winchester.    *Winchester Repeating Arms Co.*

Another system is to give the caliber and then the velocity, such as .250-3000, which refers to a .22-caliber cartridge having a bullet velocity of 3,000 feet per second. Notice that this is also an example of giving the caliber to three decimal places.

There is not much point to giving the caliber to three decimal places where the third decimal place is a zero, but in the case of a cartridge like the .257-1000 (caliber .257 and a bullet velocity of 1,000 feet per second), there is an obvious advantage to giving the third digit.

United States government cartridges are designated in a different manner. The modern .30-06 Springfield cartridge for the United States rifle, caliber .30, model of 1903, is called a ".30-06 govt." by commercial supply houses, or simply ".30-06." This refers to the fact that the bullet is .30 caliber for use in the model 1903 rifle as it was redesigned in 1906. Figure 5 shows a Winchester cartridge for this rifle, called a .30-06 Springfield by the manufacturer.

Fig. 5. .30-06 Springfield cartridge made by Winchester. *Winchester Repeating Arms Co.*

The letter M, standing for modification, is sometimes given after the caliber. An example is the U. S. government cartridge known as the .30 M1, which designates the .30-06 cartridge loaded with a boat-tailed bullet.

Fig. 6. .220 Winchester Swift cartridge. *Winchester Repeating Arms Co.*

Manufacturers sometimes add a descriptive word or phrase after the caliber for publicity purposes. Examples are the .220 Winchester Swift shown in Figure 6, and the .22 Savage High Power.

A common error is to speak of the U. S. rifle, caliber .30, model of 1903, as a .30-30. This is a certain sign of ignorance. The original .30-30 cartridge was .30 caliber, loaded with 30 grains of black powder, and used in one of the early lever-action rifles. It has nothing to do with the .30-06 cartridge or the U. S. rifle, model 1903. Figure 7 shows a modern .30-30 cartridge.

Fig. 7. A modern .30-30 cartridge. *Winchester Repeating Arms Co.*

## Choose the Correct Cartridge

Figure 8 is an illustration of a .22 short cartridge, a .22 long cartridge, and a .22 long rifle cartridge. Never fire anything but the

CARTRIDGES

Fig. 8. A .22 short, a .22 long, and a .22 long rifle cartridge. *Federal Cartridge Corporation.*

.22 long rifle cartridge in a rifle chambered for this cartridge. When a manufacturer says that one of his rifles is "chambered for .22 short, long, or long rifle," he actually means that it is chambered for the .22 long rifle cartridge but will take the other two if necessary.

.22 short cartridge in .22 long rifle chamber—bullet has to jump into rifling.

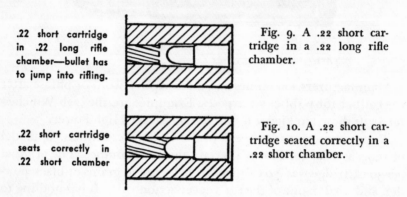

Fig. 9. A .22 short cartridge in a .22 long rifle chamber.

.22 short cartridge seats correctly in .22 short chamber

Fig. 10. A .22 short cartridge seated correctly in a .22 short chamber.

Figure 9 shows a .22 short cartridge in a .22 long rifle chamber. The bullet has to jump into the rifling. Figure 10 shows a .22 short cartridge seated correctly in a .22 short chamber. If you fire a cartridge that is not seated correctly in the chamber of the rifle, the bullet will not lie against the rifling; it jams into the rifling when the cartridge is fired, and some of the lead is scraper off and deposited in the chamber immediately behind the rifling. Eventually, you must take your rifle to a gunsmith to have the lead removed, and even then, it may be too late to cure a condition that causes inaccurate firing.

A great deal more could be said about choosing the correct cartridge. The best advice is to use only ammunition recommended by the manufacturer for your particular rifle.

## Cartridge Rims

Cartridges may be classified according to their rims as rimless, rimmed, semirimmed, and belted. A rimless cartridge has an extractor groove cut around the head of the cartridge. This type is generally used with automatic pistols and with rifles of military caliber, such as the U. S. rifle, caliber .30, model 1903.

A rimmed cartridge may be used in all types of weapons from the revolver through sporting rifles and the older military rifles. It has an external rim around the head which prevents the cartridge from entering the chamber too far.

A semirimmed cartridge closely resembles the rimless type and can be distinguished from it only by laying it on a flat surface and examining it against a strong light.

A belted cartridge is similar to the rimless type, except that the head of the case is very slightly larger than the head of a true rimless case.

Regardless of how the rim is made, its purpose is to provide a projecting edge that the extractor can grasp to withdraw the empty case after discharge.

# Chapter 4

## RIFLE SAFETY

### Safety Rules

The rules of rifle safety are few in number but each rule is vitally important to all who handle firearms. Safety should be learned at the same time that mechanical skill with the rifle is being acquired. It should be practiced at all times when firearms are handled.

1. *Treat each rifle as if it were loaded.* This is the primary safety rule upon which all other safety rules are based. When you pick up

49

any firearm, first be certain that it is empty, but even after you know that it is empty, treat it as if it were loaded.

2. *Keep the muzzle of the rifle pointing in a safe direction.* A safe direction is one in which no person, animal, or object that you do not wish to hit is within the range of your rifle bullet. Generally, the rifle should be pointed upward to keep it in a safe direction, but if you are indoors, be sure that an accidental discharge would not injure someone on an upper floor.

3. *Open the action of a rifle as soon as you pick it up and be sure that it is not loaded.* Keep the action open while you inspect the rifle and leave it open until you are ready to load under safe conditions. Make certain that it is unloaded. Someone may have accidentally loaded it while your back was turned. Be sure that you know how to unload the rifle you are using. If in doubt, consult an experienced shooter. It is easy for a beginner to make a mistake and leave a cartridge in the chamber or in the magazine where it can be fed into the chamber.

4. *Always open the action of a rifle and point the muzzle in a safe direction when passing it to another person. Do not accept a rifle from another person unless the action is open and the muzzle is pointed in a safe direction.* If the action is open, the rifle cannot be fired. This rule is similar to an old rule that you should not hand a person a knife with the point toward his body. Both rules are rules of courtesy as well as safety.

5. *Never point a rifle at anyone or anything you do not wish to shoot.* The reason for this rule is obvious to anyone who is old enough to be trusted with firearms.

6. *When loading a rifle, keep the muzzle pointed in a safe direction.* This is actually an extension of the previous rule, but it is given to emphasize the danger of accidentally shooting someone while you are loading a rifle.

7. *Be sure that you see your target and that no one is in danger, before firing.* In marksmanship, you will be penalized if you fire on the wrong target. In hunting, you not only subject yourself to criminal prosecution, but you also load your conscience with something you will never forget if you kill or wound a human being. Also, the wanton destruction of birds or animals merely for the

sake of killing them is unsportsmanlike. Equally foolish is the practice of shooting at signboards, insulators on poles, and other property that deserves to be respected. Skill in marksmanship is never acquired by random shooting.

8. *Be sure of your backstop.* On the range, a proper backstop stops the bullet behind the target. In the hunting field, some natural object should serve the same purpose. The bullet from an ordinary .22-caliber rifle cartridge can travel for one mile. The bullet from a high-velocity cartridge can travel much farther and kill or wound a man. If a bullet strikes some hard, smooth object, it may glance off (ricochet) and injure an innocent bystander. At short range, a ricochet may even injure the shooter.

9. *Know your rifle and ammunition.* To be safe, the rifle should be clean and in good operating condition. Be sure that you are using the correct ammunition for your own rifle and that you know its range, speed, and penetrating power.

10. *Do not mix alcohol and gunpowder.* An intoxicated shooter is a menace to himself and everyone near him. A drunken hunter is in the same class with the drunkard at the wheel of an automobile.

## Safety and Courtesy at a Rifle Range

The instructor or range officer at a rifle range is responsible for the enforcement of safety rules and good shooting discipline, but he cannot succeed unless he has the cooperation of everyone present. In order to conduct range shooting quickly and fairly for all, certain customs have been developed into rules.

The first group of shooters stays behind the firing line at their assigned places until the command is given: "First relay on the firing line." When they have finished shooting and leave, the instructor or range officer commands, "Second relay on the firing line." Similar commands are given for each succeeding relay until everyone has had his turn.

When a relay (group of shooters) is on the firing line and the range officer or instructor is ready for them to begin firing, he asks, "Ready on the right; ready on the left?" Any shooter who is not ready for any reason shouts, "Not ready on number two," "Not ready on number three," or whatever his firing-position number may be. The range officer or instructor waits until everyone is ready and then gives the command, "Load." No one is permitted to load his rifle until his command is given.

Assuming that all are ready and that the rifles are loaded, the command is given, "Ready on the firing line." This notifies the shooters that firing is about to begin. The next command is, "Commence firing." Until the shooters hear that, not a single shot is fired.

If some trouble develops that might cause a hazard, such as a person walking between the firing line and the target, or when the time limit for firing has expired, the command is given, "Cease firing." The shooters instantly stop firing, open the actions of their rifles, and remain quiet, waiting for further instructions. All of these commands must be obeyed regardless of any individual's notions about being as good as anyone. Range firing is dangerous unless the instructor or range officer remains the absolute boss and obtains perfect obedience from everyone.

Courtesy on the rifle range is like courtesy anywhere. Always think of others first. Avoid loud talking or anything that will distract the attention of shooters from their marksmanship. Do not boast about high scores. Help less experienced shooters. Above all, treat others as you wish to be treated.

# Chapter 5

## AIMING

### The Purpose of Sights

Sights are devices used to guide the eye in aiming a firearm. On modern rifles, sights have two purposes. First, they are used to align the bore of the rifle with the target. Second, by means of precision adjustments, usually on the rear sight, they may be used to compensate for the effect of the wind and the force of gravity on the flight of the bullet. In this chapter we shall consider only the alignment of sights.

### Sight Alignment and the Sight Picture

Figure 1 is a peep sight. Figure 2 is a post front sight. Figure 3 shows how the post front sight is centered in the rear peep sight before the rifle is aimed at the bull's eye. Figure 4 shows the bull's eye setting squarely on top of the post front sight. It is the view of the sights in relation to the target that you see when you aim the rifle. It is called the sight picture.

The rear peep sight appears as a circle when it is close to the eye. The front post sight appears as a black silhouette. The top of the post is even with an imaginary horizonal line running through the middle of the peep hole. Lining up the front and rear sights is called sight alignment. Without disturbing this alignment, the rifle is moved so that the front sight barely touches the bottom of the bull's eye, thus completing the sight picture.

Beginners often ask why the front sight is brought under the

Fig. 1. A rear peep sight. Fig. 2. A post front sight. Fig. 3. The post front sight is centered in the rear peep sight. Fig. 4. The bull's-eye sets squarely on top of the post front sight.    *National Rifle Association of America.*

bull's eye so that the bull's eye looks like an orange sitting on a fence post. The answer is that any other method of aiming would be inaccurate. If the front sight were brought into the bull's eye, you would never know how far in you had gone. If a thin line of white between the top of the front sight and the bottom of the bull's eye were permitted in aiming at a target, you would never know exactly how thin this line was. Therefore, it is always essential to have the top of the front sight barely touch the bottom of the bull's eye. This is correct for both target shooting and hunting.

In hunting you will not have a bull's eye for aiming, but you will select some portion of the body of the animal or bird for aiming, and you will follow the same principles that you have learned in target marksmanship.

The combination of a rear peep sight and a post front sight is the most satisfying sight combination for either target or game shooting, and it is best for both civilian and military rifles.

Figure 5 is a rear sight with a V-shaped notch, commonly called an open rear sight, although there are other forms of an open rear sight. Figure 6 is a post front sight. Figure 7 shows the front sight centered in the notch of the rear sight so that the top is even or level with the top of the rear sight and the front sight is an equal distance from each side of the rear sight notch. Figure 8 shows how the top of the front sight is held directly below the bottom of the bull's eye. This is how the sight picture appears to you in aiming. This combination of an open rear and a post front sight is only good for hunting. It is not used in target shooting.

Fig. 5. A rear peep sight with a V-shaped notch. Fig. 6. A post front sight. Fig. 7. The front sight is centered in the notch of the rear sight. Fig. 8. The top of the front sight is held directly below the bottom of the bull's-eye.    *National Rifle Association of America.*

Figure 9 shows the open rear sight usually found on the U. S. rifle, caliber .30, model 1903 (Springfield). Figure 10 is the post front sight commonly found on that rifle. Figure 11 illustrates the alignment of the front and rear sights. Figure 12 shows the relationship between the sights and the bull's eye. This is how the sight picture appears to you when aiming correctly. Notice that the only difference between this sight picture and the one in Figure 8 is the shape of the open rear sight. Once more, you are reminded that an open rear sight is not suitable for target marksmanship.

Fig. 9. The open rear sight usually found on the Springfield. Fig. 10. The post front sight commonly found on the Springfield. Fig. 11. The alignment of the front and rear sights. Fig. 12. The relationship between the sights and the bull's-eye.    *National Rifle Association of America.*

Figure 13 is a rear peep sight. Figure 14 is a front-aperture sight. Figure 15 shows the front-aperture sight centered in the rear peep sight before the line of aim is directed on the bull's eye. Figure 16 shows the bull's eye setting in the exact center of both the rear peep sight and the front-aperture sight. This is the sight picture you should see while aiming.

In using this combination of a rear peep sight and a front-aperture

Fig. 13. A rear peep sight. Fig. 14. A front-aperture sight. Fig. 15. The
front aperture sight centered in the rear peep sight. Fig. 16. The bull's-
eye sets in the exact center of both the rear peep sight and the front
aperture sight.    *National Rifle Association of America.*

sight, look straight through the rear peep circle and center the
front aperture in the rear peep so that you will have concentric
circles with an even band of light all around the outside rim of the
front sight. Incidentally, this outside rim of the front sight is called
a hood. The bull's eye must be in the exact center of the front sight
aperture and surrounded by an even ring of light.

If the aperture (hole) of the front sight is too small, the bull's
eye will appear fuzzy, whereas the bull's eye should be seen as a perfect, jet-black circle. Try several sizes of apertures before adopting
one as your standard. Even then, you may find that under various
conditions a change in the size of the aperture will improve your
scores.

A combination of a rear peep sight and a front-aperture sight is
best for target marksmanship. There is no argument about this
statement. However, hunters find that a rear peep sight is too
slow for finding and hitting targets in the field, especially moving
targets, and they insist that open sights are better for hunting.

If a shooter selects the proper aperture for both the rear and the
front sight, and if he learns how to use these sights, he can pick up
his target, aim accurately, and hit the target in less time than he
can with open sights. Selecting the proper aperture is simply a
matter of trial and error, as suggested before. Learning to use these
sights requires practice. When skill is attained, the front and rear
sights are aligned almost automatically, and then nothing remains
to be done except lining up the front sight with the target.

## Blackening Sights

The sights must be clean and free of fuzz or lint. In addition, they must be jet black or the proper sight picture is not presented. Wipe the sights free of dirt, oil, or grease, and then hold them over the flame from an ordinary carbide lamp, a candle, a kerosene lamp, or burning shoe paste. The smoke made by burning a small piece of camphor is excellent. If nothing else is available, burn a small piece of pine.

## The Master Eye

Every beginner asks whether he should keep his left eye open while aiming with his right eye. In the case of a left-handed shooter, he wants to know if he should keep his right eye open while aiming with the left. In general, it is better to keep both eyes open, because this method reduces eyestrain and enables the shooter to relax the muscles of his face and neck more than he can do if he closes one eye.

All rifles manufactured in quantity are designed for right-handed shooters and it is assumed that the right eye is the master eye. You can test yourself easily. Hold both eyes open and point the index finger of your right hand at some object. Close the left eye quickly. If the finger remains pointed at the object, the right eye is your master eye. If the finger moves out of alignment with the object, your left eye is your master eye.

If the right eye is your master eye and you are right-handed, you can easily acquire the habit of shooting with both eyes open. If the left eye is your master eye, you can gradually train your right eye to become the master by means of eye exercises. These should be supervised by an oculist.

A few shooters insist on closing the left eye while aiming, but they find that when they do this they partially close the right eye. The remedy is to wear a black patch over the left eye or place a cover over the left lens of shooting glasses.

## Canting

Cant means tip, tilt, slant, or incline. Canting the rifle is rolling or twisting it to the right or left so that the line of sight is not

directly above the axis of the bore. Right-handed shooters usually
cant to the right and cause the bullet to strike low and to the right.
Left-handed shooters usually cant to the left and cause the bullet
to strike low and to the left. Avoid canting by assuming a proper
firing position and holding the sights directly above the bore of the
rifle.

## Advantages and Disadvantages of Telescopic Sights

The beginner is always curious about the use of telescopic sights.
His curiosity should be satisfied, but he should be urged to use only
metallic sights, such as those already described, during his training
period.

One of the principal advantages of telescopic sights is that they
eliminate sight alignment. The shooter merely places the crosshairs
on the target and fires. The magnification of the target makes it
easier to detect errors in the sight picture, but this may be a disadvantage as well as an advantage. A telescopic sight has certain light-
gathering properties that make it easier to pick up and aim at the
target. In addition, it is easier to estimate the force and direction of
the wind with a telescopic sight.

The magnification of the target and the consequent enlargement
of errors in the sight picture frightens many shooters. The unsteadiness of the shooter's position becomes more apparent. If he is inclined to worry about hitting the target, a telescopic sight will make
him more nervous.

A target, whether it is a bull's eye on a piece of paper or an animal
in the field, is easy to hit if you take the correct shooting position,
aim properly, and squeeze the trigger, but this assumes that you
know how to set your sights and know the distance to the target. Furthermore, you must understand the effect of wind and
light. All these must be mastered whether you use metallic sights
or telescopic sights. There is no short cut to accurate rifle marksmanship.

# Chapter 6

## THE SLING

### Purpose of the Gun Sling

A gun sling has two purposes: First, it is used to carry the rifle, leaving the shooter's arms free for other things. Second, it is used in shooting to hold the rifle in a steady position and relieve the muscular strain on the arm.

The sling must be carefully adjusted for each shooting position. When the correct adjustment is found for any position, you should remember how it was made so that you can make the same adjustment again without trial and error.

The sling must fit as tightly as possible, and at the same time it must permit you to move your body freely and comfortably. These seem like opposite requirements to the beginner, and he usually complains that he can shoot better without a sling. However, you will find that you become accustomed to the sling very quickly, and thereafter make better scores than you could make without it.

### The Loop-Sling Adjustment

Figure 1 shows a sling attached to a rifle and gives the nomenclature of the principal parts. As soon as you become familiar with the names of the parts, you will be ready to go through the steps of the loop-sling adjustment to the body.

Place the butt of the rifle on your right thigh, and extend your right arm around the rifle so that the rifle rests on the inside of your right forearm, leaving both hands free to adjust the sling, as illustrated in Figure 2. Unfasten the hook of the short strap. Grasp the

## SIMPLIFIED RIFLE SHOOTING

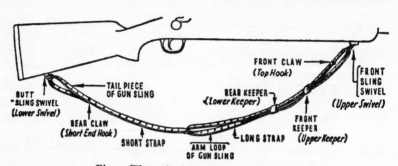

Fig. 1. The principal parts of the sling.

D-ring (metal loop) of the short strap in your right hand, pull toward the muzzle of the rifle, as illustrated in Figure 3, until the hook of the short strap is two or three inches from the butt swivel (lower swivel), and then insert the prongs of the hook into a pair of holes in the short strap, as illustrated in Figure 4.

The arm loop of the sling shown in Figure 1 is the one through which you will place your left arm. It is formed by that part of the long strap between the D-ring (metal loop) of the short strap and the lower (rear) keeper, which is merely a small leather loop. Having disengaged the short-strap hook and hooked it back into the holes in the short strap, as previously explained, you should unhook the long strap and pull the arm loop toward the butt of the rifle, as shown in Figure 5. Refasten the hook on the long strap a few holes from the end of the long strap. Push the keepers toward the upper swivel, and the arm loop should be large enough for you to insert your left arm. This procedure appears difficult in words, but if you carefully follow the directions once, the sling adjustment becomes simple in practice.

Twist the sling one-half turn to the left, as shown in Figure 6, and insert your left arm, as illustrated in Figure 7. Push the loop above the large muscle of the upper arm (bicep), as shown in Figure 8. Pull both keepers and the hook of the long strap as close to the upper arm as possible, consistent with some degree of comfort, and be sure that the arm loop is above the bicep, as shown in Figure 9.

Fig. 2. Preparing to ad-
just the sling.

Fig. 3. Unfasten the hook
of the short strap. Grasp
the D-ring of the short
strap in your right hand,
pull toward the muzzle of
the rifle . . .

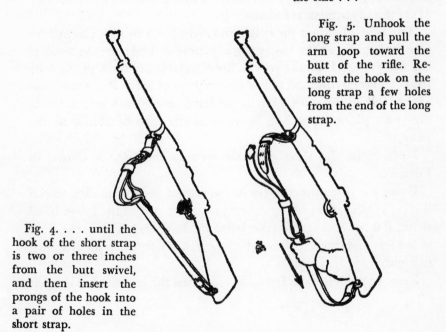

Fig. 5. Unhook the
long strap and pull the
arm loop toward the
butt of the rifle. Re-
fasten the hook on the
long strap a few holes
from the end of the long
strap.

Fig. 4. . . . until the
hook of the short strap
is two or three inches
from the butt swivel,
and then insert the
prongs of the hook into
a pair of holes in the
short strap.

Move the left hand out to the left and over the top of the sling, as shown in Figure 10. Grasp the fore end of the rifle with the left hand, illustrated in Figure 11. The left hand should be between the sling and the rifle stock.

Move the left hand forward so that the rifle is in the crotch of the hand and the sling lies flat along the back of the hand and the wrist. The short strap is not used in this adjustment, but is should be loose enough to avoid any pull on it. Neither end of the sling should be removed from either swivel. The location of the loop on the upper arm should be such that some light may be seen in the triangular space between the sling and the bend in the elbow.

The application of the loop sling to various shooting positions is illustrated in Chapter 7. Examine these positions before proceeding.

## The Hasty-Sling Adjustment

The hasty-sling adjustment is permitted for the standing position in some marksmanship matches and in firing for record under certain conditions. Although it does not provide a support as steady as the loop-sling adjustment, it is easier and quicker to use. For this reason, many hunters prefer it to the loop-sling adjustment. Make the adjustment as follows:

The rifle is held on the thigh and right forearm as explained before for beginning the loop-sling adjustment. Unfasten the hook of the short strap. Find the pair of holes nearest the hook of the long strap, and then count off ten or eleven pairs of holes. Place the claws of the hook of the short strap in the tenth or eleventh pair of holes, the exact place depending upon your size, the flexibility of the strap, etc.

Next, twist the sling one-half turn to the left, as shown in Figure 12.

Grasp the rifle immediately in the rear of the upper sling swivel if it is a typical small-bore rifle, or just in the rear of the lower band swivel if it is a Springfield rifle, using the left hand. Throw the sling to the left and catch it above the elbow, high on the arm, as shown in Figure 13.

Remove the left hand from the rifle. Pass the left hand to the left

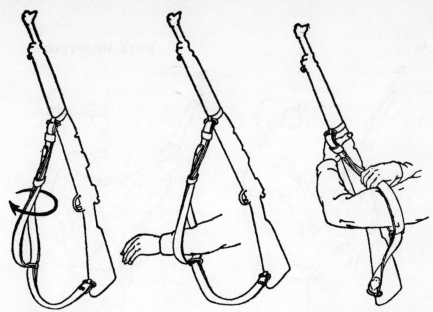

Fig. 6. Twist the sling one-half turn to the left.

Fig. 7. Insert your left arm.

Fig. 8. Push the loop above the large muscle of the upper arm.

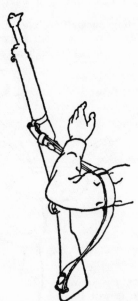

Fig. 9. Pull both keepers and the hook of the long strap as close to the upper arm as possible.

Fig. 10. Move the left hand out to the left and over the top of the sling.

Fig. 11. Grasp the fore end of the rifle with the left hand.

Fig. 12. Twist the sling one-half turn to the left.

Fig. 13. Throw the sling to the left and catch it above the elbow, high on the arm.

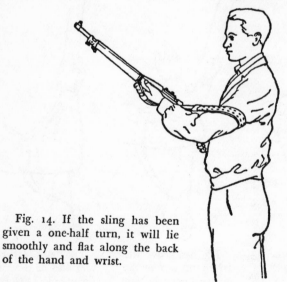

Fig. 14. If the sling has been given a one-half turn, it will lie smoothly and flat along the back of the hand and wrist.

under the sling and then to the right and over the sling. Regrasp the rifle with the left hand. If the sling has been given a one-half turn, as explained before, it will lie smoothly and flat along the back of the hand and wrist, as shown in Figure 14.

Figure 15 shows how the rifle is steadied by the hasty sling in the standing position, even without the help of the right arm. Figure 16 shows a man in the standing position firing a rifle with the hasty-sling adjustment.

## Fitting the Sling to the Man

Experiment with various sling lengths until you find the exact size that fits your body. Thereafter, make no adjustments for size, but adjust the sling looser or tighter for different positions. For example, you may want it tighter for kneeling and sitting. Observe particularly the exact distance between the butt swivel and the hook of the short strap.

If you have carefully followed these instructions, you are now ready to learn the various shooting positions. The sling may seem uncomfortable at first, but as you become accustomed to it, you will find that it provides most of the support for the rifle in the prone, sitting, and kneeling positions.

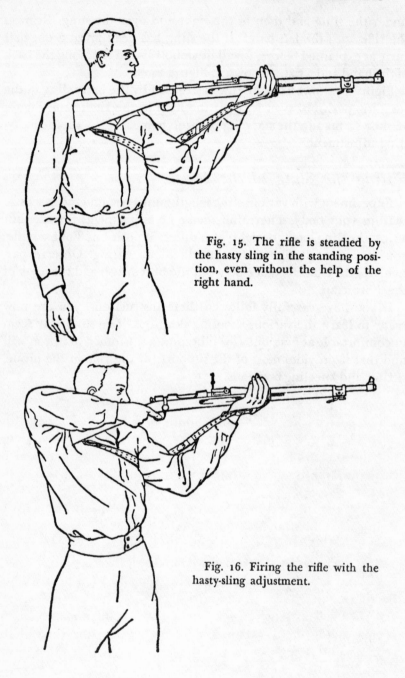

Fig. 15. The rifle is steadied by the hasty sling in the standing position, even without the help of the right hand.

Fig. 16. Firing the rifle with the hasty-sling adjustment.

# Chapter 7

## SHOOTING POSITIONS

### General Rules for All Positions

The following general rules apply to all shooting positions:

1. Half-face to the right before taking any firing position.

2. When you take a shooting position, there is some point at which the rifle aims naturally and without effort. This point should be the center of the target. If it is not the center of the target, you must move the whole body to bring the rifle into the proper alignment with the target. If you do not do this, you will subject your body to a strain during each shot you fire because you must use your muscles to pull the rifle toward the target.

3. Your right hand grasps the small of the stock. If you are firing a high-power rifle, your right thumb may be either around the small of the stock or on top of the stock, but it should not be alongside the stock. In firing a small-bore rifle, your right thumb may be either around the small of the stock or along the right side of the stock.

4. Let the rifle rest in the palm of your left hand. The wrist of your left hand is straight. Your left hand is against or near the upper sling swivel of a typical small-bore rifle or it may be either against or near the lower band swivel of a Springfield rifle.

5. Your left elbow is directly under the rifle or as nearly under the rifle as you can place it without strain.

6. The index finger of your right hand is in contact with the trigger at the most comfortable point between the tip and the second joint. The exact part of the index finger that you will use

depends on the size of your hand and the length of your arm. Try to use the second joint for squeezing the trigger, but do not worry if you must use the first joint. Keep the trigger finger away from the stock of the rifle so that all pressure will be applied to the trigger and none to the stock.

7. Rest your cheek firmly against the stock, and, if possible, on the thumb of the right hand. Relax the neck muscles and allow your head to drop slightly forward and downward, thus bringing your cheek as far forward as possible without straining and placing your eye close to the rear sight.

8. Hold the butt of the rifle firmly against your shoulder.

9. Avoid canting the rifle.

10. If you are left-handed and absolutely cannot learn to shoot right-handed, either learn to work the bolt with the left hand or have a rifle made for you with the bolt action on the left.

11. Relax. You will still live if you miss the target. Do not worry about scores. Do the best you can, and let it go at that.

12. Use your bones and not your muscles to support the rifle.

13. Do not use an artificial rest, such as a sand bag, without specific authority.

14. Adjust your gun sling before assuming a firing position or going on a line at a range. However, you may make final adjustments, such as tightening the loop, just before firing.

## The Prone Position

To assume the prone position, half-face to the right; drop to your knees, and slide your right hand back toward the butt of the rifle; lean forward, and place the rifle butt on the ground to give your body support. Place your left elbow as far forward on the ground as possible. Roll your body to the left, and slide the butt plate from the heel of your right hand into the hollow of your right shoulder. Roll your body to the right, and place your right elbow in position. Your right cheek should press firmly against the stock. You are now in the prone position illustrated in Figure 1, which is a side view. Figure 2 shows how you should look from the front.

Your body lies at an angle of about 45° with the line of aim if you are firing a small-bore rifle, or an angle of about 30° if you are firing a high-power rifle. Your spine is straight. Your legs are spread apart, and the inside surfaces of both of your feet are flat on the ground.

Fig. 1. A side view of the prone position.

Your elbows are well under your body, and they raise your chest above the ground.

Your sling should be tight enough to hold the rifle even if you relax the grasp of your hands. Never hold the rifle tightly with your hands. That is the job of the sling. Also, the sling should form the long bones of your left arm into a V-shaped support, which is clearly shown in Figure 1.

Your left elbow is directly under the rifle, thus providing support from the bones and not the muscles. After you place your left elbow correctly, do not change it during firing. If you must move your body, pivot around the elbow, but do not move your elbow.

This prone position is the first one used for instructing beginners because it is the steadiest of the standard firing positions. You should not proceed to the more difficult positions until you have mastered this position.

Fig. 2. A front view of the prone position.

The National Rifle Association of America rules describe the prone position thus:

"The body is extended on the ground, head toward the target. The fore-end and grip are held in the hands, the butt is held against the shoulder. The rifle will be supported by the shoulder and the hands only. No portion of the arms below the elbows shall rest upon the ground or any artificial support nor may any portion of the rifle or body rest against any artificial support. All parts of the rifle must be so positioned that the range officer can pass his hand from the rear of the gun between the lowest part of the rifle and the ground or ground cloth without touching the rifle."

## The Sitting Position

In changing from the prone to the sitting position you may find it necessary to shorten your sling by moving the hook the distance of two holes. You will find that the sitting position is much easier to assume correctly and almost as steady as the prone position.

To assume the sitting position, face half right and drop down, breaking your fall by extending the right arm downward and placing your right hand on the ground before you actually sit down. Work the rifle butt into the hollow of your right shoulder and lean forward to place the sling under tension. Brace your elbows against the insides of your knees and be sure that your left elbow is directly under the barrel, just as it was in the prone position. The long bones of your left arm and leg provide the principal support for the rifle. Figure 3 is a side view of the sitting position, and Figure 4 is a front view.

The National Rifle Association of America rules state: "The weight of the body must be supported only by the buttocks and the feet or ankles. The rifle is supported by both hands and one shoulder only. Arms may rest on the legs at any point above the ankles. The left hand (or in the case of a left-handed shooter, the right hand) must not rest on leg or knee. Elbows resting approximately on or just inside the knee."

You must not twist your feet and legs so that your ankle bones touch the ground. This would not give a firm position and is forbidden by shooting rules.

Fig. 3. A side view of
the sitting position.

Fig. 4. A front view
of the sitting position.

## Crossed-Ankles Sitting Position

The National Rifle Association of America rules for the sitting position also state: "Legs to be apart or crossed at the option of the shooter. When the Crossed Ankles or Cross Legged position is used, the ankle bones must be forward of a vertical line drawn from the point of the knees to the ground." Figure 5 shows the crossed-ankles sitting position.

Fig. 5. The crossed-ankles sitting position.

## The Kneeling Position

The theory of the kneeling position is that it can be used when brush or high grass would obscure the view from a sitting or prone position. The only advantage is that the kneeling position can be assumed very quickly. Actually, it is the most difficult position to assume correctly for all beginners and for the majority of experienced shooters.

To assume the kneeling position, half-face to the right and kneel on the right knee. You are expected to sit on the inside surface of your right foot. Extend the left leg as far forward as you can with comfort and still have the left foot flat on the ground. Place your left elbow near the point of your left knee, but have your knee make contact with your upper left arm about three or four inches above your elbow. The exact distance depends on the size and shape of your body. Your left elbow and left knee are directly under the rifle to give it the support of the long bones of your left arm and leg. Hold the stock high enough on your right shoulder to place the sights in line with your eyes. You are now in the correct kneeling position. Figure 6 is a side view, and Figure 7 is a front view of this position. Notice that your right elbow may be held in any comfortable position.

The above instructions describe the low position. In the high kneeling position, you sit on the heel of your right foot instead of the inside of the foot, and you pull the left foot back past the knee-cap. Either position is authorized.

Fig. 6. A side view of the kneeling position.

Fig. 7. A front view of the kneeling position.

The National Rifle Association of America rules state: "The buttocks are clear of the ground, but may rest on one foot. The rifle is supported by the hands and one shoulder only. The elbow of the left arm (or right arm in the case of the left-handed shooter) rests on the knee or leg. The elbow of the trigger arm is free from all support. The right knee of a right-handed shooter (the left knee of a left-handed shooter) must be touching the ground or mat. A soft cushion may be used. If it is used, it must be placed fully beneath the instep of the foot, with the toes and knee touching the ground or mat of the firing point."

## The Standing Position

The standing position offers less support than any other position, but it is more comfortable than the kneeling position. In this position, the rifle seems to wobble all over the landscape, but it wobbles for everyone, not merely for beginners. The remedy is to reduce the wobble as much as possible and then try to keep it uniform so that the rifle will wobble into the bull's eye as often as it wobbles out. If you will lower the rifle when it wobbles excessively, relax a few seconds, and then aim again, you will have better scores.

There are two standing positions. One is the Army standing position, and the other is the National Rifle Association standing position, usually referred to as the "N.R.A. standing position." The expression "Off-Hand" refers to any standing position, although it is applied more frequently to the Army than to the N.R.A. standing position. In both positions, the sling is not used under most shooting rules, although it is left attached to the rifle.

## The Army Standing Position

To assume the Army standing position, stand faced almost directly to the right of the line of fire, that is, you must stand almost at right angles to the target. Your left side is toward the target. Your feet are spread apart enough to provide a comfortable balance. Your body is erect although it may lean slightly backward to balance the weight of a heavy rifle. The weight of your body is distributed evenly on both hips and both feet. Turn your head to the left, and rest your cheek firmly against the stock. Do not lock your knees rigidly, but relax them.

Grasp the small of the stock with your right hand, placing the thumb of your right hand either around the small of the stock or along the right side of the stock if you are firing the typical small-bore rifle. If you are shooting a large-caliber rifle, place the thumb well around (over) the stock.

Raise the rifle on the shoulder so that about one-half of the butt is visible over the shoulder when seen from the rear. Hold your right elbow high—at least the height of the shoulder, and at an angle of 45° or more above the horizontal if possible. Exert a backward pull with your right hand to keep the butt tightly pressed against your shoulder where it fits into a pocket-like depression. If you are holding the rifle correctly with your right arm and hand, it should be possible to withdraw the left hand and still keep the rifle in a steady position, but this is only a test and not to be done while firing.

While the right hand and arm keep the rifle in position, grasp the rifle with your left hand well forward of the balance and thus provide additional vertical support. Have your left elbow approximately under the rifle, the rifle resting in the palm of the left hand, between the thumb and forefinger, and on the heel of the hand, Your left hand does not pull the rifle back toward the body as the right hand does, but merely supports and directs the rifle. Figure 8 is a front view, and Figure 9 is a side view of the Army standing position.

The National Rifle Association rules state: "Offhand Position— In the offhand position no part of the body, except the feet, touches the ground or any artificial support. The rifle is supported by the hands and one shoulder only. The forward hand will be extended,

Fig. 8. A front view of the Army standing position.   Fig. 9. A side view of the Army standing position.

so that the arm will be entirely free from touching or resting against the body. The gun sling will not be used, and may be adjusted to what is known as the 'parade' position. Including the sling within the grasp of the hand will be optional."

## The N.R.A. Standing Position

Figure 10 is a side view of the N.R.A. standing position, and Figure 11 is a front view. The National Rifle Association rules on this position state: "In the standing position no part of the body, except the feet, touches the ground or any artificial support. The rifle is supported by the hands and one shoulder only. The forward hand will be extended so that the arm will be entirely free from touching or resting against the body."

## The Hip-Rest Standing Position

Figure 12 shows a shooter resting his left elbow on his hip while firing in the hip-rest standing position.

## Field Firing Positions

The sitting position was developed for firing downhill or over low obstructions. The kneeling position is used for shooting uphill or over obstructions slightly higher than those for which the sitting position is intended. The standing position is generally used when a soldier or hunter is walking along and is surprised by the appearance of a target, in firing over high obstacles, or when it is necessary to swing the rifle to follow the movements of a moving target. The prone position is for level ground when there is plenty of time to take aim and when the shooter wishes to expose the minimum amount of his body to the enemy.

It is obvious that the four standard shooting positions (standing, kneeling, sitting, and prone) used in target marksmanship are not merely arbitrary or formal positions. Instead, they have a very practical purpose of hunting or military shooting.

The choice of which position to use depends upon the distance to the target, the time available, and the nature of the ground between the rifle and the target. In addition, accuracy and steadiness

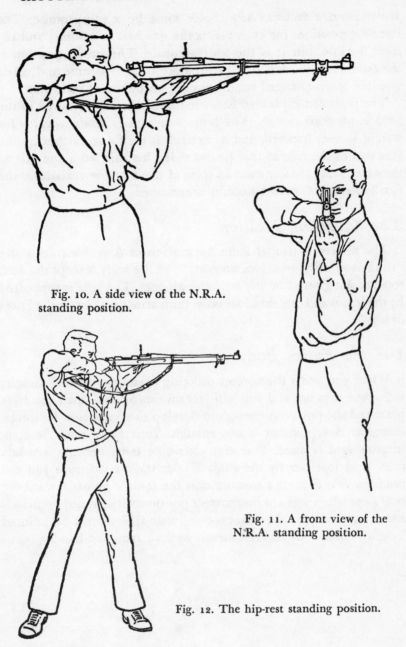

Fig. 10. A side view of the N.R.A.
standing position.

Fig. 11. A front view of the
N.R.A. standing position.

Fig. 12. The hip-rest standing position.

are important factors. Any choice must be a compromise. The standing position, for example, is the quickest to assume, and the most flexible, but it is the least accurate. The prone position is the most accurate, but it requires more time to assume and is less versatile when changed conditions are encountered suddenly.

The positions explained here are not necessarily followed in the field in all their details. The hunter or soldier tends to carry his weight farther forward, and he extends his left arm farther up the fore end of the rifle so that he can swing his rifle from one side to the other with greater ease. In spite of these minor variations, the fundamentals of correct shooting are retained.

## The Squatting Position

The revised National Rifle Association of America rules state: "In the squatting position, no portion of the body, except the feet, touches the ground or any artificial support. The rifle is supported by the hands and one shoulder only. Both arms may rest on the knees or legs."

## Use the Entire Body

When you learn the correct shooting positions, unused muscles will come into use and you will feel uncomfortable until you have practiced the positions enough to develop these muscles. However, muscular development is not enough. Your body must be comfortable and relaxed. You and your rifle must become a steady unit, held together by the sling. Under these conditions you can hold the rifle in such a manner that the muzzle points toward the bull's eye when you are in a correct position without any conscious effort on your part. In other words, your rifle should be pointed by your whole body and not merely by your arms and hands.

# Chapter 8

## SQUEEZING THE TRIGGER
## AND CALLING THE SHOT

### How to Squeeze the Trigger

When you have the sights and the target in line, do not jerk the trigger. Hold the alignment and steadily increase the pressure upon the trigger until the shot is fired. The trigger is squeezed by the steady, independent movement of the forefinger only, straight to the rear, with a smooth, steady, uniform, continuous increase of pressure so that you will not know the exact instant when the rifle will be discharged.

If you squeeze the trigger correctly, you will not become tense in anticipation of the discharge and thus lose the advantage which you gain by maintaining a relaxed position. Also, if you squeeze properly, you will not jerk or yank the trigger, thus throwing out the alignment of the sights with the target.

A beginner squeezes slowly while he is learning the technique, but there is a danger in squeezing too slowly. If you are too deliberate, your left hand may become tense, assuming that you are right-handed, and this tension in the left hand may disturb your aim.

If you squeeze too fast, there is a danger that you may not squeeze smoothly with a steadily increasing pressure, with the result that you jerk the trigger. The champions are men who have learned to squeeze fast without sacrificing smoothness.

A good trigger squeeze is acquired by practice, but ammunition is not essential. In your own room you can gain skill by dry firing, that is, going through all the motions of loading and firing with the rifle empty. Do not aim at random, but practice with a small bull's eye tacked to the wall. Practice every day but always quit before you become tired.

## Taking Up the Slack

The slack is the loose play found in the trigger before it has been moved back far enough to meet resistance. Most small-bore rifles have the slack eliminated before they are delivered from the factory, but some still have the slack. Most large-caliber rifles have the slack as a safety measure.

If your rifle has slack, take it up with a heavy pressure at first. Apply a little more pressure than the exact amount required to take up the slack. In other words, make a decisive movement with your forefinger that takes up all of the loose play in the trigger and part of the resistance offered by the trigger to its backward movement, but do not jerk the trigger. Continue to apply pressure as you squeeze the trigger steadily and smoothly and you will be suddenly surprised to find that you have fired a shot.

When you are ready to fire another shot, you will apply a slightly different amount of pressure in taking up the slack because it is almost impossible to know or control how much pressure you must give the trigger when you take up the slack. Therefore, since you cannot know how much more pressure is required beyond what you have already applied, you will not know when discharge is to take place, you will not tighten up your muscles and nerves, you will not flinch, and you will hit the bull's eye.

## Breathing

At this point we must assume that you know how to take a good shooting position, how to form the perfect sight picture in aligning your sights with the bull's eye, and how to squeeze the trigger. The latter is especially important because failure to squeeze the trigger properly will cause misses even if every other factor is absolutely correct.

Breathing is closely associated with trigger squeeze. If you breathe while aiming, the rise and fall of your chest will be transmitted to your rifle and cause the muzzle to go up and down, thus making it impossible to hold the sights in line with the bull's eye. Unless you learn to control your breathing, you will never make high scores.

After you get into position and have the sights aligned with the bull's eye, take one or two breaths, a little deeper than usual, then draw in an ordinary breath, let out a little air, and hold the remainder by closing the throat. Do not try to hold the breath by the muscular action of your diaphragm (partition between chest and abdomen); always control the breath with your throat. While you hold the breath, squeeze the trigger.

If you hold your breath too long, your position will become unsteady. Let out the breath you have been holding, take a few normal breaths until you become steady, and then repeat the process of holding the breath while you aim and fire. When you hold the breath too long, your heart will beat rapidly, you will have a fast pulse, brought on by the rapid flow of blood through the large arteries, and your shots will go wild.

You must remain relaxed. If you become irritated by something that goes wrong, if your sling is too tight, if your shirt collar is too tight, or if you think of something that happened in the past that was unpleasant, your pulse rate will increase, and you will achieve the same bad results as you would by holding your breath too long. Keep cool and take it easy!

## Calling the Shot

Calling the shot is the act of announcing the location of the shot on the target and its value immediately after you have fired the shot. You do this by noticing how your sights are aligned with the bull's eye at the instant that the shot is fired and calling out where you believe the bullet hit. You must call the shot whether you are using ammunition or not, because it is an essential part of the process of hitting the target. Champions call the shot the same as beginners, except that the experts pay more attention to it because they realize its importance.

In baseball, golf, or tennis, you are taught to keep your eye on the ball and follow through, that is, you do not stop the motion of your bat, club, or racquet the second that it makes contact with the ball, but you continue the motion of the arm or arms even after you have sent the ball flying through space. The follow through in marksmanship is attained by calling the shot.

It takes only a fraction of a second for the bullet to travel through the bore of the rifle after you have squeezed the trigger and fired the shot, but in that brief instant there is ample time for you to move the rifle so that the sights are not in perfect alignment with the target. By calling the shot, you form a habit of maintaining the sight picture after you have discharged your rifle, thus giving the bullet an opportunity to go where you want it to go.

Breaking down the firing of a shot into separate elements, we find that you align the sights with the bull's eye, squeeze the trigger, and keep your eyes watching the sight picture after the shot has been fired. Next, there is a recoil (kick) if you are firing a larger-caliber rifle, but the movement of the muzzle does not occur until the bullet has left the muzzle, hence the whipping or bouncing movement of the muzzle has no effect on accuracy.

You continue to look through the sights and hold your rifle in position. After the recoil, the sight picture will be the same as it was when you squeezed the trigger. Decide where the sights were when the shot was fired, and announce the probable location of the bullet on the target. Your instructor may tell you to do this aloud or you may announce the location of the bullet to yourself. In either case you are calling the shot.

## Locating the Shot by the Vertical Clock Face

Figure 1 shows a target with numbers on it like the numbers on the face of a clock. In reality, a target never has such numbers on it, but you always imagine that the target is a vertical clock face with twelve o'clock at the top, and the center of the clock face at the center of the bull's eye. For example, if a shot hits directly under the bull's eye it is at six o'clock; a shot directly to the left of the bull's eye is at nine o'clock; one directly above the bull's eye is at twelve o'clock; and one directly to the right is at three o'clock. Figure 2

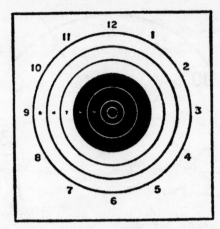

Fig. 1. A target with numbers on it like the numbers on the face of a clock.    *National Rifle Association of America.*

Fig. 2. This shot is called: "A ten at eleven o'clock."

shows a shot touching the ten ring at eleven o'clock. You would call, "A ten at eleven o'clock." Always give both the location and the value of the shot. In the beginning, call the shot aloud, but after gaining experience, call it to yourself.

The vertical clock face is used in hunting as well as in target marksmanship. Figure 3 shows how a right-quartering bird is regarded as a one-o'clock shot, according to the vertical clock system.

## Rhythmical Motions in Shooting

Rhythmical motions are necessary in baseball, tennis, golf, driving an automobile, and any other activity in which various muscles

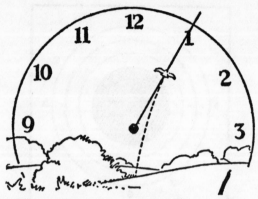

Fig. 3. The bird in this picture is regarded as a one-o'clock shot. *Sporting Arms and Ammunition Manufacturers' Institute.*

must coordinate with the eyes and brain. Shooting is no exception.

Rhythm is movement marked by regular recurrence, that is, everything must be done in the same order and in the same manner. In shooting, you must develop a fixed habit of assuming and holding a correct shooting position, loading properly, forming a perfect sight picture, squeezing the trigger, and calling the shot. All of these operations must be repeated in the same sequence and in the same way. When you have attained a smooth regularity of sequence and technique, you have acquired shooting rhythm and are on the road to successful marksmanship.

During rapid fire at paper targets, shooters appreciate the importance of rhythm because its absence shows up in exceedingly poor scores that are the sums of several individual shots. However, rhythm is just as important in slow fire, even though the shooter is receiving only one poor score at a time. If he fails to shoot with rhythm in slow fire, he will never have it in rapid fire for the simple reason that rapid fire is merely a speeded-up version of slow fire. In the case of most experts, the only difference between slow and rapid fire is the time elasping between successive shots.

This does not mean that you should hurry your shooting. While you are still learning fundamentals, take all the time that your coach or range officer will permit if you need it, but do not develop pokey habits. Take the most time with the first shot, whether you are firing slow or rapid fire, and whether you are a beginner or an expert. Your first shot should be good to establish confidence to carry you through the following shots.

Some men naturally fire faster than others. You must set your own pace by trial and error. As soon as you have mastered the fundamentals, practice dry shooting to gain smoothness, and you will be surprised how quickly you can fire well-aimed shots.

If you find yourself losing rhythm, it will be because you have violated basic principles. If you have jerked the trigger in an effort to get off a shot quickly, your whole timing pattern will be broken, and your successive shots may be bad. Likewise, if you have jerked the trigger because you saw a perfect sight picture and did not want to take the time necessary for a correct trigger squeeze, your rhythm will be interrupted.

Some interruptions of rhythm are unavoidable. For example, you may have to stop to change the tension of your sling, to adjust your sights, or to wait for a cloud of dust to rise from the vicinity of your target, but do not fall into the vicious habit of looking for such opportunities to deviate from the regular pattern of your shooting. Such interruptions destroy relaxation and create tension.

Up to this point we have discussed the separate and distinct elements of good marksmanship, but you should not think of the mechanics of shooting as separate movements while you are firing. Instead, you should first concentrate on the sight picture, squeeze the trigger while still watching the sight picture, and continue to watch the sight picture while you call the shot.

This is something like driving an automobile. You watch the traffic and the signals on the road ahead. When necessary, you engage the clutch and shift the gears, meanwhile steering the car. You are using your arms and legs in coordination with your mind, but you never for a moment take your eye off the road. When you do this smoothly, you have rhythm and good driving. When you do it poorly, you drive jerkily and have accidents. The same thing happens in shooting.

# Chapter 9

## ADJUSTING THE SIGHTS

### The Shot Group

If you have studied and applied the fundamental principles of taking good shooting positions, aiming accurately, breathing in a controlled manner, squeezing the trigger, and calling the shot, you are now ready to improve your skill by means of sight adjustment.

Early in your shooting career you should learn to group your shots, that is, keep them clustered together within very small areas. If you can do this, you need not worry much about the actual score you have made because it is better to have an apparently low score with a small group of shots than to have a high score based on shots that are widely separated. The reason is that a tight cluster of shots on the target indicates that you have attained some proficiency in marksmanship, whereas scattered shots show a lack of consistency that may mean you have not mastered basic principles.

However, you want to put all your shots in the bull's eye. To do this, you must learn to move your shot group so that the center of the group will be at the center of the bull's eye. This is accomplished by adjusting the sights up and down and right and left.

### Basic Principles of Sight Adjustment

The center of impact is the center of the group of shots on the target. The purpose of adjusting the sights is to change the rear sight so that the center of impact will be moved to the center of the bull's eye. When the center of impact coincides with the center of the

87

bull's eye, all of your shots will group evenly around the exact center of the bull's eye.

You must know two things about sight adjustment. First, you must decide how much adjustment is needed. Second, you must be able to apply this adjustment to the rear sight of the particular rifle you are firing.

The rear sight is moved up or down to adjust in elevation. It is moved right or left to adjust in windage. You can move a shot group right or left, and you can move it up or down. You cannot move it diagonally. Figure 1 is a drawing of a target. A group of ten shots is located low and to the left of the bull's eye. If you move your rear sight to the right and raise it the correct amount, you should place this group of ten shots with the center of the group at the center of the bull's eye, as shown by the group in the center of this target.

### ADJUSTING THE SIGHTS

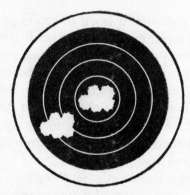 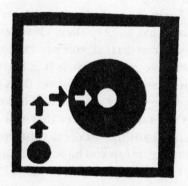

Fig. 1. Shot groups on a target. *National Rifle Association of America.*

Fig. 2. A shot group low and to the left is moved to the center. *National Rifle Association of America.*

The general rule for sight adjustment is to move the rear sight in the direction in which the center of impact is to be moved. When you want to raise the center of impact, raise the rear sight. When you want to lower the center of impact, lower the rear sight. When you want to make the shots move to the right, move the rear sight to the right. When you want to make the shots move to the left, move the rear sight to the left. As soon as you fire a few shots and adjust your sights, you will see how very easy this is. Figure 2 indicates how a group low and to the left is moved to the center.

## Micrometer-Type Rear Sights

A micrometer-type rear sight has one threaded shaft for vertical adjustments and another for horizontal adjustments. These adjustments are made by turning knurled knobs, which control the elevation and windage screws. This type of sight gets its name from

Fig. 3. The Redfield Olympic micrometer receiver sight. *Redfield Gun Sight Co.*

the micrometer, an instrument used for taking very small measurements. A micrometer-type aperture rear sight, such as the Redfield Olympic micrometer receiver sight illustrated in Figure 3, can be accurately adjusted for precision shooting, either on the target range or in the field. Figure 4 is a top view of the same sight.

A Redfield micrometer rear sight for Winchester models 54 and 70, Remington models 721 and 722, and most bolt-action high-power rifles is illustrated in Figure 5. A hunting receiver sight suitable for Springfield, Newton, Mauser, Enfield, and model-30 Remington rifles is illustrated in Figure 6. Figure 7 shows sighting disks, which are screwed into the rear sight to provide a variation of outside diameter and also a choice of aperture sizes. The latter is important because a small aperture in the rear sight permits a "finer" sight, while a large aperture makes it possible to pick up the target quicker.

Fig. 4. Top view of Redfield Olympic micrometer sight.    *Redfield Gun Sight Co.*

In order to adjust micrometer sights, we must understand a few
simple terms. A minute of angle, called a minute for short, is a
standard degree of adjustment, which will make a difference of one
inch at a distance of one hundred yards in the location of the shots
on a target. At any other distance the same ratio holds true. For
example, at fifty yards, which is one half the above distance, a minute
of angle will make a difference of one half-inch. Likewise, at one
fifth the distance (20 yards), the difference is one-fifth inch.

On the official targets of the National Rifle Association of America

### ADJUSTING THE SIGHTS

Fig. 5. Another micrometer rear
sight.    *Redfield Gun Sight Co.*

Fig. 6. A micrometer hunting rear sight. *Redfield Gun Sight Co.*

Fig. 7. Sighting disks. *Redfield Gun Sight Co.*

(abbreviated N.R.A.), the rings are one minute of angle apart. Thus, on a fifty-foot target, the rings are one sixth of an inch apart. Therefore, if the center of a shot group is in the seven ring directly under the center of the target (at six o'clock according to the vertical clock face), the shot group must be moved three rings, three sixths of an inch, or three minutes straight up.

If a group is both low and to the right, in the seven ring at five o'clock, it must first be raised until even with the ten ring, which requires about three minutes of elevation, and then it must be moved to the left until it gets into the ten ring, requiring three minutes of left windage.

The sight-adjustment knobs on micrometer rear sights turn screws in a manner similar to the turning of an ordinary screw with a screwdriver. To raise a sight, unscrew it by turning it to the left; to lower it, screw it down by turning it to the right. If right and left directions are not clear to you, simply remember that you turn in a clockwise direction to lower the sight and turn in a counterclockwise direction to raise the sight.

Most micrometer target sights have scales with pointers to indicate adjustments in elevation or windage. The scales may be divided by lines indicating minutes, and the knobs may be divided into smaller units, such as half minutes, quarter minutes, or even eighth minutes. When you turn the adjusting knob, you hear a definite click and can actually feel the spot where the click is heard. For example, if your sight is graduated in quarter minutes, you can adjust the sight one minute without looking at it by turning the adjusting knob in the proper direction through four clicks.

If you were firing at the target shown in Figure 8, you would move the shot group to the left and upward into the center of the bull's eye by adjusting the knob six clicks up in elevation and four clicks to the left on the windage adjustment to get into the ten ring.

Fig. 8. The group to the right and low is moved to the center. *National Rifle Association of America.*

## The Zero of the Rifle

The zero of a rifle for any particular range is the setting the rear sight must have in both elevation and windage in order that all of your shots may hit the center of the bull's eye on a normal day when there is no wind. In other words, the zero is the normal sight adjustment, but it applies only to one rifle. Another rifle might require an entirely different sight adjustment for the same range and under the same conditions.

For example, you might fire three or four shots with a .22-caliber rifle at fifty feet with your windage and elevation scales at dead center. Assuming that there is no wind, you might expect that all of these shots should be in the center of the bull's eye. Instead, you find that they are grouped in the six ring at seven oclock. In order to bring the group into the ten ring, you must first raise it until it is even with the ten ring, using about three minutes of elevation, and then move it to the right until it actually gets into the ten ring, using three minutes of right windage. Therefore, under ideal conditions, you will hit the bull's eye with three minutes of right windage and three minutes up elevation on your rear sight. That adjustment is the zero of your own rifle at a range of fifty feet. It will not be the zero for some other distance or for some other rifle.

## Using Crude Sights

Some low-price rifles are equipped with crude open sights that do not have a micrometer adjustment. Such rifles are not suitable for target marksmanship unless the crude sights are replaced with micrometer sights. However, it is possible to apply the same general principles in adjusting crude sights as in adjusting precision sights. Thus, if a shot is low, the rear sight is raised; if the shot is to the right, the rear sight is moved to the left. This trial-and-error method of adjustment will obtain fairly satisfactory results, but it wastes ammunition and never approaches a high degree of accuracy.

Some shooters who have rifles equipped with crude sights make the mistake of trying to compensate for errors of elevation and windage by varying their aim. For example, if the first shot is high and to the left, the shooter will aim with the top of his front sight lower than it was before and slightly to the right. He might hit the bull's eye, but it would be an accident, and he cannot repeat the same accident because he has no way of knowing exactly how he should aim to make up for the deficiencies of the sights.

## Setting Micrometer Sights with Movable Scales

Most target sights are of the micrometer type and have movable scales. Having determined your zero for any particular range, you can move the scales so that they correspond to your normal setting in elevation and windage. For example, if you find that the zero for a .22-caliber rifle at fifty feet is three minutes right windage and two minutes up elevation, you can move the scales accordingly and then have dead-center readings for that range. Sight settings for longer ranges may be found by determining the zero at each range as before, or you can obtain the approximate settings from tables prepared by the manufacturers of firearms and ammunition. However, the settings obtained from such tables are never as satisfactory as those you determine for yourself by firing the rifle.

As suggested before, if your rifle does not have movable scales, you must either memorize or record the zero for each range and then apply the indicated adjustments according to the range.

## The Flight Path of the Bullet

The line of sight from the muzzle to the target is a straight line, but the flight path of the bullet from the muzzle to the target is a curve caused by the pull of gravity. Since the force of gravity pulls a bullet down more as the distance from the muzzle increases, you must raise your rear sight more and more as the range becomes greater.

Figure 9 is the trajectory diagram for M2 armor-piercing ammunition fired from a U. S. rifle, caliber .30, model 1903 (Springfield). The trajectory is plotted for various ranges up to and including 1,000 yards. The letter H for each trajectory (flight path) represents the maximum ordinate, that is, the highest point of trajectory for that range.

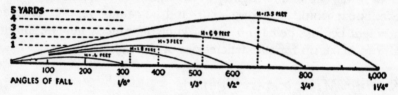

Fig. 9. Trajectory diagram for M2 armor-piercing ammunition.

Figure 10 is a trajectory diagram for regular .22 long-rifle cartridges with a muzzle velocity of 1,100 feet per second. Figure 11 is a trajectory diagram for high-speed .22 long-rifle cartridges with a muzzle velocity of 1,400 feet per second. In these two diagrams the letter M is the muzzle of the rifle, T is the target, the straight line from M to T is the base line, and the curved line is the trajectory or path of the bullet in flight. The letter S represents the height of the front sight above the axis of the bore of the rifle. The straight line from S to L is the line of aim.

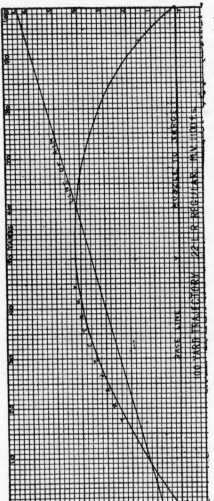

Fig. 10. Trajectory diagram for regular .22 long rifle cartridges. *Sporting Arms and Ammunition Manufacturers' Institute.*

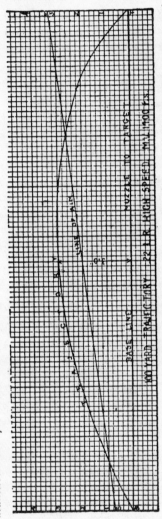

Fig. 11. Trajectory diagram for high-speed .22 long rifle cartridges. *Sporting Arms and Ammunition Manufacturers' Institute.*

Each one of the tiny squares in Figures 10 and 11 represents one yard in a horizontal direction and one-fifth inch in a vertical direction. The heavier black lines occur at intervals of five yards horizontally and one inch vertically. By referring to these diagrams and then adjusting your sights, you can improve your skill with a .22-caliber rifle either at the target range or in the field.

| Range in Yards | Angles of Elevation in Minutes | |
| --- | --- | --- |
| | .22 Long-Rifle Cartridge, Regular Velocity | .22 Long-Rifle Cartridge, High Speed |
| 25 | 3.4 | 2.3 |
| 50 | 7.1 | 4.7 |
| 100 | 15.1 | 10.5 |
| 150 | 23.8 | 17.2 |
| 200 | 33.0 | 24.6 |
| 250 | 43.2 | 32.6 |
| 300 | 53.7 | 41.3 |

Fig. 12. Angles of elevation for .22 long rifle cartridges, regular velocity; and .22 long rifle cartridges, high speed.

Figure 12 is a table giving the number of minutes a sight must be raised for increases of range (measured in yards) for the .22-caliber long-rifle cartridge of regular velocity and also for the .22-

| Range in Yards | Angles of Elevation in Minutes |
| --- | --- |
| 100 | 2.4 |
| 200 | 5.2 |
| 300 | 8.2 |
| 400 | 11.7 |
| 500 | 15.8 |
| 600 | 20.6 |
| 700 | 26.5 |
| 800 | 33.0 |
| 900 | 41.0 |
| 1,000 | 50.3 |

Fig. 13. Angles of elevation for .30-06 M2 ammunition.

caliber long-rifle cartridge of high velocity (high speed), assuming that standard factory loads are used.

Figure 13 is a table giving the number of minutes a sight must be raised for increases of range (measured in yards) for the .30-06 M2 ammunition, using factory loads.

These tables are only guides to sight setting. You must find your own zero for your own rifle at each range, using the table merely to save time and ammunition by selecting an approximate zero for the first shot at each range.

## The Effect of the Wind

The wind may deflect the bullet from its straight (although curved when viewed from the side) course between the muzzle and the target. Also, it may move the bullet up and down. Thus, a wind from the right will carry the bullet to the left, causing it to strike on the left side of the target. Wind blowing toward you may very slightly increase the resistance offered by the air to the flight of the bullet and cause it to hit lower on the target. Wind blowing toward the target from the firing line may very slightly decrease the air resistance and cause the bullet to hit a little higher. However the upward or downward movement of the bullet is seldom an important factor in marksmanship except at very long ranges, but the right or left movement is often observed at comparatively short distances.

## Wind Direction

The horizontal clock system is used in describing the direction of the wind, as illustrated in Figure 14. The firing point, where the shooter is located, is considered the center of an imaginary clock face. The target is at twelve o'clock. A three-o'clock wind would come directly from the right. A six-o'clock wind would come directly from the rear. A nine-o'clock wind would come directly from the left. In the illustration, the wind is blowing from two o'clock.

Winds from three and nine o'clock cause the greatest sideward deviation. Winds from two, four, eight, and ten o'clock have about seven eighths of the sideward force of three-and nine-o'clock winds of the same velocity. Winds from one, five, seven, and eleven o'clock

ADJUSTING THE SIGHTS

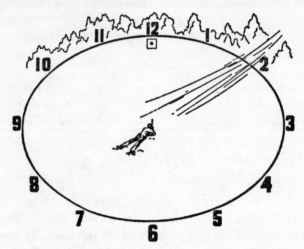

Fig. 14. The horizontal clock system.    *O. F. Moss-berg & Sons, Inc.*

have about one half the sideward effect of winds from three and nine o'clock.

## Wind Velocity

When you fire outdoors, especially at long ranges, you must estimate wind velocity in miles per hour and determine the wind direction according to the horizontal clock system. Watch for changes in the force and direction of the wind even though you are busy firing. Observe the smoke rising from chimneys, clothes hanging on a line, the danger flags of a rifle range, the smoke from a locomotive, or the effect of the wind on leaves or dirt thrown into the air.

If there is very little drift to the smoke from a fire, and if you can barely feel a slight breeze on your cheek, the wind is blowing at a velocity of about three miles an hour. Actually, you may not be able to feel the breeze on your face at all at that velocity, but when it reaches a velocity of about five miles an hour, it becomes apparent. At ten miles an hour, leaves are blown steadily along the ground and lightweight flags are beginning to be extended from their poles.

At fifteen miles an hour, dust and loose paper are raised into the air, and small loose branches are moved along the ground. At twenty miles an hour, the wind sways small bushes and trees, it tries to take your hat off, and the experienced shooters cease firing until the wind dies down.

## Formulas for Wind Compensation

When the direction and velocity of the wind are known, you can adjust your sights. The formulas that follow give the number of minutes of angle of lateral (sideward) sight adjustment required to compensate for the wind, but they are for winds blowing from two, three, four, eight, nine, and ten o'clock. If the wind blows from one, five, seven, or eleven o'clock, divide by 2. Do not use these formulas for a six-o'clock or a twelve-o'clock wind.

FORMULA FOR .22 LONG-RIFLE CARTRIDGES

$$\frac{\text{Range in yards} \times \text{wind velocity in m.p.h.}}{250} = \text{Minutes of angle}$$

Example: The wind is from 4 o'clock. The range is 50 yards. The velocity is 20 miles per hour. Hence:

$$\frac{50 \times 20}{250} = 4, \text{ hence 4 minutes right windage is required.}$$

The correction is to the right because a 4-o'clock wind is from the right and tends to blow the bullet to the left.

FORMULA FOR .30-06 RIFLE CARTRIDGES

$$\frac{\text{Range in hundreds of yards} \times \text{wind velocity in m.p.h}}{10} = \text{Minutes}$$

of angle

Example: The wind is from 3 o'clock. The range is 400 yards. The velocity is 20 miles per hour. Hence:

$$\frac{4 \times 20}{10} = 8,$$ hence 8 minutes right windage is required.

The correction is to the right because the wind is from the right and tends to blow the bullet to the left.

## Mirage

A mirage, in the usual sense of the word, is an optical effect, such as that sometimes seen on the ocean or on plains and deserts. The reflected image is seen, usually inverted, although the real object may not be in sight.

In shooting, mirage refers to heat waves and their effect on aiming. On a hot day the heat waves between the shooter and the target seem to lean toward the direction in which the wind is blowing. Thus, in Figure 15, the solid black bull's eye is the true bull's eye, whereas the shaded object is the way the bull's eye looks to the shooter when the heat waves are leaning toward the right. In this case, the wind is blowing from left to right across the range.

When there is mirage, the bull's eye will not seem perfectly round to you but will be elongated and slanting with the heat waves. You may unconsciously aim under the apparent center instead of aiming under the true center, thus placing your shots to one side of the bull's eye. Knowing that mirage exists, you can exercise care in aiming.

Fig. 15. The effect of mirage. *National Rifle Association of America.*

A B

## The Effect of Light

Wind, light, and mirage have very little effect on marksmanship with the .22-caliber rifle at a range of fifty feet, which is the usual distance at which beginners fire. Also, in firing the .30-06 cartridge in the U. S. rifle, caliber .30, model of 1903, at five hundred yards or less, the effect of weather conditions may be disregarded except for the wind.

However, the effect of light should not be disregarded. If light comes from one side and not from the other, it has the same general effect as wind from that side, although to a smaller extent. This is because the side of the front sight toward the light is more clearly defined and is unconsciously held under the center of the bull's eye, thus causing the bullet to strike away from the direction of the light.

If you are shooting a .22-caliber rifle, you can almost always disregard the effect of light at one side, but in firing the .30-06, you may find under some conditions that you will need to allow as much as one-quarter point on the U. S. rifle, model 1903, or one click on the model 1903A3.

In making this small allowance, the sight is moved toward the main source of light, whether it be the sun on an outdoor range or some source of artificial light on an indoor range.

In Figure 16, there is even light from both sides, all of the sight is visible and the hold is correct for a center shot. In Figure 17,

Fig. 16. There is even light on both sides. *National Rifle Association of America.*

Fig. 17. There is a strong light from the left. *National Rifle Association of America.*

there is strong light from the left, the left side of the sight is more prominent, the bull's eye is centered over the visible portion of the sight, and the shot would hit to the right.

## Rear Sights of Military Rifles

The rear sight of the U. S. rifle, caliber .30, model of 1903, is adjustable for windage, and the drift of the bullet to the right (caused by the rifling) is offset automatically by the construction of the rear sight leaf. The leaf is graduated from 100 to 2,850 yards. The lines extending across one or both branches of the leaf are 100-yard divisions, the longer of the short lines representing 50-yard and the shorter lines 25-yard divisions. The drift slide, which may be moved up or down on the leaf, has notches called open sights and a circular hole called the peep sight. With the leaf raised to the vertical position, the lines on either side of the peep sight and the lower notch enable the drift slide to be set accurately at any desired graduation on the leaf. When the leaf is folded down and the battle-sight notch (a V-shaped notch) in the slide cap is used, the sights are then set for 547 yards in this down position of the slide. Figure 18 shows the sight in the raised position.

The Springfield rifle has been made with several different features. For example, the M1903A3 rifle is equipped with a ramp sight consisting of a base, windage yoke, slide aperture, spring, and windage index knob, as shown in Figure 19. The range scale on the windage yoke is marked in 50-yard graduations. With the thumb and forefinger, the slide aperture can be moved up and down this scale for various ranges. Turn the windage index knob to move the yoke to the right or left to allow for windage. Each click represents a change of 1 minute of angle or a horizontal change of impact of approximately 1 inch for each 100 yards of range. Each division or mark on the windage scale represents 4 minutes of angle or a change in the point of impact of 4 inches at a range of 100 yards.

Fig. 18. The rear sight of the Springfield rifle.

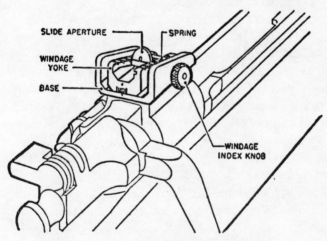

Fig. 19. The rear sight of the M1903A3 rifle.

# Chapter 10

## RAPID FIRE

### Rapid-Fire Technique

Everything that you have previously learned in slow fire is applied in rapid fire. It is very important that you understand that the aim and the trigger squeeze are the same as in slow fire. Time is gained by getting into your shooting position quickly, by working the bolt rapidly, by reloading the magazine quickly and without false motions, and by keeping your eyes on the target while you are working the bolt.

The importance of correct rapid-fire training for hunting and military shooting cannot be too strongly emphasized. This phase of instruction is often neglected. In rapid fire, you do not sacrifice accuracy for rapidity. By means of careful training, accurate fire becomes more and more rapid until you have acquired the ability to fire from 10 to 15 accurate shots per minute, but you should not attempt to fire more than 10 shots per minute until you have had long training on the rifle range and have become an experienced shot.

If you have not acquired a smooth rhythm for firing slow fire, your rapid fire will not produce the scores you have a right to expect, hence it becomes necessary for you to return to fundamental marksmanship principles and perfect your slow fire before you can progress further.

The champion rifle shooters usually fire each shot in about the same time whether they are firing rapid or slow fire. The time limits for official record practice allow about four to six seconds for each shot. If an experienced shooter takes six seconds to fire one shot at slow fire, he merely speeds up his loading procedure, he fires from the magazine of his rifle instead of firing it as a single-loader, and he economizes on time between shots. In addition, if he has been in the habit of looking at the target through a spotting telescope between shots at slow fire, he drops this step and waits until the end of the rapid-fire string to obtain his score and grouping. In other words, the expert regards rapid fire as a series of slow-fire shots tied together by short intervals and smooth timing.

Getting into position quickly is one important means of saving time in rapid fire. Practice getting into the prone, sitting, and kneeling positions from the standing position without false motions and in such a manner that when you are in position your rifle is pointing toward the bull's eye almost automatically. This seems impossible when you begin to practice positions, but after a little experience you will be pleasantly surprised to find that you can get into a comfortable position with your rifle pointing toward the bull's eye without difficulty.

Keep your eyes on the target constantly. You can do this only if you make a fixed habit of getting into position quickly. This procedure somewhat resembles driving an automobile. You watch the road ahead even while you are shifting gears and steering.

Practice dry firing. Get into position and simulate actual firing, working your bolt, changing the magazine, and doing all the other things you have previously learned, just as though you were firing cartridges. Perform each step correctly and always execute each motion in the same manner to establish proper habits.

Do not fuss around on any operation and lose time that will cause you to slight the next step in order to save time. If you can go through all the motions of rapid fire accurately and rapidly, you will soon forget that they are separate steps and will concentrate on aligning the sights with the bull's eye and calling your shots. Accuracy of individual motions comes first, then smoothness of operation, and finally speed.

In conducting rapid fire, the instructor or range officer will give the command, "Load and lock." You load the rifle and place the safety in the safe position. The next command is, "Ready on the

right? Ready on the left?" If you are not ready, call, "Not ready on
———," giving the number of your firing point. If everyone is ready,
the command, "Ready on the firing line!" is given. You move your
safety to the fire position and start firing as soon as your target is
completely visible. Do not start firing until the target is fully raised
or you will lower your score.

## Trigger Squeeze in Rapid Fire

In rapid fire, you squeeze the trigger exactly as you do in slow
fire. Exert a steadily increasing pressure upon the trigger until the
shot is fired. Breathe between shots. Do not try to hold your breath
while firing several shots because if you do the last shots of the series
will be poor. If you find that you have what seems like an irresistible
urge to hold your breath for several shots, count the shots aloud to
yourself as you fire them. Thus, after the first shot, say one; after
the second shot, say two; etc. Counting causes you to take a new
breath for each shot.

## Working the Bolt

In order to work the bolt properly, divide the operation into four
separate motions, thus: (1) raise the bolt handle; (2) pull the bolt
back; (3) push the bolt forward; and (4) turn the handle down. You
must use some muscular effort to do this properly because the bolt
must be pulled completely back to extract and eject the fired cartridge, and it must be pushed completely forward to feed a fresh
cartridge into the chamber and close the breech. However, in spite
of the force and precision of your movements, you must regard
bolt operation as a single, smooth, quick manipulation.

In theory, it is desirable to keep the rifle pointing toward the bull's
eye. However, most experts obtain a smoother and more rapid bolt
operation by lowering the muzzle and quickly canting the rifle to
the right to open the bolt. They then return the rifle to its normal
firing position at the exact instant that the bolt is closed, thus help-
ing the forward motion of the bolt.

Do not look into the chamber while you are working the bolt
because this slows up your bolt operation, causes you to lose your

own target, and may result in your firing on the wrong target. Keep your eyes on your target, and you will not be able to gaze into the chamber.

A bolt-operation exercise is an excellent means of acquiring a smooth and rapid bolt operation. Tie the trigger back to the trigger guard in order to cause the bolt action to be the same as it is when the trigger is squeezed. If the trigger is not thus tied, the rifle will remain cocked when the bolt is closed, and the amount of force required to raise the bolt again will be less than when actually firing or simulating firing.

Practice this bolt-operation exercise in all shooting positions, and do not consider yourself proficient until you can operate the bolt at least twenty times in twenty seconds while you are in the prone position.

## Reloading

In rapid fire, you fire several shots from one clip (magazine), remove the clip, reload with another clip, and fire the contents of that clip. You must practice reloading until you can do this easily, smoothly, and quickly. Time spent in reloading is part of the time allowed for firing the entire string, hence any delay subtracts from the time available for shooting.

The first step in mastering reloading is to learn the loading system of your own rifle. Having done this, obtain dummy cartridges and practice reloading, paying close attention to your bolt operation and timing exercises explained before.

If you have a U. S. rifle, caliber .30, model 1903 (Springfield), you load from a clip by placing one end of a loaded clip into its seat in the receiver. With the fingers of your right hand under the rifle against the floor plate and the base of your thumb on the powder space of the top cartridge near the clip, press the cartridges down with the thumb into the magazine with a firm, steady push until the top cartridge is caught by the right edge of the receiver. The empty clip is removed with the right hand and thrown out of the way.

After loading the magazine, to place a round in the chamber, close the bolt. As the bolt is closed the top cartridge in the magazine is

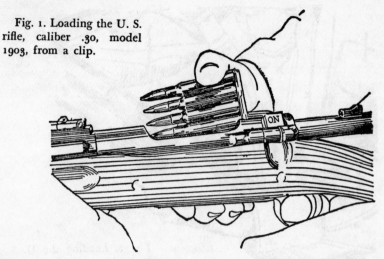

Fig. 1. Loading the U. S. rifle, caliber .30, model 1903, from a clip.

pushed forward into the chamber. Figure 1 illustrates the loading of the U. S. rifle, caliber .30, model 1903.

During your reloading exercise be sure that the cutoff is turned up so that the magazine follower will hold the bolt open when the magazine is empty. The cut-off is the small rectangular device marked "ON" in Figure 1. Count your shots as you fire or simulate firing. After the fifth shot, which is the last, bring the bolt back and reach for the second clip. Load the clip as explained above, and fire the remaining five shots of your string.

Figure 2 shows a U. S. rifle, caliber .30, model 1917, being loaded from a clip. Both this rifle and the U. S. rifle, caliber .30, model 1903, can be operated as single loaders, but for rapid fire they are loaded from clips.

In firing the U. S. rifle, caliber .30, M1 (Garand), which is a self-loading (semiautomatic) weapon, the clip itself is inserted into the magazine. As soon as the last shot is fired, the rifle automatically ejects the empty clip, the operating rod (bolt handle) is locked back, and the action remains open.

To reload the Garand, hold a loaded clip in your right hand, and place it on top of the magazine follower. Close your right hand into a fist with your thumb extended. Hold your elbow high, place the ball of your thumb on top of the clip at its forward end, about the

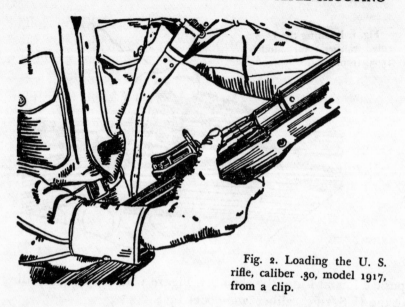

Fig. 2. Loading the U. S. rifle, caliber .30, model 1917, from a clip.

middle of the top cartridge, with your thumb pointed toward the muzzle. Then press the clip down into the receiver until it is caught by the clip latch. You must be careful to swing your thumb quickly to the right, or it will be struck by the bolt that closes as the operating rod is released. If you strike the operating rod handle with the heel of your hand, the bolt will close and lock quicker.

If you use a typical .22-caliber bolt-action rifle, the clip (magazine) is removed from the position forward of the trigger guard on the lower side of the rifle. On some .22-caliber rifles the magazine is released by pushing a button on the left; on others a knurled knob must be turned to release a catch.

Regardless of the construction of a .22-caliber bolt-action rifle, you originally load with five rounds in the magazine, remove the empty magazine during rapid fire, and insert another loaded magazine holding five rounds.

## Timing

Timing practice is difficult to manage alone. Get a friend to serve as a coach. If he is already an experienced shooter, it will be better, but even a person who knows nothing about marksmanship will be of great help to you if he makes an effort to improve your timing.

Begin by getting into one of the firing positions and aiming at a target. Pretend to fire rapid fire. Operate the bolt, hold your breath, and pretend to fire during a ten-second period, at the end of which your coach should command, "Bolt." This is the signal for you to repeat the sequence, pretending to fire a second shot. Continue until you have simulated the firing of five shots within fifty seconds.

Repeat this exercise until you become familiar with the timing of each shot and can manipulate the bolt smoothly, squeeze the trigger properly, maintain the sight picture, and call your shots, all within the ten-second period. Then cut down the time to nine seconds, then to eight, to seven, to six, and finally to five seconds.

As soon as you can simulate the firing of five shots in five seconds, practice getting into the prone, sitting, or kneeling position from a standing position as part of your timed exercise. In addition, begin to reload as soon as you have simulated the firing of the first five shots, and simulate the firing of the second clip. This will give you practice in timing the whole ten-shot string, but practice the exercise for each position until you have convinced yourself that your timing is good enough to begin firing live loads.

You will find that it requires more time to fire the first shot of each clip accurately than the remaining rounds. Therefore, allow yourself twice as much time, if you need it, for the first and sixth shots of each ten-shot string. All during these exercises, the use of dummy cartridges will add reality to the practice and make the timing more accurate.

The above instructions apply in particular to bolt-action rifles, whether .22 caliber or larger. In firing a semiautomatic rifle, such as the Garand, there is no manual bolt operation, hence shorter time intervals are possible. Begin with an interval of six seconds, cut it gradually to five, and then concentrate on a four-second interval.

The autoloading mechanism of a semiautomatic rifle depends upon the discharge of a cartridge for its functioning, hence you must instruct your coach to cock the hammer between shots by hitting the operating rod handle smartly to the rear with the heel of his hand.

## *How to Take the Prone*
## *Position Rapidly*

In preparing for rapid fire, the sequence of movements for each position is practiced slowly at first. As proficiency is acquired, speed and accuracy in assuming the positions are obtained.

In explaining how to assume the prone position we shall describe the movements in numerical order to make the sequence clear. After the sequence is learned, the position should be assumed in one continuous motion when the target appears in rapid fire or at the command, "Targets up" (commence firing), according to the orders issued by the range officer.

First assume the correct prone position and aim at the target. Mark the places for the elbows and the point on the ground just below the butt of your rifle in the firing position. Then get up, first to your knees, then to your feet, keeping your feet in place. The prone position is then assumed by the numbers in five counts as follows:

1. Being at the ready position, with sling adjusted, the left hand just below the lower band swivel (in using the Springfield rifle) and

Fig. 3. The ready position be-        Fig. 4. Dropping to the knees in
fore taking the prone position.       assuming the prone position.

the right hand at the heel of the butt, bend both knees to the ground. Figure 3 shows how you should look in the ready position. Figure 4 shows the second part of the movement when you drop to your knees.

2. Place the toe of the butt of the rifle on the ground at the point previously marked, as shown in Figure 5.

Fig. 5. Place the toe of the butt of the rifle on the ground.

3. Place the left elbow on the ground in the place previously marked, as shown in Figure 6.

Fig. 6. Place the left elbow on the ground.

4. Place the butt of the rifle against the right shoulder with the heel of the hand against the butt plate, as shown in Figure 7.

Fig. 7. Place the butt of the rifle against the right shoulder with the heel of the hand against the butt plate.

5. Grasp the small of the stock with the right hand, place the right elbow on the ground in the place previously marked, and assume the aiming position, as shown in Figure 8.

Fig. 8. Grasp the small of the stock with the right hand, place the right elbow on the ground, and assume the aiming position.

In the field, you can take the prone position rapidly after running forward by taking a short jump, landing with your feet apart, and proceeding in a manner similar to that already described.

## How to Take the Sitting
## Position Rapidly

1. To assume the sitting position rapidly, break the fall by placing the right hand on the ground to the rear of the spot upon which the buttocks are to rest.

2. Assume the correct sitting position and aim at the target. Mark and prepare the position of the heels. Mark the spot upon which the buttocks are to rest and then rise, keeping the feet in position. You are now in a ready position with the sling adjusted, as shown in Figure 9. When the target appears or when the command, "Targets up" (commence firing), is given, sit down on the marked spot, breaking the fall with the right hand, as shown in Figure 10; place the left arm in position; with the heel of the right hand on the butt plate, place the butt against the shoulder, as shown in Figure 11; grasp the small of the stock with the right hand and assume the aiming position, as shown in Figure 12. Your eye must be kept on the target throughout this exercise.

3. Another method of taking the sitting position rapidly is to take the prescribed sitting position, mark and prepare the places for the heels, then cross the left leg over the right. Rise, and stand with

Fig. 9. The ready position before taking the sitting position.

Fig. 10. Break the fall with the right hand in sitting down.

the legs crossed. Upon command or when the target appears, bend the knees and sink to the ground, uncross the legs, and place the heels in the marked places. Place the left arm in position. With the heel of the right hand on the butt plate, place the rifle butt against the right shoulder and grasp the small of the stock with the right hand. Assume the aiming position.

RAPID FIRE

Fig. 11. Place the left arm in position; with the heel of the right hand on the butt plate, place the butt against the shoulder.

Fig. 12. Grasp the small of the stock with the right hand and assume the aiming position.

## How to Take the Kneeling Position Rapidly

To take the kneeling position rapidly, assume the correct kneeling position, mark the position of the left foot and the right toe, prepare the toe hole for the right foot if required. Rise with the right toe at its marked place and the left foot in its marked place. Upon command or when the target appears, kneel with the right knee on its marked spot; place the left arm in position; with the heel of the right hand on the butt plate, place the butt to the shoulder; grasp the small of the stock with the right hand and assume the aiming position.

# Chapter 11

## FIELD MARKSMANSHIP

### The Requirements of Field Marksmanship

In hunting or in military operations the shooter must be able to estimate the distance to the target, whether it is stationary or moving, and fire his rifle in such a manner that he will hit the target. These things seem obvious, and yet they require training and experience for success.

### Methods of Range Estimation

In military service, the distance from the shooter to the target may be estimated by observing the fall of the bullets, estimation by eye, and the use of tracer bullets. In civilian life, tracer bullets are not used for hunting because the tracer is a burning composition placed in the bullet. It will set fire to grasses, bushes, and trees. Furthermore, tracers are usually loaded only in special military cartridges and are not commercially available. Therefore, hunters must depend upon either observation of fire or estimation by eye.

### Observation of Fire

Observation of fire is usually limited to dry ground where the dust will rise slightly above the striking point of the bullet. Sometimes it will succeed over wet ground where little splashes of mud and water reveal the strike of the bullet, but this is an exceptional situation.

If you depend on observation of fire over dry ground, you will learn that dust rises on the side toward which the wind is blowing. Thus, if the wind is blowing from left to right across your front, dust will rise to the right of the point where the bullet hits.

A companion hunting with you who is to one side will think that shots that are hitting beyond the target are striking toward his side of the target. Shots that are really hitting short of the target will appear to your companion as striking toward your side of the target. Unless he knows these facts, he will tell you to shoot to the right or left when he should be telling you to raise or lower your sights.

Having observed the fall of the bullets, you can change your sights if the game is not moving too fast, but if you are in a hurry there is nothing to do but to change your point of aim, that is, aim over or under or to the right or left of the target, but a hit under such conditions is problematical.

## Eye Estimation

If you attempt to estimate the range to a target without previous training and experience, it is certain that your estimation will be at least 15 per cent over or under. For example, if you estimate that the distance is 600 yards, it is reasonably certain that the range is actually somewhere between 510 yards and 690 yards. This probability of error is based on statistics compiled by the U. S. Army over a long period of time and applies to the average man. If you are a genius, you might be able to estimate distances right on the nose without training, but the odds are that you will guess wrong and miss the target if you set your sights accordingly.

Begin the study of eye estimation by measuring one hundred yards on level ground. Walk in your usual manner over this course, and divide 3,600 inches by the number of steps you take. The answer is your pace in inches. Repeat this several times until you are sure that you know your average pace for level ground. Repeat the process uphill and downhill to get your average pace for hilly country.

When you know your pace, go into rough country and estimate the range to various objects. Pace the distance to each object and compare your estimation with your paced distance.

It is advisable to become familiar with a mental unit of measurement. The best unit for most purposes is one hundred yards. Learn how this distance appears over flat and hilly country, downhill and across valleys. Check your estimations by pacing.

A handy method of measuring long distances is mentally to divide the distance in two, and split it again, thus having a distance to estimate that is only one fourth the whole. Estimate the distance and multiply by four.

If you are hunting with a companion who has had the same training, get him to form estimates of distances independently of you and then average your estimates. This will increase your accuracy.

## Eye Estimation by Subtending

Another form of visual range estimation is subtending. To subtend is to extend under or be opposite to, as, for example, a chord subtends an arc. This appears difficult at first glance, but it is very easy if you try it.

Fasten a ruler horizontally to a stick driven in the ground at a distance of one hundred yards. Aim at the ruler and observe how much of the ruler is covered by the width of the front sight, how much is covered by the width of the rear sight, and how much is covered by the width of the rifle barrel. Knowing these things, you can estimate range.

Thus, if the rear sight of your rifle covers only half the width at an unknown distance, the range is fifty yards. If it covers twice as much width, the range is two hundred yards, etc. This method is not limited to using parts of the rifle. It will apply to the width of a finger or the whole hand, or any other object which can be held before the eyes. It is even better if you have a telescopic sight made with horizontal crosswires marked off in divisions for this very purpose.

If there is no hurry about firing a shot, estimate the range first by the ordinary eye-estimation method, then with the subtending method, average the estimates, and you should have a close estimate.

There is another variation of eye estimation that is sometimes helpful. Compare the height of objects like fence posts, cornstalks, cows, horses, etc., with the height of the front sight at various ranges. Then, when you go hunting, try to compare the height of wild animals with the height of the front sight to get the range. Like the other methods, this one requires practice to approach accuracy.

## The Appearance of Objects at a Distance

In hunting, the ground is seldom perfectly flat for great distances except in certain sections of the United States, and even in the prairie and desert country much of the ground is broken by bushes, growing crops, and ditches. Under these conditions, the appearance of objects at a distance must be understood in estimating the range.

Objects seem closer: (1) when the object is in a bright light; (2) when the color of the object contrasts sharply with the color of the background; (3) when the hunter is looking over water, snow, a wheat field, or any uniform surface; (4) when the hunter is looking down from a height; (5) in the clear atmosphere of high altitudes; and (6) when the hunter is looking over a depression, most of which is hidden.

Objects seem more distant: (1) when the hunter is looking over a depression most of which is visible; (2) when there is a poor light or a fog; (3) when only a small part of the object is revealed; and (4) when the hunter is looking from low ground toward higher ground.

## The Appearance of Game Animals and Birds

Know the size, shape, and color of the animals and birds you wish to shoot. These factors vary according to the season and the locality. For example, rabbits and hares vary in length from eight inches to twenty-five inches in different parts of the United States; they vary in size and shape according to their age and physical development; and they vary in color more than most hunters realize, not only from one species to another, but also according to the season. A knowledge of these factors helps to find game and estimate its range.

# Chapter 12

## MOVING TARGETS AND FANCY SHOOTING

### Lead or Forward Allowance

In order to hit a moving target, it is necessary to aim a distance ahead of it and on its projected path so that the target and the bullet will meet at the same time and place. This distance is known as the lead or forward allowance. A lead must be applied in all firing except when the target is at an extremely close range, when it is diving directly at the shooter, or flying directly from him.

### Determination of Lead

The lead necessary to hit any moving target depends upon: (1) the speed of the target, (2) the range to the target, (3) the time of flight of the bullet, and (4) the direction of flight of the target with respect to the line of fire.

When a moving target suddenly appears, it is impossible for you to consider all of the above factors and compute accurately the lead required to hit the target. Therefore, you must determine leads in advance for the kind of targets you expect to hit and under the conditions that you expect to prevail.

### Application of Lead

Although the lead is determined originally in feet or yards, it is applied in the field in terms of target lengths. It is very difficult for you to estimate with any degree of accuracy a lead such as five or ten yards when the target is several hundred yards away. Therefore, you should train yourself to apply the length of the target, as it appears to you, along the projected path of the target to determine where to aim for each shot. Thus, you may lead a deer one half or one fourth of its length, or some other distance, with the deer's apparent length as the unit of measurement.

For example, let us imagine that we suddenly see a deer at a distance we estimate to be 200 yards. He is moving straight across our front at a speed we estimate to be 30 miles per hour. Also, we estimate that he is about five feet from his nose to his tail. The problem is to calculate how far to fire in front of him to kill him.

The rifle we are using is the U.S. rifle, caliber .30, model 1903. We are firing a cartridge that has a muzzle velocity of about 2,700 feet per second, but the velocity falls off as the distance from the muzzle increases, and we know from consulting a table supplied by the cartridge manufacturer that at a range of 200 yards it will take one fourth of a second for the bullet to reach a target.

The deer is running at a speed of 30 miles an hour. This is the same as 44 feet per second. In one-fourth second, the time that it takes for our bullet to travel 200 yards, the deer will have moved one-fourth of 44 feet, or 11 feet. Since the deer is assumed to be 5 feet long, we must lead the deer a little more than twice his length to hit him. Therefore, we aim in front of the deer a distance we believe to be slightly more than twice his length, fire the rifle, and hope we hit him.

It is obvious that hitting the deer on the nose will not kill him. If we decide that a bullet behind the shoulder will bring him down, that is our aiming point, and we therefore aim slightly more than twice his length in front of him, measured from the aiming point behind the shoulder.

## The Swing and Follow-Through

Assuming that the target is a deer running across our front, moving from left to right, begin to swing the muzzle of your rifle to the right at exactly the same speed as that at which the deer is moving. While you are swinging, get your rifle on your shoulder without changing your speed of swing in the slightest, and give the rifle enough lead to provide for the time it takes the bullet to travel from the muzzle to the target.

Meanwhile, you must start taking up any slack in the trigger and complete the trigger squeeze while the rifle is in full motion, traveling at the same speed as the deer, but leading the deer by the required forward allowance.

It is important to begin the swing at the same instant that you start to put your rifle on your shoulder. If you begin to mount your rifle first, and then start to swing, you must swing faster than the speed of the deer to catch up with it, pass it, and obtain the necessary lead. At that instant, you will be swinging your rifle faster than the deer is running, hence you must slow up in order to be swinging at the same speed that the deer is running. This involves two separate operations and wastes both time and energy.

Even after you have squeezed the trigger and fired the shot, continue the swing at the same speed and along the same path as before. This is known as the follow-through and is used in golf, tennis, baseball, swimming, and every other sport. If you stop the swing as soon as you squeeze the trigger, you will probably miss the deer because the deer continues to run after you have squeezed the trigger.

## The Standing Position in the Field

You will fire most of your shots at moving targets from a standing position, but it will not be the standing position of the rifle range. Instead, you will spread your feet farther apart to permit a freer swing from your hips, you will lean forward slightly, and you will face more directly toward your target.

The manner in which you hold your rifle will be different, too. You will extend your left arm farther forward, your left elbow may not be directly under the rifle as it is on the range, and you will probably have your right elbow lower than the usual target position. With these exceptions, you will apply all of the fundamentals of marksmanship learned on the range except that your sight picture may vary slightly.

There is room for argument on this subject, but some of the best shooters insist that in firing at moving targets you should place the front sight directly over the spot you wish to hit instead of holding the top of the front sight directly under and touching the bottom of the bull's eye. Personally, the author has always used the same sight picture in hunting as on the rifle range. Your own experience will soon tell you which is better for your own shooting.

## Safety Precautions in Shooting Moving Targets

All of the safety rules are in full effect in shooting moving targets. Do not mistake a cow for a deer, and if some hunter is wearing a coonskin hat, do not fire as soon as you see the fur. If you are hunting deer, remember that your bullets will kill men at a great distance, and be sure that there is some hill or other safe backstop to catch the bullets. For your own protection, be sure that the bullets will not strike a rock or a hard tree, glance off, and hit you or one of your companions.

## Swinging Targets

In shooting swinging targets, beginners make the mistake of following the target back and forth with the rifle. The correct method is to catch the swinging target at one end of the swing or the other, that is, at the point where it reverses direction, as shown in Figure 1, where the letter X indicates the point of aim.

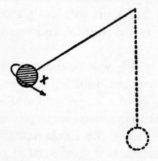

Fig. 1. Hit a moving target at the point where it reverses direction. *Winchester Repeating Arms Co.*

Fig. 2. Fire two shots at the bottom bottle to break both before the upper bottle falls to the ground. *Winchester Repeating Arms Co.*

## Breaking Bottles

A spectacular exhibition stunt is to place one bottle on top of another, step back about thirty feet, break the bottom bottle, and then break the top bottle before it falls to the ground. The trick in this is to fire two shots in rapid succession at the bottom bottle. Your aim must be accurate and rapid, or this will fail. Be sure that no one is endangered by flying glass. Figure 2 shows the bottles in position before firing.

## Shooting with a Card
## Over the Muzzle

A trick that is mystifying to most observers is to shoot with a card over the muzzle, as shown in Figure 3. Take a fairly stiff card three or four inches wide and about three or four inches long (a playing card or a calling card will do), cut a hole in the center large enough to slip it over the muzzle, and place it over the muzzle and up against the front sight, but do not bend it back over the sight. Keep both eyes open. You will then see both the target and your sights, and if you are accustomed to shooting with both eyes open, it will be easy to hit targets whether they are stationary or moving.

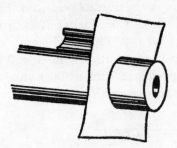

Fig. 3. If you keep both eyes open, you can hit targets with a card in front of the front sight.   *Winchester Repeating Arms Co.*

## Shooting Pictures

The first step in learning to shoot pictures is to learn how to draw pictures with dots. Start with very simple outline sketches and practice until you can draw several pictures with pencil dots very quickly. Then, using a repeating rifle, practice drawing the same pictures at close range, as shown in Figure 4. Gradually extend the range until you are at least thirty feet away from the target.

Fig. 4. Learn to shoot pictures at close range.    *Remington Arms Co., Inc.*

## Shooting with a Mirror

In order to shoot with the aid of a mirror, you must first be a reasonably good shot in the normal positions. Then practice aiming at targets with an empty rifle, facing away from the targets, and watching them in a mirror. The third step is to practice firing at bull's eyes on paper targets with the mirror. The fourth step is to fire from peculiar positions, such as over your shoulders, between your legs, over your head, etc., still using the mirror.

## Final Advice on Targets

Many men who are experts in hitting moving targets with a rifle believe that the easiest and quickest method of gaining proficiency is to learn how to hit clay targets in either skeet or trapshooting. This is explained in great detail in the author's book, *Field, Skeet and Trapshooting*. Having acquired skill with the shotgun, you can then switch to the rifle and apply what you have learned with the other weapon.

There are other experts who contend that the fundamental differences between handling a rifle and a shotgun make it very inadvisable to use a shotgun as preparation for hitting moving targets with a rifle. They correctly emphasize that a rifle is aimed whereas a shotgun is pointed. These men believe that the use of clay targets is wise, but that the shooter should do all of his practicing with a rifle.

Finally, in all fancy shooting and firing at moving targets, there is no place for the careless or inaccurate shooter. Learn how to hit the bull's eye of a paper target first and then advance to the more difficult targets.

# Chapter 13

## SIMPLIFIED BALLISTICS

### Ballistics Defined

Ballistics is the science of projectiles in motion. Interior ballistics explains what happens inside the firearm. Exterior ballistics explains what happens during the flight of the bullet from the muzzle of the rifle to the target. Forensic ballistics was a term used several years ago to describe the examination of firearms and ammunition in criminal investigation, but this is now known as firearm identification.

### Rifling

We have previously explained that rifling is a system of spiral grooves cut into the bore of a rifle to give a spin to the bullet that will give it a steady flight, nose forward, to the target. The number of grooves in a rifle varies from four to eight according to the design. These grooves are cut to depths of .002 to .006 inch, depending upon the caliber of the rifle, the relative widths of the lands and grooves, and other design factors. Remember, the lands are merely the portions of the bore left after the grooves have been cut.

The caliber of a rifle is usually designated according to the bore size before the grooves are cut, that is, it is measured between the lands and not between the grooves.

The twist is the inclination of the rifling grooves to the axis of the bore, that is, the angle the grooves make with the long dimension of the bore. The direction of twist is the direction that the grooves turn. You can see it by looking through the bore of a rifle from the breech. It may be either right or left, but most American firearms have rifling that twists to the right, the most important exception being Colt pistols and revolvers, which have a twist to the left.

The pitch is the distance that the rifling advances for each complete turn. For example, the rifling may make one complete turn in each ten inches of barrel length. Therefore, if the barrel is twenty-five inches long, the rifling makes two and one-half turns. Pitch and twist are often confused by the layman because they are closely related, but there is a distinct difference, as we have explained.

If the bullet that will be used generally in a rifle is long in proportion to its diameter, the rifling should have a quicker twist, that is, it should make a complete turn in a shorter length of the barrel in order to give the bullet a faster spin. On the other hand, if the bullet is short in proportion to its diameter, such a fast spin is not required and the rifling may have a slower twist.

## Pressure

When a cartridge is fired, the burning powder gases develop pressure in the chamber of the rifle and exert a thrust against the cartridge case, the chamber of the rifle, the bullet, and the bore of the rifle. The gases find it easier to escape by driving the bullet through the bore under normal conditions, hence the bullet leaves the muzzle and travels to the target.

If the pressure is too great, the rifle may blow up, but it must be great enough to drive the bullet through the bore and to the target, hence controlling pressure of the gas is a matter of great importance. Not only must the pressure be kept within the desired limits, but it also must be maintained reasonably uniform or the performance of the cartridges will not be consistent. All of these things require the best efforts of trained specialists in firearm and ammunition factories, but every shooter should understand something about pressure in order to make the most intelligent use of his arms and cartridges.

One of the several methods of testing pressure is by the use of a pressure gauge. A small hole is drilled through the barrel of a rifle to be tested into the chamber. A small, tight-fitting steel piston is placed in this hole. A small compression cylinder of lead or copper is placed over the piston and held in place by a steel yoke.

The rifle is then loaded with a cartridge and fired. The pressure from the burning powder gases is exerted in all directions with the same force. It drives the bullet out through the bore, but at the same time it pushes upward against the piston and compresses the copper or lead cylinder. The length of the cylinder is then measured and compared with its length before the test. The difference is an indication of the pressure in the chamber.

## Bullet Velocity

In determining bullet velocity, one method uses two photocells placed forward of the muzzle of the rifle. When a shot is fired, the first photocell closes an electric switch as the bullet goes past and starts a device that counts electric impulses. When the bullet passes the second photocell, the switch is opened and the counting stops. Since the distance between the photocells is known, it is an easy matter to compute the velocity of the bullet.

The muzzle velocity, also called initial velocity, is the speed at which the bullet travels when it leaves the muzzle of the rifle, usually given in feet per second (f.s.). As soon as the bullet leaves the muzzle it begins to lose velocity, hence the velocity that a bullet has when it hits a target is always less than the muzzle velocity.

## Point Blank Range

When people use the expression point blank range, they usually mean the distance from the muzzle at which the bullet will strike the target when the rear sight of the rifle is in its lowest position. However, this is a loose term which should be avoided by anyone who makes any pretense of understanding firearms.

## More about Trajectory

The shooter's line of sight is a straight line from his eye through both rear and front sights to the target. The line of sight is higher than the bore because the sights are above the bore. When the rifle is fired, the trajectory (flight path of the bullet) rises from the muzzle to the line of sight, crosses above the line of sight, curves over the line of sight, and finally drops to the line of sight at the target.

## Bullet Upset

The upset of a bullet is its expansion caused by the force of the powder gases at the discharge of the cartridge. When the rifle is fired, the powder gases expand and push against the base of the bullet, but the point of the bullet does not move as soon as the base, hence the base expands or upsets. This upsetting is desirable because it causes the bullet to fill the grooves of the barrel (rifling) completely and prevents the powder gases from sneaking forward around the bullet. Thus, the bullet is forced out through the bore with great speed.

## Keyholing

Keyholing is the tumbling of the bullet in flight. It may be caused by some defect in the bullet that destroys its balance, or it may be caused by the failure of the twist in the rifling to give the bullet the correct spin. If a bullet has been keyholing, it almost never strikes the target point first, hence there is a great loss of accuracy and energy.

## Sectional Density

The sectional density of a bullet is the weight compared to its diameter. If one bullet has a greater weight than another bullet of the same diameter, the first has a greater sectional density. If two bullets have the same weight, the one with the smaller diameter has more sectional density.

There is a general rule that a bullet with great sectional density has more range and penetrating power than one with less sectional density, other factors remaining the same. The reason for the rule is that a bullet of great sectional density has a smaller frontal area exposed to the resistance of the air in flight. For example, a 172-

grain, .30-caliber bullet has a greater sectional density than a 172-grain, .45-caliber bullet. The two bullets have the same weight, but the .30-caliber bullet has the smaller diameter, hence it encounters less resistance in flight and has a greater range and better penetration.

# Chapter 14

## THE .22-CALIBER
## RIFLE RANGE

### Basic Requirements

Safety is the first consideration in shooting. The easiest course for the beginner to take is to join an existing rifle club and use the facilities already in existence. There are several advantages in this. First, the range is undoubtedly safe for both the shooters and the bystanders; second, the personnel problems are largely solved, thus eliminating the difficulty of forming an efficient operating organization; and third, at a range run by a club you will meet experienced shooters who will gladly help you to progress in marksmanship.

If there is no range within easy traveling distance from your home, you can organize and operate your own. In addition to safety, which must be emphasized, the range should be attractive and accessible to your potential club members. It should be a .22-caliber range because a range for high-caliber-rifle firing requires more land, more expensive equipment, and much more elaborate safety precautions.

Of course, if you are willing to shoot by yourself, you need not worry about forming a club or building a formal range. Instead, you can fill an old packing box with sand and shoot to your heart's content in your basement. However, most people find it more fun to have some competition and the social contacts that come with organized shooting.

### An Indoor Target Range

An indoor range is sometimes called a gallery range, but this term should not be confused with the commercial shooting galleries. You can construct an indoor range anywhere that you have space at least 65 feet long to take care of the standard 50-foot indoor shooting distance. The additional 15 feet is needed for the backstop, the targets, men lying at the firing points, and enough space for a man to walk back and forth behind the firing line.

The width is determined by the number of firing points. For each firing point allow four feet, except that four and one-half feet must be allowed for the firing point at the left end of the firing line because a shooter in the prone position extends his body to the left and rear of his firing point.

Few modern homes have a basement providing 65 feet of unobstructed view, hence it may be necessary to obtain space in the basement of a municipal or county building, a school, a garage, or some other large public or commercial building. The sheriff or the chief of police will help you in finding such space if he is a publicspirited citizen.

Be sure that you do not shoot toward any doors or windows. All firing should be toward a solid masonry wall that is backed by the earth. If there are any windows or doors in front of the firing line, they must be bricked in or coverel with steel plate and permanently closed. The steel plate should be at least $\frac{1}{4}$-inch thick, but $\frac{1}{8}$-inch steel plate is satisfactory if it is faced with wood 1 inch thick. Even with these precautions, do not allow anyone to fire cartridges more powerful than the .22 long rifle.

## The Backstop

Figure 1 shows a simple backstop made by filling a packing box with sand. The box should be large enough to be filled with sand 24 inches deep and 18 inches in thickness. Remove the original boards from the front and replace with boards about 1 inch thick. The bullets will cut these boards away, and they must be replaced frequently if you do much shooting. Also it is necessary to remove the fired bullets from the sand frequently so that they will not form clusters of lead that will cause ricochets.

Figure 2 shows a semiportable backstop, which is especially desirable if the room you are using as an indoor range must be cleared

Fig. 1. A simple backstop made by filling a packing box with sand.    *National Rifle Association of America and O. F. Mossberg & Sons, Inc.*

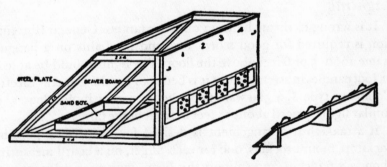

Fig. 2. A semiportable backstop.    *Sporting Arms and Ammunition Manufacturers' Institute.*

for other purposes. The framework is made of 2- x 4-inch boards, faced with a sheet of beaver board and backed by ¼-inch steel plate set at an angle of 45°. In the bottom, there is a box holding sand to a depth of 3 or 4 inches for catching the fired bullets. This sand box is simply a separate tray that can be removed when you move the backstop around. The beaver board is replaced when the bullets have cut large holes in it behind the targets. The height of the backstop is about 5 feet. The length depends upon the number of shooters. For four shooters, it should be about 9 feet long.

You might think that a wooden, stone, brick, or concrete wall behind the targets would provide all the safety that anyone could expect, but the bullets will cut holes into such construction, the lead will accumulate, and then when you fire there is a danger of ricochets.

If you have permanent possession of the room where you are establishing your range, install steel plates about 3/8 inch thick from one side of the range to the other, but have them slant backward at an angle of 45°. In front of the steel plates, lay portable wooden trays holding sand to a depth of about 6 inches. These trays should be about 5 or 6 feet wide. You need enough trays to catch the bullets from the full extent of the steel plates, but be careful that each tray is short enough so that it can be moved easily. Sift the sand frequently to remove the bullets, both for the sake of safety and to obtain the money the bullets will bring as junk.

## Lighting

It is wrong to throw light on only the targets. General illumination is required for good scores. Suspend the lights on a hanging frame about 5 or 6 feet above the floor. The lights should be at least 75 foot candles in strength, but it is better to use the General Electric Company type L-9 500-watt flood lights with stippled lenses, or similar lights, placed about 15 feet in front of the targets.

If a makeshift arrangement is desired for use with a portable backstop, mount sockets, one for each target, on a board measuring about 2 x 6 inches, and support this board with triangular wooden pieces that will hold it at a suitable angle for properly illuminating the targets, as illustrated in Figure 2. Use at least 60-watt Mazda bulbs, and tack heavy white paper or cardboard behind the lights to provide reflection. This unit is placed about 5 feet in front of the targets, but since it is portable, trial and error will determine the best distance.

It is a good idea to have indirect lighting over the firing line and the space behind the firing points, with increasingly bright lights along the range as you approach the backstop. The light on the targets should be more intense than anywhere else in the room, but there must be no sharp contrast or glare.

## Target Carriers

If your indoor range is permanent, target carriers will save labor and increase the pleasure of shooting. They are merely devices to which the paper targets are attached. At the firing point, a man turns a crank, which operates a system of wires or cables that carry a target back and forth between the firing point and the backstop. This makes it unnecessary to halt firing while someone goes forward to change targets or replace one that has come loose. Carrier systems can be bought from the Caswell Target Carriers, Anoka, Minnesota; through any large sporting goods dealer; or they can be made locally by any metalsmith.

## The Indoor Firing Line

At each firing point a numeral should be painted on the floor or on a wooden upright to correspond with the same numeral painted above the target corresponding to that firing point.

The floor is too hard for comfortable shooting. Provide some kind of a mat at each firing point. Some clubs use gymnasium mats, but they are usually too deep and soft. Second-hand single-bed mattresses are more popular, although a few experts object to a mat which is more than an inch thick.

Indicate a "ready line" by a line painted on the floor, a rope, a line of benches, a wooden rail, or some other means of showing that those not firing are to stay behind the firing line, preferably at a distance of at least 10 feet.

## Mounting Indoor Targets

In Figure 2, the targets are tacked to wooden racks with thumbtacks. Two racks are provided for each backstop so that one set of fresh targets is always in place for firing while the other set is being changed. Additional details regarding the mounting of targets are given under the discussion of outdoor ranges.

## Requirements for an Outdoor Rifle Range

The first requirement for an outdoor rifle range is a safe backstop. A steep hill makes an ideal backstop, but it must be free of rocks from which bullets might ricochet, and it should be high enough so that bullets will not pass over the top. Also, it is desirable that people and animals should not be able to approach the targets from the back or sides of the hill without being seen by the shooters. If these features are not already present, the cost of clearing the ground of trees and bushes, moving dirt and performing other work must be considered in evaluating any prospective site for a range.

The ground between the firing line and the backstop should be reasonably level, and the direction of shooting should be toward the north or northeast to avoid having the sun shining into the faces of the shooters, but the direction of fire is always secondary in importance to the necessity of having a safe backstop.

The second important requirement is accessibility. The range should be easily reached by the people who will use it, but it should not be located in a thickly populated section where the neighbors will complain about the noise or where there will be any slight possibility of people wandering across the line of fire.

The third requirement is the legal right to use the land. Waste land is often entirely suitable for a rifle range and may be obtained at a low rental rate. However, regardless of the friendliness of the owner, any agreement to use land should be in writing, and particular attention should be paid to the right of the shooters to remove any buildings they may erect on the range.

The fourth requirement is that the range be large enough to accomplish its purpose. Beginners fire at 50 feet. Most experienced .22-caliber rifle shooters fire at 50 or 100 yards. If firing is to be done at 100 yards, the range itself must be at least 110 yards long, not including the land for the backstop.

In determining the width, allow at least 5 feet for each firing point. In addition, it is advisable to allow land at each end of the firing line for paths to the backstop to be used while firing is not in progress.

## Target Butts and Frames

The cheapest and simplest arrangement of target butts and frames for .22-caliber firing consists of a row of posts about 8 feet apart in front of the backstop and horizontal wooden frames hung from hooks or nails driven into the posts. Targets are clipped or tacked to the frames. The hooks or nails in the posts are placed at two levels so that the targets are about 1½ feet from the ground for the prone, sitting, and kneeling positions; and about 5 feet, 3 inches from the ground for the standing position. At these heights, the targets are at the level of the shooter's eyes for standing and slightly higher than eye level for the other positions.

Figure 3 is a front view of a target frame, and Figure 4 is a side view of the same frame. Blank cards, the same size as targets, are placed behind the true targets. These are called backing cards or backing targets. If they are placed the proper distance behind the true targets it is possible to examine them and determine the firing point from which a crossfire shot was fired. This is a required feature of target frames for official .22-caliber rifle matches at ranges of 50 yards or more.

Although the frame shown in Figures 3 and 4 is primarily intended for outdoor ranges, the same design or a variation of it can be used under some conditions for an indoor range.

Beginners sometimes ask about the use of target carriers on an outdoor range to avoid the trouble of moving from the firing line to the butts to examine and replace targets. However, experience has shown that these devices are practicable only on the 50-foot indoor range.

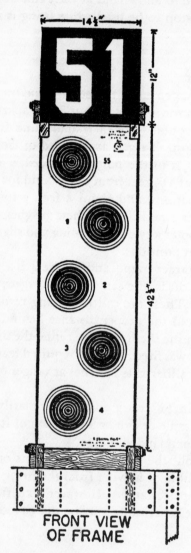

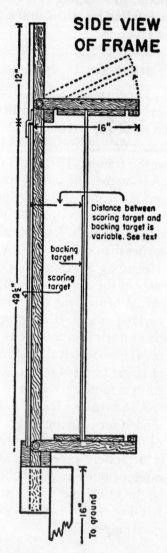

Fig. 3. Front view of a double target system. *Sporting Arms and Ammunition Manufacturers' Institute.*

Fig. 4. Side view of a double target system. *Sporting Arms and Ammunition Manufacturers' Institute.*

# Chapter 15

## THE LANGUAGE OF
## THE RIFLE RANGE

### The Shooters

Rifle shooting, like any other sport, has its own language. Some of the words are strictly technical words, while others are definitely slang. Many of them are ancient members of our spoken language, and yet they seldom appear in print. In order that you may feel at home on your first visit to a range, the more common shooting expressions are explained here.

A *tyro* is any beginner. If he fires with the first group of men to go on the firing line, he is in the *first* relay. If he attends an official tournament, he *registers* by stating that he wishes to compete and paying the required sum to the official empowered to collect registration fees. This is his first act at a tournament, but it does not entitle him to enter the separate events. In order to compete in the separate matches included within the tournament, he tells the proper official that he wants to compete and pays an *entry fee*. Thus, if there are three separate matches in a tournament, he must pay one registration and three entry fees if he wants to participate in everything.

An experienced shooter may be classified by the N.R.A according to his average tournament scores. Then, in future tournaments, he competes with other shooters in the same classification, and he is known as a *classified shooter*.

Classified shooters may be classified, in ascending order, as *marksman, sharpshooter, expert,* or *master,* but these terms are not to be confused with the qualification ratings established by the armed services of the United States. The latter are determined according to total scores received under certain specified conditions and do not depend upon average scores or tournament competitions.

A shooter may wear a *brassard*. Originally, this was merely a badge worn on the arm, but today it may be sewed to any part of a coat, sweater, or shooting jacket. Emblems and letters indicate the wearer's membership in shooting organizations or his marksmanship qualification.

## The Rifles

The term *small bore* has a loose, general reference to all firearms of small caliber, but in organized target shooting, it is restricted to the .22-caliber rimfire cartridge firearms.

The rifle, pistol, shotgun, or other firearm, may be referred to as an *arm* or a *piece*. These words are used in military shooting more than in civilian marksmanship.

A *bull pup* is a rifle having a barrel of normal length and a special stock in which the action is located immediately forward of the butt plate. This results in a rifle having a short over-all length and makes it necessary for the shooter to place his cheek along the side of the action. A *bull gun* is a target rifle with a heavy barrel and sights that are adjustable for long-range shooting.

A *double rifle* is one with two separate barrels, usually arranged side by side, and somewhat similar in construction to a double-barrel shotgun.

A *double-set trigger* is an arrangement of two triggers on a rifle, one forward of the other. When one trigger, usually the rear trigger, is pulled, the other is set on a delicate sear so that a very light touch on the second trigger is enough to discharge the rifle.

A *free rifle* is any rifle the shooter may wish to use, without the usual restrictions regarding barrel length, weight, set triggers, butt plates, palm rests, or accessories that may govern the normal selection and use of a rifle in the standard marksmanship events. An American free rifle is of the so-called Schuetzen type, which was popular with German-American rifle clubs about 1900. A European or Olympic free rifle is usually heavier and has a more complicated construction than the American free rifle.

A *palm rest* is permitted in free rifle competitions only. It is shaped something like an egg or a doorknob and may be made of wood or any other material. It is attached to an adjustable stem in front of the trigger guard. In the standing position of a free rifle match, the shooter holds the palm rest in the palm of his left hand and rests his left elbow against his side. As previously suggested, this device is used only on the various forms of free rifles, but not on rifles fired in regular competitions.

*Muzzle-loading rifles* are extensively fired in special matches all over the United States today. Both flintlock and percussion rifles are used, although not necessarily in the same match. These rifles are sometimes called *charcoal burners,* although the same term is also applied to muzzle-loader shooters. It refers to the fact that the old-fashioned black powder is used in muzzle loaders.

## Getting Ready to Shoot for Record

The shooter who wants a good score practices dry shooting, as mentioned before. He practices with an unloaded rifle or with dummy cartridges to improve his skill in taking proper positions, breathing, squeezing the trigger, etc.

He *dopes the wind* by observing its direction and force, estimating its effect on the flight of the bullet, and making the necessary sight adjustments. He also observes changes in light and the appearance of any mirage in making sight adjustments.

*Fouling shots,* also called *warming shots,* are often fired before firing the sighting and record shots because a clean barrel does not shoot the same as one which has been in use for several shots.

*Sighting shots* are those fired at a target for the purpose of accurately setting the sights. Such shots are allowed in some matches immediately before the beginning of record fire.

The shooter may have a *spotting scope.* This is a telescope of comparatively high power, which may be mounted on a tripod and placed near the shooter or his coach and used to observe the location of shot holes on the target. This eliminates any need for waiting for information from the target butts and makes it possible to adjust the sights properly after each shot.

A *loading block* is often merely a wooden block with holes in it for cartridges. The shooter can look at it and tell how many shots he has fired already and how many he has left, thus eliminating any possibility of firing too few or too many shots in a record event.

A *trigger weight* is a weight fastened to a hook and temporarily attached to the trigger of a rifle held in a vertical position to determine the trigger pull required to fire the rifle. For example, the trigger of a small-bore rifle used in official competitions must hold a weight of not less than three pounds without discharging.

## Match Firing

An *aggregate match* is one that consists of two or more separate matches. The score for the aggregate match is found by adding the separate scores of the included matches.

The *course of fire* consists of the requirements of a match regarding the number of shots at each range, the position in which the shots must be fired, and other restricting rules.

*Crossfiring* is shooting on the wrong target. This is usually penalized sufficiently to discourage carelessness. The use of the backing targets previously mentioned is a means of detecting the origin of crossfire.

A *flier* is a wild shot on a target. The shooter may have a good group otherwise, but because of a poor position, improper breathing, jerking the trigger, incorrect sight adjustment, or some other reason, he places one shot outside of the group.

When a shooter is making a perfect score, he may say that he is *going clean,* or *in the black,* although the latter expression does not necessarily mean that he is firing all his shots into the ten circle.

In a *handicap match,* an experienced shooter may be penalized by subtracting extra points from his actual score in order to give other shooters an equal opportunity of winning an award.

A *hang-fire* is a cartridge that does not fire when the trigger is squeezed but fires shortly after the firing pin hits the primer. When a hang-fire occurs, the wise shooter waits a few seconds, keeping his rifle pointed toward the target.

A *keyhole* is a hole of irregular shape made in the target by a bullet that tumbles through the air. The same word is also used as a verb. For example, a shooter may say, "The last shot keyholed."

A *misfire* is a cartridge that does not discharge when the firing pin strikes the primer. A hang-fire discharges eventually but a misfire fails to fire from one blow of the firing pin. Sometimes it is possible to recock the rifle and fire again, thus discharging a misfire, but this is not recommended in shooting for record.

If a shot hole barely breaks a scoring ring on a target, it is known as a *nipper*.

A shot hitting the target exactly in the center of the bull's eye is a *pinwheel*.

*Plinking* is random or informal shooting at miscellaneous targets other than paper targets, such as signboards, insulators on electric or telephone poles, tin cans, etc. It is strongly discouraged by all experienced shooters because it destroys property, endangers lives, and does not add to the shooter's skill.

A *possible,* sometimes called a *straight,* exists when all shots are in the 10-ring.

The X ring, which is an additional circle inside the ten ring of some targets, is used to decide tie scores without changing the scores. For example, if two men have the same score and have the same number of shots in the ten ring, the one having more of his ten-ring shots in the X ring will be the winner.

## Match Terms

When rifle clubs compete with each other on the same range, they are sometimes described as firing *shoulder to shoulder,* although it is obvious to anyone who understands shooting positions that it is impossible actually to fire that close together.

It is also possible for a club to compete with a club at a distance. The targets to be used by both clubs are prepared in advance and marked for identification so that additional targets cannot be fired on to raise the score. The fired targets are then exchanged by mail after each club has fired on its home range. This is known as a *mail match, postal match,* or *home-range match.* If the scores are exchanged by telegrams and the targets exchanged later by mail, the event is known as a *telegraphic match.*

In some competitions between individuals, a shooter may enter the competition two or more times, select the targets having the highest scores, and submit a prescribed number of these for his total score. This is known as a *reentry* match. It is especially popular with rifle clubs that are trying to raise money, because they can charge a fee for each re-entry and award a prize that costs far less than the sum of the fees.

## Stage and String

When a rifle match is fired in more than one shooting position or at more than one range, the firing at each position of range is called a *stage*. For example, if ten shots are fired at two hundred yards in the sitting position and ten shots in the prone position at the same distance, there are two stages because there are two positions. Likewise, if ten shots are fired in the prone position at two hundred yards and ten shots are fired in the sitting position at three hundred yards, there are still two stages.

A *string* is a series of shots forming part of a stage.

## Miscellaneous Shooting Terms

A *bench rest* is a special form of a table on which the shooter leans with both elbows while the barrel or the fore end of the rifle rests on some special support, such as a sandbag. It is used to obtain increased accuracy, especially when a shooter wants to "sight in" his rifle very carefully.

A *crisp trigger* is one that allows the firing pin or hammer to operate smoothly and quickly, with no apparent lost motion.

A *doby* is a bronze medal awarded in a shooting competition. The plural is *dobies*. This is purely a slang term and probably originated with western shooters who thought that bronze medals resembled the adobe of which frontier homes were sometimes made.

A *dumdum bullet* is one that expands on impact and tears up the body tissue of any person or animal it hits. The name originated in Dumdum, India, where such bullets were originally made. The use of these bullets in warfare is forbidden by international treaties.

*English,* in shooting, has a meaning somewhat like the one it has in pool or billards. When the shooter says that he gives it a little English or puts English on it, he means that he holds his rifle to the right or left of the target instead of adjusting the sight. This is generally regarded as bad practice, although an expert rifleman can sometimes correct quicker for a sudden change of wind by aiming slightly right or left, or up or down, instead of adjusting his sights. Another name for the same thing is *Kentucky windage.*

A *false muzzle* is a short section of barrel placed temporarily over the muzzle of a muzzle-loading rifle in order to start the lead bullet properly into the bore. It is taken off before firing.

A *fishtail wind* is one that changes from side to side behind the shooter, that is, at six o'clock on the horizontal clock face. It is a great source of trouble in firing at long ranges.

The *hip-rest position* is one in which the left elbow rests against the side of the body above the hip in firing from the standing position.

*Horizontal spread,* also called *horizontal dispersion,* is the horizontal distance between the bullet holes on the right and left of a shot group on a target.

*Hulls,* are empty, fired cartridge cases. For example, a range officer or instructor may order the shooters to "pick up your hulls," or he may say, "Pick up your brass." The fired cartridges are picked up by each shooter at his firing point and thrown into a receptacle provided for that purpose. Later, they are sold for junk or sometimes reloaded.

*Leading* is the accumulation of lead in the bore of a rifle left by a lead (nonjacketed) bullet.

A *marker* is a tin disk on the end of a pole used to signal the value of a shot from the target butts to the firing line. A white disk indicates a five, a red disk is a four, a black and white disk is a three, a solid black disk is a two, and a miss is signaled by waving a red flag. These values are for military targets. The slang terms for the same values are: "bull's eye" for five; "center" for four; "magpie" for three; "outer" for two; and "swabo" for a miss. There is no ring having a value of one on a military target.

A *muzzle brake* is a device placed on the muzzle of a rifle or shotgun to deflect the escaping powder gases to the sides or the rear in order to reduce the recoil. The Cutts Compensator is an example of a muzzle brake.

A *paster* is a small square of paper that is pasted over the bullet hole in a target after the value of the shot has been signaled to the shooter. Black pasters are pasted on the bull's eye and white pasters elsewhere on the target.

The *pattern* is the distribution of shot from a shotgun on a target perpendicular to the barrel at a given distance. The usual practice is to use a circle having a thirty-inch diameter, and then record the percentage of shot pellets falling within the circle, as well as the evenness of their distribution. Although this is not a rifle term, it is explained here because it is often used erroneously by riflemen in discussing their shot groups.

*Progressive powder* is a smokeless gunpowder that burns slowly at first when ignited by the primer and then burns faster as the pressure from the expanding gases is built up inside the cartridge or shotgun shell. This term is used to distinguish modern powder from the older powders, which burn at a comparatively constant speed regardless of how much pressure is built up in the cartridge case or shell.

A *spotter* is a cardboard or tin disk fastened around a sharp stick that is plunged into a bullet hole in a target to indicate to the shooter the exact location of his shot. It is usually white on one side and black on the other. When the shot is in the bull's eye, the white side is toward the shooter; when the shot is elsewhere on the target, the black side is toward the firing line.

A *Spitzer bullet* is one having a long, sharp point. The word comes from the German *Spitzgeschoss,* meaning a pointed bullet. An example is the U.S. Government, caliber .30, 173-grain, boat-tailed bullet, fired in the 1903 (Springfield) rifle.

A *wildcat cartridge* is a cartridge designed or manufactured by a private individual and not commercially distributed by a principal ammunition manufacturer. Some of the best cartridges used today were originally classified as wildcats. Examples are the .257 Roberts and the .220 Swift.

# Chapter 16

## HOW TO SELECT A
## .22-CALIBER RIFLE

### General Requirements

The first consideration in selecting your .22-caliber rifle is your size and weight. Your rifle should be chosen to fit your body instead of trying to adapt your body to the rifle. Visit a firearms dealer, and practice aiming several different rifles at targets until you find one that seems to point itself naturally and comfortably from the various shooting positions.

The second consideration is the degree of accuracy you expect to attain. There is no advantage in buying an expensive target rifle if you do not intend to practice marksmanship long enough and carefully enough eventually to shoot high scores consistently. If you merely intend to fool around, an inexpensive rifle is good enough.

The third consideration is the cost. The small singleshot, lightweight training rifles are the cheapest in price, but they are primarily intended for boys and young men of small size and light weight. The best advice for most people is to buy the very best rifle that their budget will permit. The reason is that if you buy a cheap rifle you will never be satisfied with it, and you will probably quit shooting before you are well started. On the other hand, if you invest in a comparatively expensive weapon, you will obtain better results from the first and you will tend to continue your practice to get your money's worth.

Safety is always an important consideration in any phase of firearm activity. Semiautomatic rifles, trombone or slide-action rifles, and lever-action repeaters with tubular magazines are never recommended by men experienced in the training of junior shooters, and they are not highly regarded by those who specialize in training adults. The reason for rejecting these types of rifles for training purposes is that their magazines are so constructed that it is possible for you to leave a cartridge in the magazine without knowing it. Then, if someone picks up your rifle and pulls the trigger, he may accidentally kill or wound a bystander or himself.

The best .22-caliber rifles are always chambered for the .22 long-rifle cartridge. Never fire anything but this cartridge in a rifle chambered for it. If you fire a .22 short cartridge in a rifle chambered for the .22 long rifle, lead will be scraped off the bullet by the chamber because the bullet must jump from the cartridge case into the rifling of the bore. The lead left by bullets in this manner accumulates and may eventually make it impossible for you to load a cartridge into the rifle.

There are several good lever-action single-shot rifles, but the bolt-action type is preferred by most experienced instructors and coaches.

If you have a choice of weights, always take the heavier rifle because it is easier to hold steady, and it prepares you for holding the heavier rifle you will eventually fire in hunting or in military service.

The choice of sights is very important in selecting a target rifle. Figure 1 shows a ramp-type front sight with a hood. Figure 2 shows a ramp-type front sight without a hood. Figure 3 illustrates a target-type hooded front sight with interchangeable inserts. Figure 4 shows another target-type front sight of the hooded type, also available with a variety of inserts, although the inserts are not shown in the illustration. The inserts make it possible to choose a post and an aperture suitable for each shooting condition. If you cannot obtain a rifle equipped with a hooded front sight having interchangeable inserts and cannot afford to have one installed to replace the sight already on the rifle, then your second choice for a front sight is a plain post-type sight such as the one illustrated in Figure 5.

Although they are not recommended for beginners, or for accurate target shooters, bead front sights are installed on some rifles.

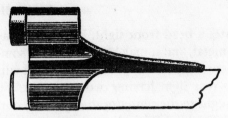

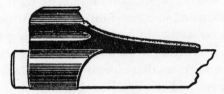

Fig. 1. A ramp-type front sight with a hood.
*Redfield Gun Sight Co.*

Fig. 2. A ramp-type front sight without a hood.
*Redfield Gun Sight Co.*

Fig. 3. A target-type hooded front sight with interchangeable inserts. *Redfield Gun Sight Co.*

Fig. 4. A target-type hooded front sight. *Redfield Gun Sight Co.*

Fig. 5. A plain post-type front sight.

Fig. 6. A bead-type front sight.

Fig. 7. How to aim when a rifle is equipped with a bead-type front sight and a rear sight having two apertures.

Figure 6 illustrates a bead front sight. The bead may be made of ivory, plastic, or metal, and it may be red, gold, or some other color. Figure 7 shows how to aim when a rifle is equipped with a bead-type front sight and a rear sight having two apertures. The top of the front sight is brought to the center of the aperture in the rear sight, and then, with the sights held in line, the top of the front sight is brought directly under the spot on the target that is to be hit.

The rear sight should be an adjustable peep sight. Sights of this type have been discussed in a previous chapter. Although it is not recommended for target shooting or accurate hunting, some shooters like a semi-buckhorn rear sight, such as the one illustrated in Figure 8, which is shown with smaller drawings to explain the five-step elevation adjustment and the receiver disks.

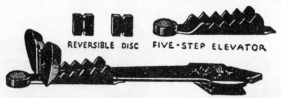

REVERSIBLE DISC    FIVE-STEP ELEVATOR

Fig. 8. A semibuckhorn rear sight.    *Redfield Gun Sight Co.*

## Cost Classifications

The highest quality, heavyweight, .22-caliber target rifles have adjustable sights, specially designed stocks, sling straps, and other accessories that contribute to success. The next lower class consists of medium-weight, moderately priced, .22-caliber target rifles, which are generally similar to the better grade except for weight and price. The lightweight, low-cost, .22-caliber training rifles are suitable for general and short-range target shooting, for beginners and for all inexpensive shooting. Rifles of this bottom grade are available in single-shot and repeating models.

The rifles described and illustrated in this chapter are not necessarily the only ones that belong in each weight and price class, but they are the ones which have been found desirable by the author and his associates.

## High-Quality, Heavy .22-Caliber
## Target Rifles

The Remington model 37, Rangemaster target rifle, illustrated in Figure 9, is a bolt-action rifle with a five-shot magazine, 28-inch barrel, micrometer rear sight with quarter-minute clicks, globe front sight with seven interchangeable inserts, and a sling strap with an adjustable front swivel. It weighs about twelve pounds.

Fig. 9. Remington model 37, Rangemaster target rifle. *Remington Arms Co., Inc.*

The Winchester model 52, standard barrel, target rifle, shown in Figure 10, has a bolt-action, 5-shot magazine, 28-inch barrel, micrometer rear sight with quarter minute clicks, interchangeable disk front sight, scope blocks, and sling swivels. It weighs about ten pounds.

Fig. 10. Winchester model 52, standard barrel, target rifle. *Winchester Repeating Arms Co.*

The Winchester model 52, heavy barrel, target rifle, illustrated in Figure 11, has a bolt-action, 5-shot magazine, 28-inch heavy target barrel, micrometer extension rear sight adjustment to quarter minutes, quick detachable front sight, Springfield-type sling and

Fig. 11. Winchester model 52, heavy barrel, target rifle. *Winchester Repeating Arms Co.*

adjustable sling swivels with a hand protector, full beavertail fore-arm, and a high comb. It weighs about twelve pounds.

The Winchester model 52, Bull Gun, shown in Figure 12, has a speed lock, bolt action, extra heavyweight 28-inch barrel, Vaver W11a front sight, Vaver 5237 extension rear sight with one-eighth-minute clicks, Marksman No. 1 stock, adjustable front sling swivels, and telescope bases. It weighs about thirteen and one-half pounds.

Fig. 12. Winchester model 52, Bull Gun.      *Winchester Repeating Arms Co.*

In addition to these commercially available rifles, the United States Government manufactures in its arsenal at Springfield, Massachusetts, two models of .22-caliber rifles, M1 and M2, which weigh about ten and one-half pounds. These rifles are available in limited quantities to rifle clubs belonging to the National Rifle Association and are regularly issued to the armed services of the United States for target practice.

## Medium-Quality, Mediumweight .22-Caliber Target Rifles

The Mossberg G.I. model 44US rifle, illustrated in Figure 13, has a bolt action, 7-shot magazine, 13/16-inch heavy-type 26-inch barrel, Mossberg No. S100 receiver peep sight with one-half-minute click adjustments for windage and elevation, ramp-type front sight with a choice of four inserts, an adjustable trigger pull, and

Fig. 13. Mossberg G. I., model 44US rifle.      *O. F. Mossberg & Sons, Inc.*

quick detachable sling swivels. It weighs about eight and one-half pounds.

The Remington model 513TR Matchmaster rifle, shown in Figure 14, has a bolt action, 6-shot box magazine, 27-inch barrel, micrometer rear sight adjustable to quarter minutes, globe front sight with seven interchangeable inserts, and a sling strap with an adjustable front sling. It weighs about eight and one-half pounds.

Fig. 14. Remington model 513TR Matchmaster rifle.     *Remington Arms Co., Inc.*

The Winchester model 75 target rifle, shown in Figure 15, has a bolt action with speed lock, 5-shot magazine, 28-inch tapered barrel, pistol-grip stock with semibeavertail fore end, high comb, Winchester No. 105 front sight, Lyman 58-E receiver sight with quarter-minute clicks for windage and elevation, side lever safety, adjustable sling swivel base, and an Army-type tan leather sling strap. It weighs about eight pounds, ten ounces.

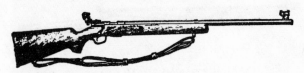

Fig. 15. Winchester model 75 target rifle.     *Winchester Repeating Arms Co.*

## Low-Cost, Lightweight .22-Caliber Training Rifles

The Marlin model 80-DL repeating rifle, shown in Figure 16, has a bolt action, 7-shot magazine, 13/16-inch heavy-type 26-inch rear sight, ramp front sight with hood, and swivels, It weighs about six pounds.

Fig. 16. Marlin model 80-DL repeating rifle.    *Marlin Firearms Co.*

The Marlin model 101-DL rifle, shown in Figure 17, is a bolt-action, single-shot, self-cocking rifle with a 24-inch round barrel. It weighs about five pounds.

Fig. 17. Marlin model 101-DL rifle.    *Marlin Firearms Co.*

The Mossberg model 42M rifle, shown in Figure 18, has a bolt-action, 7-shot magazine, 23-inch barrel, receiver peep sight, and quick detachable swivels. It weighs about six and three-fourths pounds.

Fig. 18. Mossberg model 42M rifle.    *O. F. Mossberg & Sons, Inc.*

The Winchester model 6940 target rifle, illustrated in Figure 19, is a bolt-action rifle chambered for .22 long-rifle rimfire cartridges only. It has a 25-inch barrel, American walnut stock, pistol grip, semibeavertail fore end, a Winchester No. 93 blade front sight, and a No. 80 peep rear sight on the end of the receiver with graduated windage and elevation adjustments. It is furnished with an Army-type leather sling strap. The weight is about five and one-half pounds.

Fig. 19. Winchester model 6940 target rifle.   *Winchester Repeating Arms Co.*

The Winchester model 6941 match rifle, illustrated in Figure 20, is like the model 6940 except that it has a Lyman 57E receiver sight with micrometer adjustments for windage and elevation. Both of these models are supplied with a 5-shot .22 long-rifle box magazine and a .22 long-rifle single-shot adapter.

Fig. 20. Winchester model 6941 match rifle.   *Winchester Repeating Arms Co.*

# Chapter 17

## HOW TO SELECT YOUR HUNTING RIFLE

### Killing Power

The selection of your hunting rifle depends largely upon the ammunition you intend to use in hunting. This involves killing power, which is the ability of the rifle and its cartridge to kill an animal cleanly and humanely. The wound should not cause unnecessary suffering, and it should not be large enough to spoil the meat by tearing up a large area.

Many modern cartridges are designed to produce very high velocity with light bullets which have a comparatively flat trajectory, long range, accuracy, and a theoretically great killing power. The shocking power of the lightweight bullet depends largely on the paralyzing effect of its high speed, hence it is possible under some conditions for a light, fast bullet to have more killing power than a heavier but slower bullet. When high speed, accuracy, and a fairly flat trajectory are combined in one bullet, the game may be killed more cleanly and be less mutilated.

However, two important factors in killing power are penetration and expansion. If the bullet does not go into the body deep enough to hit a vital organ and if it does not expand materially on impact, the animal may escape and later die a slow and painful death.

Some hunting is done at short ranges in thick brush while other hunting is conducted at long ranges over flat country. Light bullets driven at high velocities do not always cut accurately through brush, but the same bullets may be well suited to hunting in open country where the high velocity and flat trajectory are essential qualities.

All of these factors must be weighed in determining the rifle you will need. There is no such thing as a good all-round hunting rifle, and there never will be. At the best, any choice is a compromise.

## A Brief Discussion of Cartridges

The power of a rifle is in its cartridge and not in the rifle itself. In this chapter, rifles are discussed largely according to their cartridges. For this reason, we shall refer to illustrations of a few of the many cartridges adapted to hunting before proceeding to examine the rifles.

The .22 Remington-Winchester Special cartridge made by Remington is shown in Figure 1. The 25-caliber Remington cartridge with a soft-point, 117-grain bullet is illustrated in Figure 2. The Winchester .30-06 Springfield (not Super-Speed) cartridge with a 150-grain, full-patch bullet is shown in Figure 3. The Remington .30-06 Springfield cartridge with a soft-point, 220-grain bullet is shown in Figure 4.

Full-patch military ammunition for hunting is outlawed in many parts of the United States.

The Winchester .33-caliber cartridge with a 220-grain, soft-point bullet, adapted to Winchester model 86 and Marlin model 1895 rifles, is illustrated in Figure 5. The .348-caliber Winchester Super-Speed cartridge with nonmercuric priming, illustrated in Figure 6, adapted to Winchester model 71 rifle, is available with either a 200-grain, soft-point bullet or a 150-grain, soft-point bullet. The .351-caliber Winchester self-loading cartridge with nonmercuric priming, illustrated in Figure 7, is adapted to Winchester model 07 rifle, and is available with either a 180-grain, full-patch bullet, or a 180-grain, soft-point bullet.

## Varmint Rifles

In ordinary language, varmints are noxious or disgusting animals, such as rats, mice, weasels, etc., and sometimes hawks and owls, but in hunting language this term is applied to all small animals and birds that are not protected by game laws and are regarded as nuisances.

**HI-SPEED**

Fig. 1. The .22 Remington-Winchester Special cartridge. *Remington Arms Co., Inc.*

**SOFT POINT "CORE-LOKT", 117 GRAINS**

Fig. 2. The .25-caliber Remington cartridge with a soft-point, 117-grain bullet. *Remington Arms Co., Inc.*

Fig. 3. The Winchester .30-06 Springfield cartridge with a 150-grain, full-patch bullet. *Winchester Repeating Arms Co.*

**SOFT POINT "CORE-LOKT", 220 GRAINS**

Fig. 4. The Remington .30-06 Springfield cartridge with a soft-point, 220-grain bullet. *Remington Arms Co., Inc.*

Fig. 5. The Winchester .33-caliber with a .220-grain, soft-point bullet. *Winchester Repeating Arms Co.*

Fig. 6. The Winchester .348-caliber Super-Speed cartridge with nonmercuric priming, available with either a 200-grain, or a 150-grain, soft-point bullet. *Winchester Repeating Arms Co.*

Fig. 7. The Winchester .351-caliber self-loading cartridge with nonmercuric priming, adapted to Winchester model 07 rifle, available with either a 180-grain, full-patch bullet, or a 180-grain, soft-point bullet. *Winchester Repeating Arms Co.*

Examples are woodchucks, crows, prairie dogs, ground squirrels, the various species of rabbits, and coyotes.

Many of the varmints can be killed at short ranges with the high-speed .22 long-rifle cartridge fired in any of the .22-caliber rifles described in this book. However, some experienced hunters prefer the .22 Winchester rimfire cartridge, illustrated in Figure 1, usually designated as .22 W.R.F., and also known as the .22 Remington Special. It has more killing power than a high-speed .22 long-rifle but it is not so accurate. The rifles chambered for this cartridge include the Winchester model 67, single-shot, illustrated in Figure 8; Winchester model 68, single-shot; Winchester model 61, slide-action repeating shown in Figure 9; Winchester model 1890, slide-action repeating; Stevens "Favorite," single-shot; and Remington model 121, slide-action repeating, illustrated in Figure 10.

Although rifles chambered for the .22 long-rifle cartridge and the .22 W.R.F. are suitable for squirrels, crows, rabbits, sparrows, rats,

Fig. 8. Winchester model 67 single-shot rifle.    *Winchester Repeating Arms Co.*

Fig. 9. Winchester model 61, slide-action repeating rifle.    *Winchester Repeating Arms Co.*

Fig. 10. Remington model 121, slide-action repeating rifle.    *Remington Arms Co., Inc.*

and the smaller pests at medium and short ranges, those who hunt woodchucks, foxes, coyotes, ground squirrels, and similar animals prefer rifles chambered for the .218 Bee, .219 Zipper, .220 Swift, .22 Hornet, .257 Roberts, .25-35, .25-20, .250/3000 Savage, .32-20, and even the .30-06 cartridges. Various rifles manufactured by Remington, Winchester, Savage, and other makers are designed to handle these cartridges in bolt, lever, and pump actions.

## Characteristics of Deer Rifles

Cartridges for deer rifles may be divided into two groups—for brush and open shooting. Many of the cartridges suitable for brush hunting are also satisfactory for open shooting. Bullets designed especially for expanding on inpact produce better results on the heavier, thick-skinned animals that require deeper penetration.

Thick woods and brushy country that provide only quick, short-range shooting require a lighter, shorter, handier rifle with power and accuracy up to about one hundred and fifty yards, although most deer are killed at one hundred yards or less in such country.

Open plains, hilly country, and mountainous terrain that offer long-range shots that can be taken slowly and deliberately call for a powerful bolt-action rifle equipped with a telescope sight and chambered for cartridges that are powerful and accurate up to at least three hundred yards.

Cartridges suitable for brush shooting include the following: .250 Savage, 100-grain; .257 Roberts, 117-grain; .270 Winchester, 150-grain; 7-mm. Mauser, 175-grain; .30-30 Winchester, 170-grain; .30-40 Krag, 180-grain; .300 Savage, 180-grain; .30 Remington, 170-grain; .30-06 Springfield, 180 grain; .303 Savage, 190-grain; .303 British, 215-grain; .32 Remington, 170-grain; .32 Winchester, 170-grain; .33 Winchester, 200-grain; 8 mm. Mannlicher-Schoenauer, 220-grain; 8 mm. Mauser, 170-grain; .348 Winchester, 150-grain; .35 Remington, 200-grain.

Cartridges suitable for open shooting include some of the above plus the following: .257 Roberts, 100-grain; 270 Winchester, 130-grain; .30-30 Winchester, 150-grain; .30-06 Springfield, 150-grain; and the .300 Savage, 150-grain.

## Deer Rifles for Brush Shooting

Lever-action and slide-action rifles chambered for the proper cartridges are suitable for shooting deer in brush country at fairly short ranges. Examples are the Savage model 99, lever-action repeating rifle, illustrated in Figure 11, made in calibers .250/3000 (called .250 Savage) and .300 Savage; Remington model 141, Gamemaster, slide-action repeating rifle, illustrated in Figure 12, made in calibers .30 Remington, .32 Remington and .35 Remington; the Winchester model 94, lever-action repeating rifle, shown in Figure 13, made in calibers .25-35 Winchester, .30-30 Winchester, and .32 Winchester Special; and the Winchester model 64, lever-action repeating rifle, made in calibers .30-30 Winchester and .32 Winchester Special, which is illustrated in Figure 14.

The Remington model 81, Woodsmaster, shown in Figure 15, listed as an automatic or autoloading rifle, but actually semiautomatic, is made in calibers .30 Remington, .35 Remington, and .300 Savage. It is suitable for hunting deer in brush country if you want a semiautomatic, but some states have laws forbidding the use of any semiautomatic rifle. Regardless of laws, only an experienced and thoroughly trained shooter should use a semiautomatic in hunting.

Many hunters find that the lever-action rifles are easier to carry on horseback and handier to operate in the brush than bolt-action rifles. In addition to lever-action and slide-action rifles chambered for the appropriate cartridges, any bolt-action rifle chambered for the cartridges recommended for brush firing will prove satisfactory. If you have been trained in target marksmanship with a bolt-action rifle, you may prefer the same type in hunting, regardless of other considerations.

## Deer Rifles for Open Shooting

Assuming that deer hunting in the open will be at the longer ranges and provide an opportunity for taking a more careful aim in many instances, the best type of rifle is a bolt-action with a telescopic sight. Lever-action, slide-action, and semiautomatic rifles are defi-

Fig. 11. Savage model 99, lever-action repeating rifle. *Savage Arms Corporation.*

Fig. 12. Remington model 141, Gamemaster, slide-action repeating rifle. *Remington Arms Co., Inc.*

Fig. 13. Winchester model 94, lever-action repeating rifle. *Winchester Repeating Arms Co.*

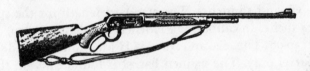

Fig. 14. Winchester model 64, lever-action repeating rifle. *Winchester Repeating Arms Co.*

Fig. 15. Remington model 81, Woodmaster, semiautomatic rifle. *Remington Arms Co., Inc.*

nitely not in the same class with bolt-action rifles for accurate fire at long ranges with high-power cartridges.

The U. S. rifle, caliber .30, model of 1903, commonly called the Springfield, and the U. S. rifle, caliber .30, model of 1917, commonly called the Enfield, both fire the .30-06 cartridge sometimes called the '06-Govt. or .30-06 Springfield; and they are both suitable for deer hunting in either the brush or the open.

One of the best deer rifles for open shooting is the Remington model 721, bolt-action repeating rifle, illustrated in Figure 16. It is made in calibers .270 Winchester, .30-06 Springfield, and .300 H&H Magnum. For deer hunting you will probably find the .30-06 Springfield cartridge best. The .300 H&H Magnum is intended for heavier game. The .270 and .30-06 rifles have a 24-inch barrel. The .300 Magnum is made with a 26-inch barrel. The weight of the rifle is about seven and one-fourth pounds. The magazine capacity is four cartridges in the .270 and .30-06 and three cartridges in the .300 Magnum caliber.

The Winchester model 70, bolt-action repeating rifle, which is equal in quality to the Remington 721, is made in calibers .22 Hornet, .220 Swift, .250 Savage, .257 Roberts, .270 Winchester, 7-mm., .30-06 Springfield, .300 H&H Magnum, and .375 H&H Magnum. This rifle, which is illustrated in Figure 17, is made in barrel lengths of 24, 25, 26, and 28 inches. The standard length for the sporting styles is 24 inches in calibers .22 Hornet, .250 Savage, .270, .257, 7-mm., and .30-06. The .220 and .300 H&H Magnum are made with a 26-inch barrel only. The 25-inch barrel is found only on the .375 H&H. The 28-inch barrel is on the Bull Gun and this style is available in calibers .30-06 and .300 H&H.

The Bull Gun, shown in Figure 18, weighs about thirteen and a quarter pounds; the standard weight of the model 70 is about eight pounds; the super grade weighs about eight and one-half pounds; the national match model weighs about nine and one-half pounds; and the target model weighs about ten and one-half pounds.

The magazine capacity of the model 70 is five cartridges in all models except calibers .300 H&H and .375 H&H, which have a four-shot capacity. Different types of stocks and combinations of sights provide a wide variety of selections in all forms of this rifle.

## HOW TO SELECT YOUR HUNTING RIFLE

Fig. 16. Remington model 721, bolt-action repeating rifle.     *Remington Arms Co., Inc.*

Fig. 17. Winchester model 70, bolt-action repeating rifle.     *Winchester Repeating Arms Co.*

Fig. 18. Winchester model 70, Bull Gun.     *Winchester Repeating Arms Co.*

Although these two outstanding modern rifles are available in many different calibers, you must be sure to buy one chambered for the cartridge you intend to shoot. Obviously, the availability of ammunition in the neighborhood where you will be hunting is an important consideration unless you have a pack horse to carry a reserve supply.

## Rifles for Larger Game

The larger American game may be regarded as including moose, elk, grizzly and Kodiak bears, walrus, etc. Cartridges suitable for this game may be used on deer at long ranges but they are generally too powerful for deer and are especially dangerous where there are many hunters in the vicinity.

Some hunters use the .270 Winchester with a 150-grain soft-point or a 130-grain expanding-point bullet, and others use the .30-40 Krag with a 220-grain expanding or a 180-grain expanding bullet. Still better is the .30-06 Springfield with a 150-grain or 180-grain expanding bullet, but the 220-grain soft-point is preferred. However, the author believes that none of the above-mentioned cartridges is as generally effective on larger game as the .300 H&H Magnum with a 180-grain expanding or 220-grain expanding bullet; the .348 Winchester with a 250-grain expanding or a 200-grain soft-point bullet; or the .375 H&H Magnum with a 300-grain expanding or a 270-grain soft-point bullet.

Among our modern rifles, the Winchester model 70 can handle the .300 H&M Magnum or the .375 H&H Magnum. The Remington model 721 can handle the .300 H&H Magnum. Of course, if you wish to take a chance at shorter ranges on the lighter loads listed for this class of game, several of the rifles already mentioned are chambered for the appropriate cartridges.

## Superpowerful Rifles

There is considerable overlapping in the selection of rifles according to the game to be hunted. Thus, the rifles chambered for the .300 H&H Magnum with either a 220-grain or a 180-grain expanding bullet, or the .375 H&H with the 300-grain expanding, 270-grain soft-point, or 270-grain full-patch bullet may be classified as superpowerful weapons which can be used for any big game in the world with the possible exception of elephant, water buffalo, and rhinoceros. At short ranges, well-aimed shots may bring down the last mentioned animals, but they are not available to the average shooter. When you are ready to hunt game in Africa and Asia, you should be experienced enough to know what rifle and ammunition you require without much advice from other hunters.

# Chapter 18

## ACCESSORIES FOR
## THE RIFLEMAN

### Shooting Glasses

You should never engage in any form of shooting without wearing glasses, whether it is pistol or rifle target marksmanship, skeet shooting, trap shooting, or hunting. Glasses protect your eyes from glare, dust, dirt, broken or chipped pieces of clay targets, shot pellets, ricochet bullets, broken primers, powder gas, and flying fragments from burst barrels.

For many years the author thought, as many others do, that wearing glasses was all right for old people and college professors, but that they were just a little sissified for a normal man. After seeing several of his shooting companions lose the sight of at least one eye from broken primers, he changed his mind.

Ordinary sunglasses, such as those usually sold in dime stores and chain drugstores, are not satisfactory. There are no bargains in glasses that are suitable for wearing at the target range or in the field. They should be manufactured by opticians or optical companies who know what the shooter needs. Examples of reliable manufacturers are: The American Optical Co., Southbridge, Massachusetts; Bausch & Lomb Optical Co., Rochester, New York; and Belz Opticians, New York City.

The most satisfactory shooting glasses are annealed to give the lenses the additional strength required to stand up under blowbacks, ricochets, etc., but where the shooter desires the utmost in eye protection, case-hardened lenses are recommended. These are much harder and can be used with safety under the most hazardous conditions.

The case-hardening of lenses is a special tempering process that makes the lenses almost nonbreakable. Actually, there is no such thing as an absolutely nonbreakable lens, except plastic lenses, which are not satisfactory in their present state of development because they scratch easily and reduce the vision.

The so-called shatterproof lenses are laminated lenses made on the same principle as automobile and airplane windshields. Two lenses are laminated on a transparent binding substance, but they tend to disintegrate and become cloudy, hence they are not recommended.

Some doctors of medicine warn against wearing tinted glasses habitually. At the same time, they agree that a good pair of tinted glasses provide protection in driving an automobile over concrete roads, in water sports, in shooting, and under other conditions where the eyes are subject to glare.

If an oculist advises you to wear glasses to improve your vision, obtain the necessary optical correction to your shooting glasses as well as your reading spectacles. You should tell your oculist about your working and recreational habits so that these may be considered in prescribing lenses. For example, you may find that the front sight of your rifle seems hazy. The oculist can then equip your shooting glasses with a small segment of sufficient focal power so that the sight will appear clear and sharp, although there may be slight haze on the target. It is not possible to make a lens that will be equally sharp on both the sights and the target. It is more important to see the sights clearly than the target.

If you wear spectacles at work or while reading, have a doctor who understands marksmanship prescribe the lens you should wear in shooting.

If you have normal vision, you do not need the services of an eye doctor, but you should choose your glasses with care. In general, your shooting glasses should have large lenses and light color tints. The best all-around shade for a shooting lens is one that has a yellow-green formula. The yellow gives the sharpness and definition in vision and accentuates the black and white. The green gives you the necessary protection against glare without reducing vision.

Most shooters wear glasses in conventional sunglass tints of medium and dark green shades, which are much too dark for shooting and often prove to be more of a handicap than a help because they lack intensifying properties. If you want the maximum amount of intensification and if you are not unusually sensitive to the glare of the sun, you can wear a canary yellow lens that provides the highest amount of brilliance. Actually, this lens acts as a filter and helps you to pick up game much more quickly when it blends in with the foliage.

If your left eye is your master eye, in firing from the right shoulder and trying to aim with the right eye, you should partially close the left eye. If you try to keep both eyes fully open, the left eye will take the leadership in sighting and will cause you to crossfire. This trouble can be met by equipping the shooting glasses with a small opaque segment over the left lens. This enables you to shoot with both eyes open without crossfiring. When you place your cheek against the rifle, the left eye automatically falls behind the opaque segment and crossfiring is eliminated.

It must be clearly understood that the master eye is not always the eye that has the clearest, sharpest vision. In many cases the master eye is much more deficient in vision than the other eye and yet it is the dominant controlling eye in lining up objects, whether or not prescription glasses are worn. As previously explained in this book, in order to aim a rifle with both eyes open, the sights and bull's eye are brought into alignment with one eye, and that is the master, controlling, dominant eye.

Assuming that you have well-fitted, correctly prescribed shooting glasses, you may still find that when you try to shoot with these glasses, particularly in a prone position, you look through the extreme outer edges of the lenses. This causes marginal distortion and prismatic displacement, throwing off the accuracy of the glasses. The lenses should have an extra wide angle and the nose piece should be designed to give a large amount of glass toward your nose. This enables you to look close to the center of the lenses in aiming the rifle and maintains a clear, sharp, corrected vision.

In addition to the features already mentioned, good shooting glasses should have a frame equipped with a plastic perspiration bar, which rests on your forehead and keeps the lenses from steaming and getting soiled from the eyebrows and eyelashes. The bar holds the lenses sufficiently far away from the face to allow a circulation of air, thus preventing the moisture from condensing on the lenses. Figure 1 is a drawing that shows the construction features of well-designed shooting glasses.

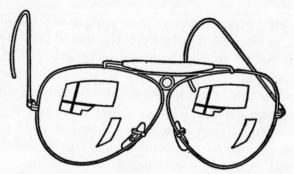

Fig. 1. The construction features of well-designed shooting glasses.     *Bausch & Lomb Optical Co.*

## Noise Suppression

Most shooters are bothered by the noise in firing large caliber rifles. The simplest remedy is to stuff cotton in your ears, but patented ear plugs are sold by most sporting-goods houses and appeal to anyone who objects to the unsightliness of wisps of cotton protruding from their ears. However, cotton is better.

## Shooting Coats

In firing a .22-caliber rifle, you do not need padding because there is not enough recoil to cause any discomfort. However, a properly designed shooting coat provides comfort because it keeps you from rubbing the skin off your elbows in the prone position.

In firing large-caliber rifles, a shooting coat is almost a necessity. You can get by without one by fastening a turkish towel under your shirt with safety pins, making certain that is extends high on the shoulder and over part of the arm.

You can make a shooting coat from an old jacket or suit coat by padding the elbows, the upper arm where the sling fits tight, and the right shoulder where the butt of the rifle rests. Pieces of sheepskin for padding may be bought from some sporting-goods houses. Sew them in place with the smooth side outside and the rough side (with the fur still on) against the coat.

## The Shooting Glove

A padded, fingerless glove for the left hand protects the hand against the tension of the gun sling. This is recommended for all rifle shooters, whether they are firing a .22-caliber rifle or a larger one. You can make one from an old glove that will be better than nothing, but it is better to buy one designed and manufactured especially for shooters.

## The Loading Block

A loading block is merely a piece of hard wood in which holes are bored for fitting the cartridges you will fire on a target range. Drill the holes so that the cartridges fit snugly but not so tight that you cannot get them out quickly. If you are not handy with tools, buy a loading block from any gun-supply house. The better types have hinged covers.

## The Gun Rest

A gun rest is merely a U-shaped piece of metal with a projection that you jab into the ground. The rifle is placed in the U at your firing point on an outdoor target range to keep it off the ground.

## Shooting Mats

Shooting mats were discussed in the chapter on ranges and are mentioned again merely to remind you that comfort is always an aid to good shooting. Figure 2 shows the use of shooting mats and other equipment on an outdoor range.

Fig. 2. Equipment in use in an outdoor range.    *Remington Arms Co., Inc.*

## Gun Cases and Scabbards

A wool-lined, waterproof gun cover, preferably with a zipper opening, a leather sling, and leather reinforcements, protects your rifle against damage in transportation, but it must not be used as a storage container because it gathers moisture and induces rusting. If you hunt big game from horseback, a leather scabbard of the type used by the horse cavalry is recommended.

## The Spotting Telescope

Many target shooters regard the spotting telescope as the most essential accessory for success on the rifle because it enables the shooter or his coach to see where each shot hits the target without waiting for any signal from the target butts.

A spotting telescope can be used at all ranges. The magnifying power is usually about twenty diameters, technically expressed as "20 X." The construction is weather proof and water resistant; it has a focusing adjustment and provides a sharp image.

A specially designed stand should be used with the spotting telescope so that the shooter can adjust the telescope with one hand if he does not have a coach or instructor with him.

# Chapter 19

## THE CARE AND CLEANING OF RIFLES

### Removing Obstructions

If you do not use the proper cleaning rags and patches, you may have a cleaning patch stuck in the bore. Also, you may accidentally scoop up sand, mud, snow, or some other obstruction in your barrel. Do not try to shoot out the obstruction by firing a live round. This will at least ruin the barrel, and it may cause a rupture of the rifle that will seriously injure you. Instead, use a cleaning rod with a little penetrating oil to help loosen the obstruction.

If the obstruction is a bullet, pour mercury into the bore and wait until it forms an amalgam with the lead, after which the amalgam can be poured out. If this fails, the bullet must be drilled out. This operation is rather difficult for a beginner and should be performed by a gunsmith unless you have some skill with tools. The details of this process are given in the author's book, *Gun Care and Repair—a Manual of Gunsmithing*.

If the obstruction is a cleaning patch or rag, do not drill it out. Plug one end of the barrel, pour kerosene or penetrating oil into the other end and insert a second plug when the barrel is apparently full. Then, turn the barrel upside down, remove the first plug, and pour in more oil so that the bore will be full. Unless you do this, the bore will not be actually full. Plug the barrel, put the rifle away overnight, and in the morning poke the rag out with a drill rod almost the diameter of the bore. If that fails, weld a corkscrew to the end of a steel cleaning rod, and remove the rag as you would a cork from a bottle.

## Removing a Bullet from the Chamber

If a bullet becomes stuck in the throat of the chamber of your rifle, and the cartridge case is pulled out, spilling powder grains in the chamber, the following procedure for removing the bullet will succeed if you are very cautious, but be sure to obey all safety precautions:

First, blow the powder out of the magazine and receiver. Second, twist the bullet out of another cartridge case and insert the cartridge case (minus the bullet of course) in the chamber, being careful that you do not spill the powder. Third, raise the muzzle of the rifle to an angle of about 60°, close the bolt, point the rifle toward the backstop of the rifle range, and squeeze the trigger. Keep your face away from the receiver of the rifle while you fire. This drives out the bullet without causing the damage that might come from a cleaning rod or a corkscrew on the end of a rod.

## Removing a Ruptured Cartridge Case

If you are equipped with the U. S. rifle, caliber .30, model 1903 (Springfield), the base of a cartridge might be torn off by the extractor, leaving the body of the case in the chamber. When this happens, obtain a device called a ruptured cartridge extractor, which looks something like a .30-caliber dummy cartridge. Insert it through the opening of the rupture case, and push it well forward into the chamber. Close the bolt so that the extractor of the rifle engages the head of the ruptured cartridge extractor, draw the bolt to the rear, and extract both the ruptured cartridge extractor and the ruptured cartridge as you would an ordinary fired cartridge case.

## Bent Barrels and Sights

Do not toss your rifle around or lean it against a tree where it will fall down or be knocked over. If the rifle falls or is struck against some object, the barrel may bend. A skilled gunsmith may be able to straighten it at considerable expense to you, but it often happens that a bent barrel is beyond repair. In this case, you must buy a new barrel and have it installed by a gunsmith.

A fall or a blow may knock the sights out of alignment. This is the least that may happen. Sometimes a blow injures the sights beyond repair.

## Tighten the Guard Screws

Examine your rifle, and you will see that the barrel is held to the stock by two or more screws. These are called guard screws. Carry a screwdriver with you, and tighten these screws if they become loose, or your rifle will not fire accurately.

## Use the Correct Ammunition

Anyone with any experience in shooting will advise you to buy a rifle chambered for .22 long-rifle cartridges and not one chambered for the .22 long or the .22 short. Some manufacturers advertise that their rifles are chambered for all three of these cartridges, but what they actually mean is that their weapons are chambered for the .22 long rifle but will take the other two.

If you load a .22 short or a .22 long cartridge, in a rifle chambered for the .22 long-rifle cartridge, the bullet will not go into the rifling properly. Instead, the bullet jumps through the chamber and slams against the beginning of the rifling. At this instant, the bullet has expanded very slightly from the force of the powder gases acting on its base, hence some of its lead is scraped off and left in the chamber behind the starting point of the rifling. Eventually, you may not be able to load any cartridge in your rifle. Meanwhile, the accuracy of fire has been decreased greatly.

## Removing Rust Spots

If a rust spot appears in the bore, use a brass-bristle brush on the end of a cleaning rod, stroke it back and forth the full length of the bore several times, and then run several cloth patches dipped in oil through the bore.

## Removing Lead

When little lumps of lead appear in the bore, usually immediately forward of the chamber, use a brass-bristle brush in the manner explained for removing rust spots, except that it should be dipped in kerosene before running it through the bore.

If the barrel is moderately rusted or leaded, remove all oil and grease from the bore and then pour mercury into the bore and wait until it forms an amalgam with the lead, after which the amalgam can be poured out. Some shooters prefer to use blue ointment, a mercury preparation obtainable at any drugstore, to loosen the lead fouling but the former method is more effective.

If the previous methods fail, especially if the bore is badly rusted or leaded, take the rifle to a gunsmith and have him put on a new barrel. This is necessary if the outlines of the rifling do not appear distinct when viewed with a strong light. It is dangerous to fire a rifle if the barrel is in this condition because a bullet may become stuck in the bore, causing the rifle to rupture. The best cure is prevention. A barrel that is properly used and cleaned will not rust or lead.

## Cleaning Equipment

A combined rifle rack and scoring table is shown in Figure 1. A knob-type tip of a cleaning rod is shown in Figure 2. Slotted, button, and jagged tips for cleaning rods are illustrated in Figure 3.

## How to Clean a Rifle

To clean a rifle, use a solid steel rod from the breech and not from the muzzle. Cleaning from the muzzle changes the location of the shot group.

Remove the bolt or otherwise open the action (depending upon the construction of your rifle), and push the cleaning rod with a brush or patches on it through the bore from the chamber to the muzzle. If the rifle is so constructed that it is impossible to clean from the breech, use the fingers to guide the cleaning rod so that it will not injure the rifling at the muzzle.

The remainder of the cleaning procedure depends upon the type of ammunition you are using. If you are using the modern non-corrosive cartridges, they will not leave a corrosive primer deposit in the bore. Instead, they leave a protective film that guards against

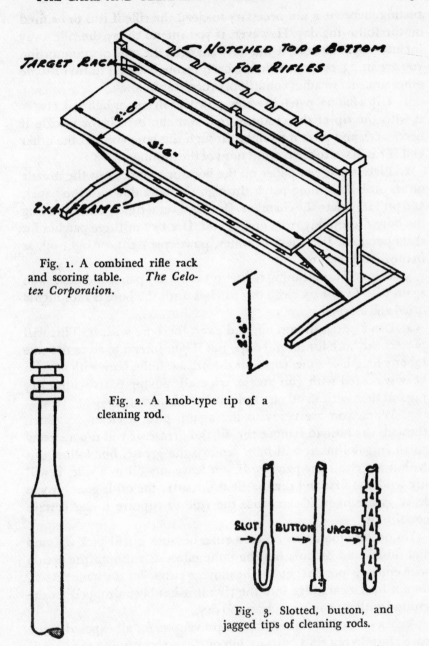

Fig. 1. A combined rifle rack and scoring table. *The Celotex Corporation.*

Fig. 2. A knob-type tip of a cleaning rod.

Fig. 3. Slotted, button, and jagged tips of cleaning rods.

rusting, hence it is not necessary to clean the rifle if it is to be fired on the following day. However, if you intend to lay the rifle away for any length of time, if you have changed the type of ammunition you are using, or if the rifle has been through a sand storm or some other unusual weather condition, proceed as follows:

1. Dip a flannel patch in water, powder solvent, or light oil, center it with the tip of the cleaning rod over the breech (or muzzle if necessary), and push it straight through the bore and out the other end. This first stroke takes out most of the fouling.

2. Place a piece of paper on the floor or ground, rest the muzzle on it, push a cleaning patch through the bore down to the paper, and pull it back to the chamber. Do this several times, thus swabbing the bore thoroughly from end to end. Use two or three patches for this operation. Dip them in water, powder solvent, or light oil, as in the first operation.

3. Wipe off the cleaning rod with a clean dry patch and then swab again with five or six clean dry patches until the bore is thoroughly dried and cleaned.

4. Dip a patch in gun oil, and swab the bore with it. This will protect the bore for several days, but if you intend to store the rifle for any length of time, wipe out the oil, swab the bore with a patch heavily coated with gun grease, wipe all moving parts with a dry rag and then with an oil rag, and put the rifle away.

5. When you are ready to fire again, push a clean dry patch through the bore to remove the oil and grease. If you dip a second patch in gasoline, it will help remove the grease, but follow this with more clean dry patches. If you leave any oil in a rifle, it will fire wildly at first and then settle down after the oil is gone. If you leave grease in it, it can cause the rifle to rupture under certain conditions.

Do not use too much oil on a rifle, because it will pick up sand and dust. Sand or dust has the same effect as rubbing the action with emery paper if it gets on the moving parts. For the same reason, do not load a cartridge into the rifle if it has been dropped on the ground without wiping it clean and dry.

A thin coat of oil is the best rust preventive for all exposed metal parts, but do not do a halfway job of cleaning or oiling the bore if you intend to fire on the following day. Either leave the bore alone or do a complete cleaning job as explained before. The reason for this is that any attempted cleaning will remove the protective film left by the firing of the modern noncorrosive ammunition.

We have mentioned the fact that unusual weather conditions justify a complete cleaning. An example of this is any sudden and violent change in temperature because this causes the rifle to "sweat," thus inducing rusting.

Weather affects ammunition. Extreme temperature changes have an unfavorable effect on the powder even though it is sealed within the brass case. If the cartridges are corroded even slightly or if they are very old, throw them in a river or bury them, and buy new ammunition.

## How to Clean a Rifle after Firing Old-Style Ammunition

If the ammunition you are using has the old corrosive-type primers, the bore is subjected to rusting from moisture absorbed by the residue left from the powder and also from moisture absorbed by the residue left from the primer. The residue left from the primer is especially bad. It is almost the same as common table salt and cannot be dissolved in oil but dissolves well in water. Therefore, water is used to clean the primer residue out of the bore. The residue left in the bore by the powder is easily pushed out by a few strokes of a cleaning patch on the end of a rod.

After using old-style cartridges with corrosive primers, carry out the following procedure:

1. Dip a flannel patch in water, preferably hot soapy water, and push it through the bore and out the other end, working from the breech if possible. You can save work if you fill a bucket with hot soapy water, place the bucket on the floor or ground, place the rifle in the bucket with the muzzle down, and work the cleaning rod up and down in a vertical plane. Run several patches through the bore to pump the water in and out.

2. Now run a cleaning rod with a brass-bristle brush on the end back and forth through the bore several times, being careful that

the brush goes all the way through the bore before you reverse its direction.

3. Run several patches soaked in water through the bore, but remove each patch as it comes out at the muzzle and replace it with another wet patch.

4. Run several clean dry patches through the bore until the last one comes out clean and dry. Examine the bore. If it is not clean and free from all residue, repeat the cleaning process, starting with the first step.

5. If the bore is now clean, soak a patch in a light oil and push it through the bore to deposit a light film.

The above procedure should be followed immediately after firing and never later than the end of the day of firing. *If the rifle is to be fired on the next day,* carry out the following procedure:

1. Disassemble the rifle as far as its construction requires for cleaning purposes. In the case of an ordinary .22-caliber rifle, this means that the gun sling is removed. In the case of a large-caliber bolt-action rifle, several parts, including the bolt, are removed.

2. Clean the bore and chamber, but do not oil the chamber.

3. Clean all metal parts, and apply a light coat of oil to those parts that do not come into contact with ammunition. Use a light preservative lubricating oil but not grease. Apply a light coat of oil to all working surfaces, cams, and the bolt mechanism.

*If the rifle is not to be fired within the next few days,* clean it as explained previously for a rifle in which corrosive-primer ammunition has been fired, and then carry out the following procedure:

1. Use a small stick covered with a corner of a patch soaked in water to clean the chamber. Twist it around the chamber to get into all the corners. Follow by using several dry patches on the stick. If the chamber is now clean and dry, insert your little finger and twist it around the chamber. If your finger comes out clean and dry, oil the chamber lightly with a light preservative lubricating oil, but remove this oil with a dry patch if you fire the rifle.

2. Wipe off the outside of the rifle with a clean dry rag to remove perspiration, dampness, and dirt. Wipe all metal parts with a rag soaked in a light oil. Wipe off the wooden parts with raw linseed oil. Wipe the leather gun sling with neat's-foot oil.

3. Clean the face of the bolt with a wet patch, dry it, and then coat with a light oil.

Be sure that no water is left in the rifle, especially in the action, where it is difficult to remove and may cause rusting even though the barrel is clean and dry.

## Cleaning Patches

Cleaning patches can be bought from any sporting-goods dealer or made at home. They should be made of mediumweight canton flannel, previously moistened thoroughly with water and wrung out several times to make it more absorbent. The flannel is then cut into squares. The correct size for a .22-caliber rifle is from three-fourths to one and one-half inches square. For a .30-caliber rifle, the correct size is about two and one-half inches square.

## Do Not Use Antirust Ropes

An antirust rope is a rope saturated with oil. In theory, the oil or grease excludes air and moisture, thus reducing rusting. In practice, the owner trusts the antirust rope, fails to inspect the bore, and finds that he has a badly rusted barrel when the next shooting season opens. Do not use this device under any conditions.

## Gun Cases and Covers

An airtight wooden cabinet is a good storage medium for the average gun owner, but a steel cabinet provides protection against fire and theft and is best if it can be made airtight. Do not store firearms in canvas, leather, sheepskin, or wooden gun cases or covers because they absorb moisture and cause rusting. They are satisfactory for transporting firearms but not for storing them. Avoid all muzzle covers, gun covers, rack covers, and plugs. These are merely catchpenny devices promoted for the profit of the sellers and the detriment of the gun owner. Finally, store the rifle in a horizontal position if you must, but it is better to store it with the muzzle down so that any moisture will drain out.

# Chapter 20

## WHAT THE N.R.A.
## CAN DO FOR YOU

### What the N.R.A. Is

The National Rifle Association of America, commonly referred to as the N.R.A., was organized in 1871 by shooters to help shooters. It is the oldest national organization of sportsmen in the United States. It is a nonprofit corporation chartered by the Congress of the United States as a membership organization. It is not affiliated with organizations of arms and ammunition manufacturers, receives no subsidies from the arms trade, and serves as the governing body for shooting activities in much the same capacity that the Amateur Athletic Union and the National Amateur Athletic Federation serve other sportsmen. All rifle and pistol shooters who engage in official competitions, and several thousand local shooting clubs, support the N.R.A.

The purposes of the N.R.A. are summarized in the following paragraph from the By-Laws:

"The objects of the Association shall be to educate the nation in marksmanship, to encourage marksmanship throughout the United States, particularly among civilians, both as a sport and for the purposes of qualifying as finished marksmen those individuals who may be called upon to serve in time of war; to encourage competition in marksmanship between teams and individuals in all parts of the United States; to encourage legislation for the establishment and maintenance of suitable ranges; to secure the issuance of arms and ammunition to those practicing on such ranges; and to create a public sentiment for the encouragement of rifle practice both as a sport and as a necessary means of national defense."

## Competitive Program

Approximately one third of a million men and boys belong to the N.R.A., and there are more than seven thousand local clubs. In order to meet the demands of these clubs and individuals for organized competition, the N.R.A. supervises local tournaments; state, regional, and national championships; and international competitions, including the shooting program of the Olympic Games.

In addition to the above events, there are around-the-calendar competition and qualification courses for senior and junior clubs, high-school teams, college teams, summer camps, and other local organizations. The winners of these matches have an opportunity to advance to national competitions.

## Army Cooperation

Since the N.R.A. is chartered by Congress and aids the national defense, it has a semigovernmental status that enables its members and clubs to receive special benefits from the Department of the

Army. Individual members can qualify for Army medals and ratings by firing prescribed courses. The Department of the Army extends assistance to clubs in the loan of arms when the Army supply justifies such action. Individual N.R.A. members are permitted to purchase surplus ordnance supplies, including rifles and ammunition through the Army's Director of Civilian Marksmanship, when arms and ammunition are available for sale.

## Service Functions of the N.R.A. Headquarters

The N.R.A. maintains a national headquarters in its own building at 1600 Rhode Island Avenue, N.W., Washington 6, D. C. The headquarters staff is composed of outstanding specialists who direct civilian shooting activities and supply information to individual members and clubs.

The Technical Service gives information and experimental data to members and also to manufacturers and dealers in an effort to improve the quality of arms and ammunition.

Prospective members of clubs are given advice and material for forming an organization, supplied with plans for constructing rifle ranges, and furnished with instruction aids, including the latest type of visual aids.

Members are kept informed of proposed local, state, or national legislation which tends to violate the provision of the Bill of Rights of the Constitution of the United States that guarantees the rights of American citizens to keep and bear arms.

The N.R.A. publishes *The American Rifleman,* a monthly magazine of high quality devoted entirely to firearms subjects, and sends each individual member a copy. It is not restricted to modern rifle shooting, but includes articles on pistol shooting, hunting, muzzle-loading shooting, gun collecting, and other firearm topics. The material is well written by experienced arms experts, checked carefully by the N.R.A. staff, and generously illustrated.

## The Governing Body of the N.R.A.

The N.R.A. is governed by a board of sixty directors, one third of whom are elected each year. The directors then elect an Executive

Committee of ten members, who exercise the active control of the organization. All officers serve without pay except the Executive Vice-President and the Executive Director. The technical and administrative staff, of course, are well paid.

## Individual Membership

Any man or woman eighteen years of age or older may become a senior member if his application is endorsed by an N.R.A. member, an officer of an N.R.A. club, or some public official. There are three principal classes of membership: Annual, Associate, and Life.

An annual member pays four dollars per year and receives a free subscription to *The American Rifleman*. He may receive free advice on technical matters direct from the N.R.A. headquarters. He receives reduced entry fees at certain marksmanship tournaments and other benefits.

An associate member pays two dollars and is admitted in this status only if he or she is a dependent member of the family of an annual or life member. An associate member does not receive the magazine.

A life member pays fifty dollars. He receives all the privileges of an annual member plus the right to vote, to be elected to the board of directors, and to serve as an officer of the association.

## Junior Membership

A boy or girl less than nineteen years of age may be recommended for a junior individual annual membership, which costs fifty cents. He receives membership credentials, a handbook written especially for him, and announcements of competitions for which he is eligible. As a junior member, he does not receive the magazine, but he may subscribe at a reduced rate.

## N.R.A. Clubs

As in any other sport or hobby, the greatest pleasure can be derived from shooting by becoming a member of a club devoted to rifle and pistol activities. By all means join one of the clubs in your community. If, by chance, no such club now exists take the initiative to start one.

Any group of ten or more American citizens, eighteen years of age or older, may apply for an N.R.A. Senior Club charter. The only fees paid to the N.R.A. are annual dues of three dollars per active club member. These dues not only establish N.R.A. affiliation for the club as an organization but also pay for individual N.R.A. membership for each club member, including an annual subscription to *The American Rifleman*. This special club rate is a reduction from the regular four dollar N.R.A. individual membership.

Junior rifle clubs may be established by ten or more boys or girls under nineteen years of age. Each junior club is under the direct supervision of an adult instructor. Such clubs pay an annual affiliation fee of five dollars, regardless of the number of club members. The N.R.A. has a special program of safety education, instruction, qualification firing and competition for these younger shooters. Manuals on instruction and club operation are furnished each junior club instructor. All club members are issued a pocket *Junior Rifle Handbook*.

Some junior clubs are independent, but the majority are organized within existing youth organizations, such as schools, Boy Scout Troops, Girl Scout Troops, Y.M.C.A.'s, Y.M.H.A.'s Sons of the Legion, Sons of the V.F.W., 4-H Clubs, etc.

College shooters can also obtain an N.R.A. club charter under an arrangement rather similar to the junior club affiliation. There is a series of special N.R.A. competitions for such groups.

Members of N.R.A. affiliated junior and college clubs may subscribe to *The American Rifleman* at special reduced rates.

Full information on organizing any of these types of clubs can be secured by writing to the Club Activities Division, National Rifle Association of America, 1600 Rhode Island Avenue, Washington 6, D.C.

# Part II

## PISTOL AND
## REVOLVER SHOOTING

# Chapter 1

## THE DEVELOPMENT
## OF SINGLE-SHOT PISTOLS

### Why Men Like Pistol Shooting

Civilian shooters like to fire pistols because their cost is low, they are easy to carry, the ammunition is relatively inexpensive, and it is usually easy to find the space required for a private range or a club. Pistol shooting develops control of the nerves, co-ordination of the muscles, and concentration of the mind, and at the same time it provides more complete relaxation than tennis, golf, baseball, or the other better-known sports.

Policemen and sheriffs depend upon success in pistol marksmanship to save their lives in their daily contact with armed criminals. The criminal usually will not engage in gun play with a law-enforcement officer who is known to be a good shot, but if the criminal is foolish enough to draw on the officer, the latter can win if he has been trained properly. Furthermore, the public has more confidence in its defenders if they gain and maintain their skill with arms by means of constant and organized marksmanship practice.

Members of the armed services not armed with shoulder weapons need hand guns for personal protection when engaged with the enemy at close quarters, and even those who are required to carry shoulder weapons have found that a hand gun can be fired faster, more easily, and often more accurately at short ranges than other weapons.

### The Sport for the Average Man

You need not be a genius or an athlete to become a good pistol shot. If you have good health, normal vision (natural or corrected by glasses), and ordinary intelligence, you can easily and quickly master the essentials of pistol marksmanship. After learning the fundamentals, you can go on to become a regional or even a national champion if you have the desire to win. Your mental attitude is the most important factor in success with hand guns.

## Pistols and Revolvers

The word *pistol* has several meanings. First, it refers to all hand guns, weapons that are fired from the hand, such as single-shot pistols, revolvers, and semiautomatic pistols. A single-shot pistol is designed to be loaded with only one cartridge at a time. The revolver has one barrel, behind which is a cylinder containing several chambers, usually five or six, although some .22-caliber revolvers have eight or nine. Each time that the hammer is cocked (pulled all the way back), the cylinder is automatically revolved, bringing a new chamber in line with the barrel so that several shots can be fired in succession without reloading.

In automatic weapons, either the recoil (kick) of the gun or the pressure developed by the gases from the combustion of the powder in the cartridge can be used to open the breech (rear of the barrel) after each shot is fired, at the same time extracting and ejecting the empty cartridge case; a new cartridge is loaded into the chamber; the chamber is closed by a spring; and the gun is ready to fire when the trigger is pulled again.

When a gun of this type is made so that it will continue to fire as long as the trigger is held back and it receives ammunition, it is fully automatic. When a new pull on the trigger is required to fire each shot, it is correctly described as an autoloading, self-loading, or semiautomatic weapon. Thus, the ordinary automatic pistol is actually semiautomatic.

With this brief introduction to hand guns, it might be expected that we would immediately plunge into the methods of holding, aiming, and firing, but generations of shooters have found that they can handle their weapons better if they have a good understanding of their development, construction, and operation. Therefore, we shall begin with the early development of single-shot pistols and then examine the progress made in the design of revolvers, semiautomatic pistols, and ammunition.

## Gunpowder

We do not know where or when gunpowder was invented, but it is certain that a monk, Roger Bacon, mentioned it in his writings sometime before 1267, probably as early as 1249, and there is an ancient manuscript which indicates that gunpowder was in existence as early as 846. The first record of its use in Europe was made by Bishop Albertus Magnus, who said in 1280 that gunpowder was employed during the siege of Seville, Spain, in 1247. Other records show that various kinds of guns and cannon were extensively used before 1350 A.D.

Gunpowder is a mixture of saltpeter, sulphur, and charcoal. From its discovery until the invention of guncotton in 1846, it was the only explosive in common use. It is still used today for blasting and other purposes and usually consists of 75 parts saltpeter by weight, 10 parts sulphur, and 15 parts charcoal.

Fig. 1. A German peasant holding a hand cannon.

Fig. 2. A German soldier firing a hand cannon.

Fig. 3. A French soldier firing a hand cannon.

## Primitive Firearms

The earliest firearms were probably rockets fired from a bamboo tube to give them direction and elevation. The next step was the construction of wooden cannon bound with iron hoops, and from those primitive fieldpieces it was a short transition to cannon of iron and bronze.

We do not know whether the large cannon came first or the small hand cannon, such as the one shown in Figure 1. This illustration is a reproduction of a drawing found in an ancient manuscript. It shows a German peasant of about the year 1400 holding in his left hand a short iron tube fastened to a wooden handle. He filled the little cannon with gunpowder, dropped in an iron or lead ball, and held a flaming torch at the muzzle. When the powder in the tube caught fire, it burned and hurled the ball into space.

Figure 2 shows a German soldier of about the same period, but his hand cannon has a hole in it at a distance from the muzzle, thus making it possible to light the charge of powder with less danger to the shooter.

Figure 3 shows a French soldier of about the year 1450. His gun is mounted on the end of a stick, which is held under the left arm during firing, and the touchhole, where the powder is lighted, has been moved farther back so that the powder will burn from the rear toward the front.

Fig. 4. A cavalryman in armor about to fire a petronel from horseback.

All of the early firearms were not fired on foot. Figure 4 is a picture from an ancient manuscript showing a cavalryman in armor about to fire a little gun called a petronel. This was simply a short iron cylinder with a stock of the same metal and a ring at the end. The touchhole was on the top side. The weapon was strung on a leather strap passed over the horseman's head so that the gun would hang against his side when not in use. A short forked rest supported the gun for firing at one end and was fastened at the other end to the saddle. In the illustration, the horseman holds a burning wick called a match in his right hand, while his left steadies the gun for discharge. This gun was probably used about the year 1425.

Fig. 5. A small hand cannon called a hand culverin.

The ancestors of our modern pistols were small hand cannon, such as the one in Figure 5, called a hand culverin. The fork fastened to the gun about two thirds of the distance from the muzzle to the rear of the barrel was used to steady the weapon in the left hand.

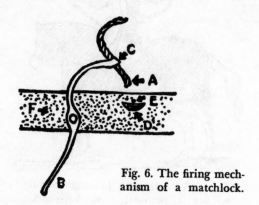

Fig. 6. The firing mechanism of a matchlock.

## The Matchlock

Men were not satisfied with their early guns. They continued to experiment until they developed the matchlock in Europe about 1450. Figure 6 shows the firing mechanism of an early gun of this type. A lighted wick (match), the burning end of which is marked

*A* in the drawing, was carried in the clamp (marked *C*) at the end of a curved piece of metal called a *serpentine* because it resembled a snake. This serpentine was simply a primitive form of our modern trigger and is marked *B* in the drawing. When the lower end was pulled, the burning end of the wick was lowered into a pan containing powder, marked *D,* The main charge of powder in the gun was thus ignited through the small touchhole marked *E*. The powder in the gun burned, generated gas, and threw out the iron or lead ball.

In order to be sure that the slowly burning match would light the powder, the gunner had to blow on the match before firing his gun. Various substances were tried in an effort to make a match that would burn steadily and not require blowing on it. The best substance was saltpeter. The match was soaked in a saltpeter solution, dried, and then cut into lengths of four or five feet. One end was attached to the serpentine, and the rest was left dangling or else it was wrapped around the stock. When the soldier pulled the serpentine, he not only had to lift the lighted end of the match, but he also had to lift at least part of the weight of the slack portion of the match.

These difficulties were met by developing a snapping matchlock. This had a spring and lever arrangement so that the serpentine would be held back by a spring until released by pulling. The pull of the trigger (serpentine) caused the upper end to fall with a quick blow that lighted the priming powder in the pan and at the same time knocked the ashes off the glowing end of the match. Figure 7 shows a Chinese matchlock pistol of the snapping type. In Europe the serpentine was now called a cock because its new shape suggested the head of a rooster.

The snapping mechanism of the improved matchlock was not a new discovery. It had been used before on the crossbow for discharging darts and arrows. Throughout the history of firearms men have gone back to some earlier weapon to get inspiration for putting the old ideas into new forms for new purposes. This is one reason we should know something about the history of firearm progress. History is a light out of the past that can light our footsteps in the future.

## Early Attempts to Make a Repeater

Centuries ago men wanted firearms that would fire more than one shot without reloading. Figure 8 shows a multi-shot hand cannon with its barrels side by side. Figure 9 shows a hand cannon made with two barrels side by side and a third barrel on top. These were probably designed and made about the year 1500. Although the firing mechanism was not shown in the ancient manuscripts from which these drawings were copied, it is probable that they were matchlocks.

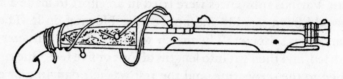

Fig. 7. A Chinese matchlock pistol.

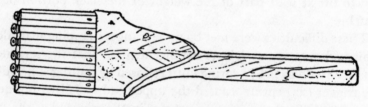

Fig. 8. A multishot hand cannon with its barrels side by side.

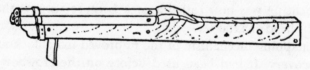

Fig. 9. A hand cannon with two barrels side by side and a third on top.

## Guns Help the Rise of the Common Man

In the year 1430, an Italian writer described the siege of the city of Lucca thus:

"The Luccanians invented a new weapon. In their hands, they

held a block of wood about one and one-half yards long, fastened to which was an iron tube filled with sulfur and saltpeter which threw iron bullets by the force of fire. The blow, when it struck, brought certain death, and neither armor nor shield was a sufficient protection; then, not seldom did a single bullet penetrate a file of two or three men."

It was this ability of the ordinary man, armed with a gun, to kill knights in armor that later led to the decline of knighthood and the rise of the foot soldier as the chief reliance of the king. Knights had been recruited from the upper classes, but foot soldiers were peasants who gradually grew in power until, centuries later, they were able to gain a fair degree of freedom and prepare the way for the rise of the republican form of government.

## The Wheel Lock

The wheel lock was probably developed in Germany about 1515. The firing mechanism was based on the principle of making sparks by striking steel against flint and consisted of a notched wheel with

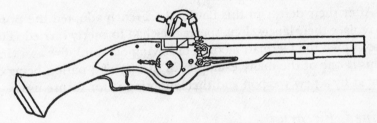

Fig. 10. A martial wheellock pistol.

a spring, which was something like a clock spring. The wheel was wound with a keylike object called a *spanner*. When the trigger was pulled, the wheel was released and revolved rapidly against a piece of flint held in the jaws of a cock. This produced sparks, which lighted the priming powder in the pan and set off the main charge of powder in the barrel. Figure 10 shows a martial wheel-lock pistol.

Figure 11 includes two views of the wheel-lock firing mechanism. The notched wheel (*A*) rotates in the direction indicated by the arrow and strikes sparks from a piece of flint (*B*), which is held firmly against the wheel by the clamp (*C*) and the spring (*E*). When the lock is cocked, the cam (*G*) presses against the arm (*F*) and holds the cover (*D*) away from the pan holding the powder. Pulling the trigger releases the catch (*J*), which holds the wheel in the locked position, and the spring (*K*) rotates the wheel when it returns to its normal position indicated in the dotted lines of the lower view. If we think of the mechanism as resembling that of a modern cigarette lighter, the whole thing becomes easy to understand.

## Origin of the Word Pistol

About the year 1540, a short, lightweight wheel lock was developed in the city of Pistoia, Italy, and called a pistol. This weapon was small and handy enough to be carried by mounted men. At the Battle of Renty, fought in 1544, German cavalry used the pistol successfully for the first time in the history of warfare when they charged the French in squadrons fifteen to twenty ranks deep. The cavalrymen halted as soon as they came close enough to fire, each rank firing in turn and wheeling to the left or right, falling in again at the rear and reloading their pistols.

After their defeat in this battle, the French adopted the pistols to replace their lances, long spears they had formerly carried. They also copied the German method of having one rank fire at a time. This is one of the many examples in history of a nation being defeated by a new weapon and then adopting it for future use.

## Rifled Firearms

For many centuries most firearms were smoothbores, that is, the barrel was simply a hollow tube, smooth inside. It is believed that during the early days of the wheel lock, probably between 1515 and 1550, gunsmiths in Germany began to cut grooves inside the gun barrels, thus producing what we now call *rifling*. These grooves were usually cut in a spiral to give the bullet a spin that would insure its steady flight, point on, toward the target, but some of the very early rifled arms had straight grooves. In what is now the United States, rifled weapons of all kinds—pistols, rifles, and carbines—came into general use while we were still under the British flag, but in Europe

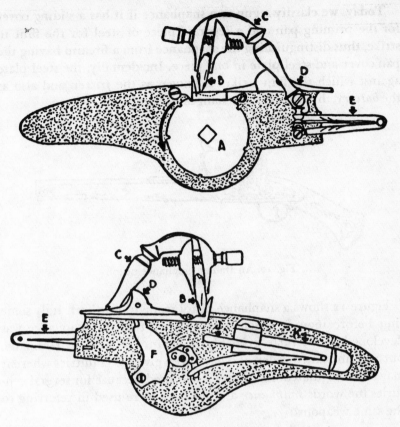

Fig. 11. Two views of the wheellock firing mechanism.

smoothbores—guns without rifling—were common until well into the nineteenth century.

## The Snaphance

The word *snaphance*, also spelled *snaphaunce*, is of Dutch or German origin and comes from the fact that the hammer, connected to a spring, falls forward with a snap, sending sparks into a pan containing priming powder and connected through a touchhole with the main charge of powder in the barrel. The jaws holding the flint were called the *cock*, and the piece of steel against which the flint strikes to make fire was called the *hen*.

Today, we classify a gun as a snaphance if it has a sliding cover for the priming pan and a separate piece of steel for the flint to strike, thus distinguishing the snaphance from a firearm having the pan cover and steel plate in one piece. Incidentally, the steel plate against which the flint strikes is known as the *frizzen* and also as the *battery*, these being interchangeable words.

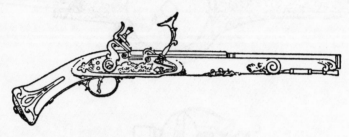

Fig. 12. An Italian snaphance pistol.

Figure 12 shows a snaphance pistol made in northern Italy some time before 1600. It is generally believed that the snaphance was developed about 1550, probably in Spain, Holland, or Germany, but Scotland and Sweden also have been given as countries where it may have originated. Its history is confused because for several centuries the words *snaphance* and *flintlock* were used in referring to the same weapons.

## The Miquelet

The word *miquelet* comes from a corps of armed men known as "Miquelites," who performed duty as escorts for distinguished persons and shipments of valuable cargoes in Spain. They were named for one of their leaders, Miquel de Prats, an armed retainer of the notorious Cesare Borgia.

The miquelet lock has a heavy outside mainspring and hammer (cock) assembly, as distinguished from the snaphance lock with its lock mechanism inside a lock plate where it cannot be injured easily. In this feature the miquelet is inferior to the snaphance, but the miquelet has the advantage of having a frizzen (battery) and pan cover in one piece, so that the pan is uncovered when the flint hits the frizzen.

Another feature of the miquelet is a safety catch, made necessary by a faulty design permitting the cock to slip when in the half-cock position. This safety catch consists of a bolt at right angles to the lock plate, and a nose on the front of the cock that rests on the bolt at the half-cock. The first part of the pull on the trigger releases the bolt and leaves the cock free to strike the frizzen. Another distinguishing feature is that the miquelet always has a hammer that is straight and not S-shaped.

Both pistols and shoulder arms with miquelet locks were used for many centuries in countries bordering or adjacent to the Mediterranean. We do not know when or where this weapon was developed, but we do know that it is one of the transition pieces between the wheel lock and the flintlock. Figure 13 shows an Arabian miquelet pistol.

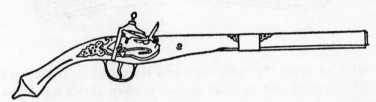

Fig. 13. An Arabian miquelet pistol.

## The Flintlock

The flintlock, like other early weapons, was not definitely invented at some particular time and place by a single person. Instead, it was a gradual development, the product of many gun designers, but it began to emerge as a distinct type about 1630 and reached its final form about 1675. In its last stage it had a frizzen (battery) that was made in one piece with the cover of the priming pan. When the trigger was pulled, the hammer (cock) struck the frizzen to make sparks and at the same time knocked the cover of the priming pan out of the way so that the sparks could ignite the powder in the pan.

The flintlock was the weapon of our ancestors who fought under the British flag in the French and Indian Wars of colonial days and against the British in the Revolution and the War of 1812. It remained the common weapon of warfare and hunting until the percussion (cap-and-ball) system of ignition came into general use sometime between 1835 and 1845.

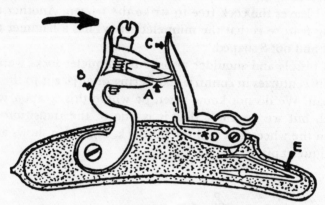

Fig. 14. The firing mechanism of a flintlock.

Figure 14 shows the mechanism of a typical flintlock. When the trigger is pulled, the hammer (cock), marked *B*, springs forward and strikes the flint, marked *A*, against the battery (frizzen), marked *C*. The battery flies forward, taking with it the pan cover, and the sparks drop into the priming pan, marked *D*, where they set fire to the priming powder. The fire in the pan then passes through the touchhole in the side of the barrel and fires the main charge of powder. The spring for the battery is marked *E*.

Flintlock pistols made in the United States armories at Harpers Ferry, Virginia, and Springfield, Massachusetts, or by private individuals and companies under contract with the United States, for use by the federal military and naval forces or for distribution to state forces under federal jurisdiction are classified by collectors as U.S. martial flintlock pistols. Figure 15 shows one of these hand guns, which played an important part in making and preserving us a nation.

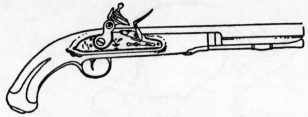

Fig. 15. A U.S. martial flintlock pistol.

## Kentucky Flintlock Pistols

A true Kentucky pistol is a short arm made by one of the same gunsmiths who made the well-known Kentucky rifle. These weapons are similar in design and construction to the Kentucky rifles, having the same slender stocks and "furniture," the rifles' trigger guards, ramrod thimbles, muzzle caps, etc. They are full stocked, that is, the wooden stock extends to the muzzle. No two are alike because they were not made to a standard pattern. Like the Kentucky flintlock rifles, they were seldom made in Kentucky but were made mostly in eastern Pennsylvania, although a few were made in New York, New Jersey, and Ohio. A typical Kentucky flintlock pistol is shown in Figure 16.

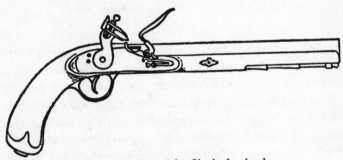

Fig. 16. A Kentucky flintlock pistol.

## Percussion (Cap-and-Ball) Pistols

In 1807, a Scotch Presbyterian minister of Belhelvie, in Aberdeenshire, received a patent for a specially designed lock, in which a

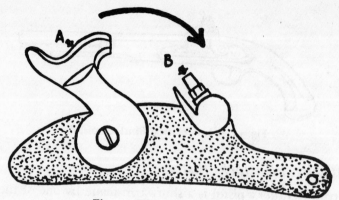

Fig. 17. The percussion lock.

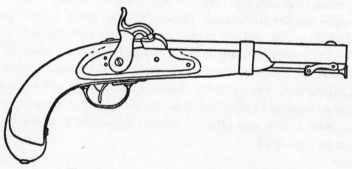

Fig. 18. A U.S. martial percussion pistol.

steel hammer or striker would explode a small quantity of detonating powder placed in the pan of the gun. This invention, next to the discovery of gunpowder, was the most important development in the history of weapons up to that time, for it is the basic principle underlying the evolution of the metallic cartridge, successful breech-loading firearms, and all other modern gun improvements.

Forsythe found that a very sensitive compound, such as fulminate of mercury, could be exploded with a blow. He mixed the fulminate of mercury with powdered glass and loaded the mixture into copper or brass caps, which we now call primers. These caps were placed in a nipple over a vent hole leading into the powder charge in the barrel. When the hammer hit the cap, the flame from the primer went through the vent and ignited the main powder charge. In modern cartridges, the priming mixture is built into the base or head of the cartridge.

Figure 17 shows a later form of the percussion lock. When the trigger is pulled, the hammer, marked *A*, falls forward and strikes the anvil, marked *B*, with enough force to set off a percussion cap containing the primer charge.

## U.S. Martial Single-Shot Percussion Pistols

Single-shot percussion pistols were made for the armed services of the United States during the second quarter of the nineteenth century in the United States armories at Harpers Ferry, Virginia, and Springfield, Massachusetts, and by various private contractors. One of these pistols is shown in Figure 18.

## Deringer and Derringers

A *Deringer* is any of the guns made by a Philadelphia family of that name, from pistols to carbines, but when the word is spelled *Derringer* (with two r's), it includes all short-barreled pocket pistols of large caliber. Deringer was the originator of the type that took his name, and his guns were extremely popular. To trade on his reputation, competitors brought out similar models, which they called Derringers to avoid lawsuits.

## Dueling Pistols

Dueling pistols from about 1750 to 1800 were standardized as single-barrel flintlocks with a smooth bore .5 inch in diameter or caliber .50, as we would term it today. The barrel could not exceed 10.5 inches or be less than 9 inches in length. The sights had to be fixed, and the trigger pull could not exceed 3 pounds. Otherwise, the grip, safety, and trigger system could be of any design and construction. The wooden portion extended to the muzzle in the earlier specimens, but the later models often had half stocks. Sights were provided for target practice, but the code of dueling prohibited taking deliberate aim, that is, the opponents were to aim and fire on signal or on command, as determined by the seconds.

Hair triggers were invented so that it would be possible to fire the pistol by a slight pressure on the trigger, so light that it would not disturb the aim. A small, powerful spring was first compressed or set by pressing the trigger forward. Years later, set triggers were made so that they could be set by means of a button.

Percussion dueling pistols were similar in construction to the flintlock pistols except for the ignition system. Dueling went out of style in America before the general introduction of cartridge pistols, hence there are no true American cartridge dueling pistols and very few European models in that category.

## Single-Shot Cartridge Pistols

Single-shot cartridge pistols can be used only for target shooting. Because of their limited use, they are manufactured commercially in limited quantities and today are made principally on special order.

# Chapter 2

## PERCUSSION REVOLVERS

### Early Revolvers

For many centuries, men experimented with various methods of making a pistol so that more than one shot could be fired without reloading. A simple multishot pistol was made by having several barrels with a firing device for each. Another type of gun had only one barrel, which was loaded with several charges of powder and balls, one charge on top of another like a Roman candle. Still another design consisted of a single barrel and a magazine (storage container) with a mechanism for feeding charges into the barrel by the operation of either a lever or a slide. None of these systems was found very satisfactory.

The first step toward the creation of a revolver came when a revolving mechanism was designed for bringing either several barrels or several chambers at the breech of the barrel successively into line for firing. For example, a flintlock pistol would have several barrels, each with its own priming pan and frizzen, which were revolved to bring each one successively into place for firing by the single hammer of the gun. Later, in percussion days, this type of weapon was known as a pepperbox pistol. Obviously, the addition of barrels increased the number of shots that could be fired without reloading, but the weight and difficulty of firing accurately were also increased.

The finest multishot weapon made before the invention of the Colt revolver was the Collier flintlock revolver, patented in 1818 by Elisha Haydon Collier of Boston, Massachusetts, an American citizen who spent several years in England, where he made and sold most of his firearms. A typical Collier revolver was caliber .34, 5 shot, with a 9-inch octagon barrel and a total length of 17½ inches, although other barrel lengths were used.

In most Collier revolvers, the cylinder was rotated by hand, although some specimens had a spring arrangement for rotation. Ignition was supplied by a single flintlock firing device with a magazine for powder in the back of the frizzen, making it possible to re-cock for each shot without stopping to prime. The Collier-type revolvers were expensive to make, fragile, slow in operation, and awkward to carry.

## Samuel Colt and His Invention

Samuel Colt was born in Hartford, Connecticut, July 19, 1814. As a boy he worked hard on a farm and in various small industrial plants, but he dreamed of success as a firearms manufacturer and he made his dreams come true. Today, the word *Colt* is a synonym for *revolver* all over the world, although to many people it conveys the idea of any hand gun, revolver, or semiautomatic pistol.

In 1832, when he was barely nineteen years old, he sent a description of his basic idea to the United States Patent Office. In 1833, by lecturing on laughing gas he earned the money to construct both a pistol and a revolver, and on their principle he obtained French and English patents in 1835 when he visited Europe. On his return to the United States he received his first patent on February 25, 1836. This

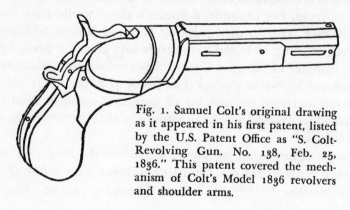

Fig. 1. Samuel Colt's original drawing as it appeared in his first patent, listed by the U.S. Patent Office as "S. Colt-Revolving Gun. No. 138, Feb. 25, 1836." This patent covered the mechanism of Colt's Model 1836 revolvers and shoulder arms.

patent covered the mechanism of his Model 1836 revolvers and revolving shoulder arms. His original drawing is shown in Figure 1.

## Colt's First Company

On March 5, 1836, Colt formed the Patent Arms Manufacturing Company, at Paterson, New Jersey, at the foot of the falls of the Passaic River, where he could obtain water power to run the machinery. Here at Paterson were made the famous revolvers, revolving rifles, and revolving shotguns so highly regarded by modern gun

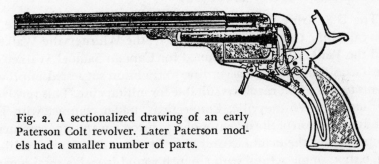

Fig. 2. A sectionalized drawing of an early Paterson Colt revolver. Later Paterson models had a smaller number of parts.

collectors. Figure 2 illustrates a sectionalized drawing of an early Paterson revolver. Later Paterson models had fewer parts. Figure 3 shows a Paterson revolver with a long barrel. Figure 4 is a drawing made by a Colt artist of a revolver similar to the U.S. Army Revolver, Model 1847, which was not made at Paterson but which was probably designed by Colt while operating his original factory.

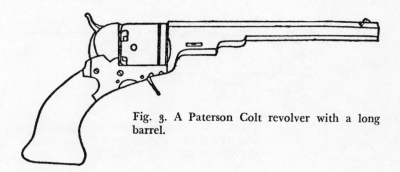

Fig. 3. A Paterson Colt revolver with a long barrel.

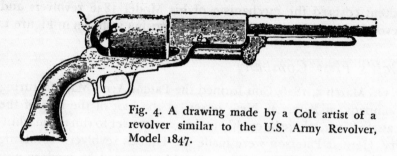

Fig. 4. A drawing made by a Colt artist of a revolver similar to the U.S. Army Revolver, Model 1847.

## The Whitneyville Revolver

The U.S. Army Revolver, Model 1847, illustrated in Figure 5, also called the Colt-Walker Model 1847, the Whitneyville Walker, and the Walker Pistol, was named for Captain Samuel Walker of the Texas Rangers, who according to tradition suggested improvements to make Colt revolvers suitable for military use. This revolver was made at Whitneyville, Connecticut, under contract with Eli Whitney, the son of the inventor of the cotton gin and a government contractor for the manufacturer of military muskets. It was caliber .44, 6 shot, single action, with a 9-inch round barrel, a total length of 15½ inches, and a weight of 9 ounces. A hinged-lever ramrod, usually called a loading lever, was mounted under the barrel for seating the bullets in the chambers, since all charges of powder and bullets were loaded from the front of the cylinder. This weapon was a favorite arm of mounted men for years after its invention and won its place in the gallery of American history after its use by our cavalry in the Mexican War.

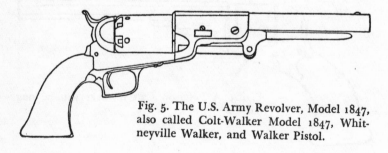

Fig. 5. The U.S. Army Revolver, Model 1847, also called Colt-Walker Model 1847, Whitneyville Walker, and Walker Pistol.

## The Hartford Arms

Colt made revolvers at his Paterson plant from 1836 to 1842, when his original corporation failed financially. The Whitneyville contract was only a stopgap. In 1848 Colt established his factory at Hartford, where he began to make a long series of revolvers for the armed services of the United States as well as for the pioneers who were pushing back the frontier.

One of his many Hartford models was the Colt Model 1851 Navy Revolver, also called Old Model Belt Pistol, Old Model Navy Pistol, Model of 1851 Navy, and Model of 1851 Navy Pistol. An exploded view of the Colt Model 1851 Navy Revolver is shown in Figure 6. This was caliber .36, 6 shot, single action, with a 7½-inch octagon

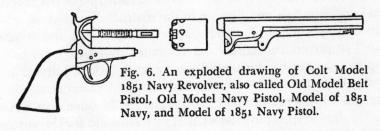

Fig. 6. An exploded drawing of Colt Model 1851 Navy Revolver, also called Old Model Belt Pistol, Old Model Navy Pistol, Model of 1851 Navy, and Model of 1851 Navy Pistol.

barrel, a total length of 13 inches, and a weight of 2 pounds, 10 ounces.

## Colt Arms in the Civil War

Samuel Colt was one of the few men who foresaw the coming of the Civil War. He enlarged his factory, installed additional machinery, and made his estimates on a basis of one million Union soldiers fighting for a period of five years, which was a close guess made long before hostilities opened. Without regard for profit, he put all his energies into the Union cause and worked so hard that he died on January 10, 1862, aged forty-eight, in the prime of his life. For three days he lay in state, and on the fourth day he was buried with the full military honors of his rank, a lieutenant colonel of the Connecticut Militia. To the slow tap of muffled drums, troops with reversed arms followed his casket to the grave between long double lines of bareheaded employees of the company he founded.

After the Civil War, Colt percussion revolvers were converted to fire metallic cartridges until new models were designed especially for the use of such loads. The corporation continued in business for many years as Colt's Patent Fire Arms Manufacturing Company, the name given it by its founder, but a few years ago it adopted its present name of Colt's Manufacturing Company, because it makes many objects other than firearms.

## Colt's Place in History

Without detracting in the least from the honor due to Samuel Colt, it should be clearly understood that he did not invent the revolver in the strict sense of the term. The principle of the revolver was known in Asia and Europe in the matchlock period, as shown by many specimens of matchlock revolving pistols and muskets found in private collections and museums. What Colt did was to improve the design mechanically to make it practical, develop assembly-line mass-production methods, and, most important, publicize and sell his product in great quantities. In other words, Colt did for the firearms business what Henry Ford did for the automobile industry.

## Other Famous Makers of Percussion Revolvers

Colt was not the only manufacturer of percussion revolvers for the United States during the Civil War. Allen and Wheelock, Joslyn, Pettingill, Remington, Rogers and Spencer, Savage, and Whitney revolvers were purchased for Federal forces. In addition, revolvers were imported in large quantities from Europe. The full story of the part played in our history by percussion and other arms is beyond the scope of this text, but is treated at great length in the author's *Gun Collecting*. Detailed descriptions, illustrations, and values of arms for collectors are given in the author's *The Gun Collector's Handbook of Values*.

# Chapter 3

## MODERN CARTRIDGE REVOLVERS

### General Types

Figure 1 is a drawing of an earlier type of revolver designed for the use of metallic cartridges. It is variously known as the break-frame, hinged-frame, hinged-action, break-open, top-breaking, or tip-up type. The top strap is unlatched from the breech and the barrel swung downward to open the revolver. When the action is open, the empty cartridges may be pushed out by a star-shaped extractor that is mounted on a central stem in the cylinder and fits around a portion of each cartridge. Revolvers of this type are still made for light sporting purposes but not for target shooting.

Figure 2 is a drawing of a solid-frame, swing-out type of revolver,

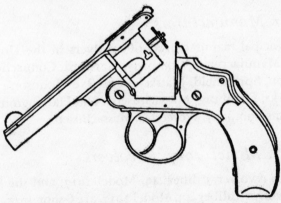

Fig. 1. A revolver known as the break-frame, hinged-frame, hinged-action, break-open, top-breaking, or tip-up type.

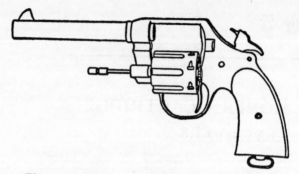

Fig. 2. A solid-frame swing-out type of revolver.

which is in general use today. The frame is not hinged or jointed. To extract the empty cartridge cases, the cylinder is swung out to one side and the empty cartridges pushed out by the extractor.

In some of the obsolete models of the solid-frame type, the cylinder is not hinged and cannot swing out, but may be removed for loading and unloading. In still other obsolete solid-frame revolvers, the cylinder does not have an extractor. Instead, the cartridges are put into the cylinder one at a time through a loading gate in the side of the frame, and the empty cartridge cases are pushed out, one by one, through the same gate by means of a ramrod or loading lever attached to the lower side of the barrel.

## Revolver Manufacturers

The principal manufacturers of revolvers in the United States are Colt's Manufacturing Company, Hartford, Connecticut; Smith and Wesson, Springfield, Massachusetts; Iver Johnson's Arms and Cycle Works, Fitchburg, Massachusetts; and Harrington and Richardson Arms Company, Worcester, Massachusetts.

## The U.S. Model 1917 Revolvers

The Colt revolver, caliber .45, Model 1917, and the Smith and Wesson revolver, caliber .45, Model 1917, are 6-shot, breech-loading, solid-frame, swing-out hand weapons issued to certain members of the armed forces of the United States and sold to civilians through the regular channels of trade. The construction features of the two guns are similar. A study of these arms gives the shooter a fundamental understanding of modern revolver design.

Each has a cylinder having six chambers arranged about a central axis so that six shots may be fired before reloading is necessary. The chambers of the cylinder are loaded with six cartridges in two clips of three rounds each. When the cylinder is closed, the revolver is ready for firing.

These revolvers are designed to fire the caliber .45 Model 1911 ball cartridge. The action of cocking the hammer causes the cylinder to rotate and align the next chamber with the barrel.

To fire single action, with the revolver fully loaded with ammunition, cock the revolver with the thumb and squeeze the trigger for each shot. Double-action firing is similar to single-action except that the revolver is cocked by pressing on the trigger, releasing the trigger and pressing again, continuously until the desired number of shots is fired.

If one or more of the chambers is empty, the cylinder should be rotated so that a loaded chamber will be moved into line with the barrel when the revolver is cocked. The closed cylinder may be rotated to its proper position by holding the hammer back at about one fourth of full cock. With the hammer of the Colt revolver down, the first loaded chamber should be next on the left of the chamber aligned with the barrel since the cylinder rotates clockwise. With the hammer of the Smith and Wesson revolver down, the first loaded

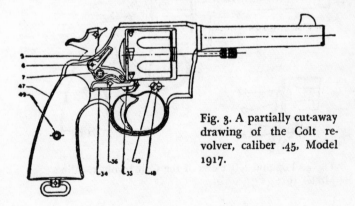

Fig. 3. A partially cut-away drawing of the Colt revolver, caliber .45, Model 1917.

chamber should be next on the right of the chamber aligned with the barrel since the cylinder of the Smith and Wesson rotates counterclockwise.

The rate of fire is limited by the dexterity of the shooter in reloading the cylinder and by his ability to aim and squeeze the trigger.

## Revolver Nomenclature

Figure 3 is a partially cut-away drawing of a Colt revolver, caliber .45, Model 1917. The numbers refer to the parts as follows: (5) safety, (6) spring, (7) lever, (47) rear strap, (49) escutcheon, (34) latch bolt, (36) bolt screw, (35) bolt spring, (19) screw, and (18) lock.

Figure 4 shows the top and left views of the same revolver and details in the lower left corner. The numbers refer to parts as follows: (21) spring, (20) latch, (42) screw, (41) plate, (48) rear strap, (50) escutcheon, (40) screw, (27) ratchet, (13) hand, (24) trigger, and (42) screw. The numbers in Figures 3 and 4 are neither consecutive nor complete because the illustrations were copied from drawings numbered for purposes of disassembling and assembling the revolver.

### MODERN CARTRIDGE REVOLVERS

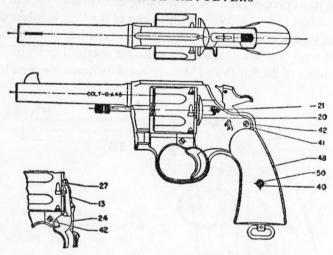

Fig. 4. Top and left views of the Colt revolver, caliber .45, Model 1917.

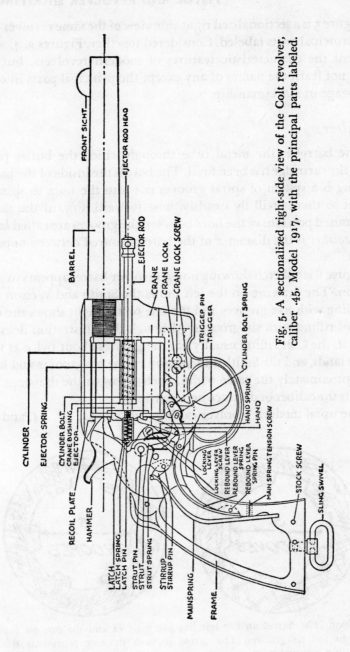

Fig. 5. A sectionalized right-side view of the Colt revolver, caliber 45, Model 1917, with the principal parts labeled.

Figure 5 is a sectionalized right-side view of the same revolver with the principal parts labeled. Considered together, Figures 3, 4, and 5 present the characteristic features of modern revolvers, but you need not learn the names of any except the principal parts in order to engage in marksmanship.

## Caliber

The barrel is the metal tube through which the bullet passes after the cartridge has been fired. The bore is the inside of the barrel. Rifling is a system of spiral grooves cut into the bore to spin the bullet so that it will fly steadily, nose forward, toward the target. The raised portions of the bore between the grooves are called *lands*. The *caliber* is the diameter of the bore measured between opposite lands.

Figure 6 is a sketch showing how a revolver barrel appears in cross section. The drawing on the left shows the Smith and Wesson type of rifling with five grooves and the one on the right shows the Colt type of rifling with six grooves. Although the illustration does not show it, the Colt rifling usually has the grooves about twice as wide as the lands, and the Smith and Wesson rifling has grooves and lands of approximately the same width. Each arrow in the drawings represents the caliber or distance between lands.

The usual modern revolver calibers are .22, .32, .38, .44, and .45.

Fig. 6. The barrel on the left has five grooves and the one on the right has six grooves. The arrow in each drawing represents the caliber measurement.

Caliber may be expressed in decimal fractions of an inch or in milli-meters when the latter usage is definitely indicated. Caliber does not indicate speed or power. Also, the mere fact that a revolver is designated by a certain caliber does not necessarily mean that the diameter between the lands in the bore will be that many hun-dredths of an inch. For example, the .38 Special Revolver made by Colt measures .346 inch between lands and .353 inch between grooves. The bullet has a diameter of .359 inch, hence it is apparent that the actual caliber is closer to .36 than it is to .38.

## Important Parts

Important parts of the revolver are the barrel, already discussed; the action, including the cylinder; the frame; and the stocks. The action is the mechanism that fires the cartridge. It consists of several moving parts. The firing pin is a sharp-pointed steel rod, which strikes the primer in the base of the cartridge to fire it. The firing pin may be a separate part or it may be part of the hammer. The trigger is a curved metal lever which is part of the action. When it is squeezed by the shooter's finger, it disengages a sear and discharges the revolver. The sear is essentially a small lever connected with the trigger for the purpose of releasing the hammer at the moment of firing. When the firing pin and hammer are separate parts, the ham-mer strikes the firing pin in a revolver of simple construction. A mainspring drives the hammer and firing pin forward when the trigger is squeezed.

The rear opening of the barrel is the breech into which the car-tridge is loaded. The muzzle is the mouth or front end of the barrel. The cylinder is the barrel-like object that revolves and holds the cartridges, one at a time, in line with the barrel for firing. The chambers of the cylinder are the holes into which the cartridges are loaded.

The frame is merely the structure that holds the other parts to-gether. The handle may be made of one piece, or it may be made of two pieces fastened on each side of the rear end of the frame. In many revolvers there are two pieces of wood, hard rubber, plastic, or ivory. These may be referred to as grips or stocks, but sometimes the word *stock* or the word *butt* is used in referring to the whole rear portion of the revolver held in the shooter's hand. This subject is discussed more fully in another chapter.

## The Iver Johnson "Hammer-the-Hammer" Safety Device

Figure 7 is a cross-sectional view showing the construction of a typical revolver made by Iver Johnson's Arms and Cycle Works and embodying their famous "hammer-the-hammer" safety device. An important part of this safety feature is drawn in solid black in the illustration and is marked "the famous safety lifter." It is merely a lever operated by the trigger. The firing pin is separate from the hammer, and the hammer is cut away so that it cannot strike the firing pin directly. The lever is attached to the trigger in such a manner that when the trigger is pulled the lever moves up between the hammer and the firing pin. The blow of the hammer is transmitted through the lever to the firing pin. Thus, the cartridge cannot be fired by hammering the hammer but only by pulling the trigger.

## Colt and Smith and Wesson Safety Features

The Iver Johnson device was so popular that Colt and Smith and Wesson followed with devices of their own to accomplish a similar purpose. Colt revolvers are made with a lever attached to the trigger in such a manner that a block of metal moves between the face of the hammer and the frame of the revolver to prevent the firing pin from striking the primer of the cartridge until the trigger draws the metal block out of the way. This is known as the Colt Positive Lock.

Smith and Wesson called their device, which was somewhat similar to the Colt design, the New Patent Safety Hammer Block. It should be understood that these particular safety features are not necessarily found on all models of Iver Johnson, Colt, and Smith and Wesson revolvers, and that there are other devices in all makes of revolvers that are intended to reduce accidents.

Sights are the devices on a gun for aiming. The revolver sights on semimodern revolvers had a U-shaped notch for the rear sight and

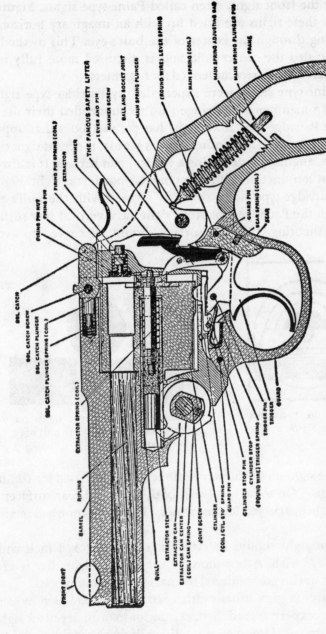

Fig. 7. A cross-sectional view showing the construction of a typical
Iver Johnson revolver. (*Courtesy Iver Johnson Arms & Cycle Works*)

a bead for the front sight, often called Paine-type sights. Figure 8 shows how these sights are lined up with an imaginary horizontal line running through the center of the bull's-eye. This method of aiming is called the center hold and is discussed more fully in a later chapter. It is not recommended for beginners.

The Paine-type sights were superseded by Patridge-type sights, named for a man named Patridge who recommended their use in 1898. The Patridge-type front sight has parallel sides that appear rectangular when you are aiming. For target use, the front sight consists of a rectangular blade having a vertical rear surface. It is always mounted in conjunction with a rectangular-notch rear sight. Figure 9 shows Patridge-type sights correctly aligned with the bull's-eye.

Although the Patridge-type front sight has a vertical rear surface for target shooting, the rear surface should be curved to avoid

Fig. 8. Paine-type sights. (*Courtesy Smith & Wesson*)

Fig. 9. Partridge-type sights correctly aligned with the bull's-eye. (*Courtesy N.R.A.*)

catching the sight on the holster if the revolver is carried for combat or self-defense. On some revolvers, both front and rear surfaces of the front sight are curved for this reason. These are known as service-type sights.

The front sight should be either 1/10 inch or 1/8 inch wide, preferably 1/8 inch. A few shooters use a front sight that is 3/32 inch wide, but this is considered too narrow by most experts.

Colored front sights, usually either red or white, are used by some shooters, but experts regard them as inferior to ordinary black sights for most purposes. However, a small chalk mark on the tip of the front sight, placed there after the sight has been thoroughly blackened, is recommended by a few shooters, especially those who like the "center hold," because it gives them a clearer view of the relationship between the front and rear sights when they are aiming at the center of the bull's-eye.

Fixed sights are lined up at the factory and permanently mounted to meet the requirements of the average shooter at the average distance. Adjustable sights may be moved up and down or right and left. On some revolvers, both sights are adjustable and on others only one can be moved. Among the regional and national champions, about one third use the sights with which the revolver is equipped at the factory, while the others buy special sights and have them installed by a gunsmith who specializes in this work. Most shooters can do as well or better with factory sights.

## Barrel Length and Sight Radius

The barrel must be long enough for all the powder in the cartridge to burn before the bullet leaves the muzzle. If the barrel extends beyond that length, the extra barrel decreases the speed of the bullet slightly because it offers friction. However, most cartridges are so loaded that they continue to exert some push on the base of the bullet through the length of the barrel.

The sight radius is the distance between the front and rear sights. A revolver with a long barrel may be aimed more accurately than one with a short barrel because a better alignment can be obtained. However, when firing a long-barreled revolver, you observe your errors of aiming more easily and may hesitate to squeeze the trigger because you are afraid that you will miss the bull's-eye. For this reason, it is usually better for a beginner to have a barrel of moderate length.

## The Advantages of the Revolver

The advantages of the revolver, compared with a semiautomatic pistol, are:

(1) It is safer for beginners to carry and fire.

(2) The revolver does not fail to function when a cartridge misfires.

## Disadvantages of the Revolver

The disadvantages of the revolver, compared with a semiautomatic pistol, are:

(1) It is slower to load and fire. (This is an advantage for a beginner, but not for the skilled shooter.)

(2) The grip (stock, butt, or handle) is usually not as good.

(3) It is more difficult to clean after firing.

(4) It is more bulky and hence awkward to carry.

(5) The accuracy may be less than that of a semiautomatic pistol because the cylinder does not line up with the barrel, especially in the case of a worn revolver, or an inexpensive one that was not rejected in the factory for defects.

(6) A corroded or worn barrel must be replaced at the factory.

(7) Defective parts are more difficult to replace.

NOTE: *The above statements are general comments that are subject to some exceptions. For example, a corroded or worn barrel of some semiautomatic pistols must be replaced at the factory, hence the revolver is not always at a disadvantage when compared with a semiautomatic pistol.*

# Chapter 4

## SEMIAUTOMATIC PISTOLS

### Manufacturers of Semiautomatic Pistols

In the United States, the principal manufacturers of semiautomatic pistols are Colt's Manufacturing Company, Hartford, Connecticut; and the High Standard Manufacturing Corporation, Hamden, Connecticut. Colt makes semiautomatic pistols in calibers .45, .38, and .22 Long Rifle. High Standard makes semiautomatic pistols in calibers .38 and .22 Long Rifle.

### Colt Government Models

The most widely used sidearm of the armed services of the United States is the Colt semiautomatic pistol, caliber .45. There are two

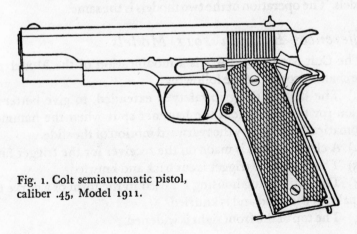

Fig. 1. Colt semiautomatic pistol, caliber .45, Model 1911.

233

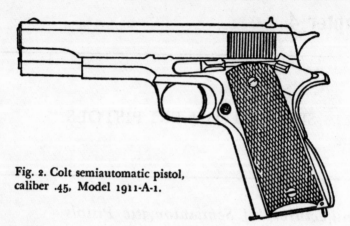

Fig. 2. Colt semiautomatic pistol,
caliber .45, Model 1911-A-1.

models. The older pistol, Model 1911, is illustrated in Figure 1. The newer weapon, Model 1911-A-1, is shown in Figure 2.

Both models are recoil-operated magazine-fed self-loading hand weapons. The gas generated in a cartridge fired in the pistol is utilized to perform the functions of extracting and ejecting the empty cartridge case, cocking the hammer, and forcing the slide to the rearmost position, thereby compressing the recoil spring. The action of the recoil spring forces the slide forward, feeding a live cartridge from the magazine into the chamber, leaving the weapon ready to fire again. Figure 3 is a sectionalized drawing of the Model 1911-A-1, but the nomenclature is essentially the same for both models. The operation of the two models is the same.

## Differences Between 1911 Models

The Colt Model 1911-A-1 is a modification of the Model 1911. The changes consist of the following:

(1) The tang of the grip safety is extended, to give better protection for the hand from the hammer spur when the hammer is automatically cocked by the rearward motion of the slide.

(2) A clearance cut is made on the receiver for the trigger finger.

(3) The face of the trigger is cut back and knurled.

(4) The mainspring housing is raised in the form of a curve to fit the palm of the hand and is knurled.

(5) The top of the front sight is widened.

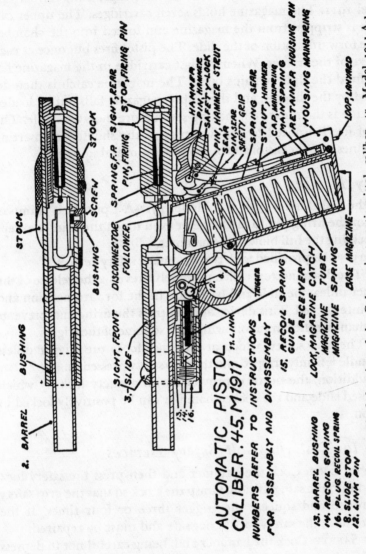

AUTOMATIC PISTOL
CALIBER .45, M1911

NUMBERS REFER TO INSTRUCTIONS
FOR ASSEMBLY AND DISASSEMBLY

2. BARREL

BARREL BUSHING

STOCK

STOCK

BUSHING SCREW

STOCK

DISCONNECTOR

FOLLOWER

SPRING, F.R. SIGHT, REAR

PIN, FIRING

STOP, FIRING PIN

HAMMER

PIN, HAMMER

SAFETY-LOCK

SEAR

PIN, SEAR

SAFETY GRIP

SPRING SEAR

STRUT, HAMMER

CAP, MAINSPRING

MAINSPRING

RETAINER HOUSING PIN

HOUSING MAINSPRING

LOOP, LANYARD

SIGHT, FRONT

3. SLIDE

TRIGGER

LOCK, MAGAZINE CATCH

MAGAZINE TUBE

MAGAZINE SPRING

BASE MAGAZINE

15. RECOIL SPRING
GUIDE

1. RECEIVER

13. BARREL BUSHING

14. RECOIL SPRING

16. PLUG RECOIL SPRING

8. SLIDE STOP

12. LINK PIN

Fig. 3. A sectionalized drawing of the Colt semiautomatic pistol, caliber .45. Model 1911-A-1.

## Ammunition and Magazine

The Colt pistol is designed to fire cartridge, ball, caliber .45, Model 1911. The magazine holds seven cartridges. The upper cartridge is stripped from the magazine and forced into the chamber by the forward motion of the slide. The pistol fires but once at each squeeze of the trigger. When the last cartridge in the magazine has been fired the slide remains open. The magazine catch is then depressed by the shooter, and the empty magazine falls out. A loaded magazine is then inserted, making seven more shots available. The rate of fire is limited by the dexterity of the shooter in inserting magazines into the pistol and his ability to aim and squeeze.

## Safety Devices

In the Colt Model 1911 and Model 1911-A-1 pistols, it is impossible for the firing pin to discharge or even touch the primer except on receiving the full blow of the hammer.

The pistol is provided with two automatic safety devices:

(1) The disconnector, which positively prevents the release of the hammer unless the slide and barrel are in the forward position and safely interlocked. This device also controls the firing and prevents more than one shot from following each squeeze of the trigger.

(2) The grip safety, which at all times locks the trigger unless the handle is firmly grasped and the grip safety pressed in.

In addition, the pistol is provided with a safety lock by which the closed slide and the cocked hammer can be positively locked in position.

## How to Test the Colt Safety Devices

SAFETY LOCK. Cock the hammer and then press the safety lock upward into the safe position. Grasp the stock so that the grip safety is depressed and squeeze the trigger three or four times. If the hammer falls, the safety lock is not safe and must be repaired.

GRIP SAFETY. Cock the hammer and, being careful not to depress the grip safety, point the pistol downward and squeeze the trigger three or four times. If the hammer falls or the grip safety is depressed by its own weight, the grip safety is not safe and must be repaired.

HALF-COCK NOTCH. Draw back the hammer until the safe engages the half-cock notch and squeeze the trigger. If the hammer falls, the hammer or sear must be replaced or repaired. Draw the hammer back nearly to full cock and then let it slip. It should fall only to half cock.

DISCONNECTOR. Cock the hammer. Shove the slide one quarter inch to the rear, hold the slide in that position, and squeeze the trigger. If the hammer falls, the disconnector is worn on top and must be replaced. Pull the slide all the way to the rear and engage the slide stop. Squeeze the trigger and at the same time release the slide. The hammer should not fall. Release the pressure on the trigger and then squeeze it. The hammer should then fall. The disconnector prevents the release of the hammer unless the slide and barrel are safely interlocked in the forward position. It also prevents more than one shot following each squeeze of the trigger.

## General Data on Colt Models 1911 and 1911-A-1

The barrel is 5 inches long. The over-all length is 8.593 inches. The pistol weighs 2.437 pounds with the magazine. The loaded magazine, holding seven rounds, weighs about .481 pound. The empty magazine weighs about .156 pound.

The Model 1911-A-1 is known commercially as the Government Model .45 Automatic Pistol. The sights are of the fixed type, ramp style, and glare proofed. The trigger is grooved. The hammer spur is checkered. The stocks are checkered. The finish is a dual-tone blue, glare proofed.

## The Colt .22 Conversion Unit

A unit formerly designed solely for owners of Government Model .45 Automatic Pistols is now available for both the .45 and the Super .38 automatic pistols. The unit parts, consisting of a special slide assembly, barrel, floating chamber, ejector, recoil spring, magazine, and slide stop, are interchanged with those of the .45 or the Super .38 without the use of tools, thus making it possible to fire .22-caliber cartridges for target practice in your regular sidearm.

## The Colt Super .38 Automatic Pistol

The Colt Super .38 Automatic Pistol is used by many big-game hunters and explorers. It is patterned after the Government Model .45 Automatic Pistol and includes the same safety features. It is chambered for the powerful Super .38 Automatic High Speed cartridge with a muzzle velocity of 1,300 feet per second. The magazine carries 9 cartridges. The barrel is 5 inches long, the total length is 8½ inches, and the weight is 39 ounces. Like the .45 Automatic, it has fixed-type ramp-style sights, glare proofed, an arched housing, grooved trigger, checkered hammer spur, checkered stocks, and is a dual-tone blue, glare proofed.

## The Colt Woodsman Semiautomatic Pistols

The Colt Woodsman semiautomatic pistols are made in three models; Sport Model, Target Model, illustrated in Figure 4, and Match Target Model. All three fire .22-caliber Long Rifle cartridges, regular or high speed. The magazine capacity of each pistol is 10 cartridges, but a 5-shot magazine is also available for the Match Target Model.

Fig. 4. Colt Woodsman Target Model semiautomatic .22-caliber pistol.

The Match Target and Target models each have a 6-inch barrel; the Sport Model has a 4½-inch barrel. The overall length is 10½ inches for the Match Target, 10½ inches for the Target, and 9 inches for the Sport Model. The weight is 41 ounces for the Match Target; the Target Model weighs 33 ounces; and the Sport Model weighs 31 ounces. Each has an adjustable rear sight and a Patridge-type front sight. The trigger is grooved; the stocks are checkered plastic; and the finish is a dual-tone blue, glare proofed, for each model. Two sizes of grip adapters are supplied with each Woodsman pistol.

## High Standard Semiautomatic Pistols

The High Standard Manufacturing Corporation is the youngest of the large manufacturers of hand guns, but it has been a leader in the production of .22-caliber semiautomatic pistols for a long time. It was the first to realize that target shooters needed a semiautomatic with more weight in the barrel and a longer grip to fit the hand better. It was the first to provide an automatic slide lock for the .22-caliber semiautomatic pistol to hold the slide open and indicate when the last cartridge has been fired from the magazine. This also operates as a lock on the action when the magazine is empty and holds the slide open when the pistol is used at the target range as a single-shot. Figure 5 shows a typical pistol made by this company.

Fig. 5. A typical semiautomatic .22-caliber pistol made by High Standard Mfg. Co.

## High Standard Model H-D Military

The High Standard Model H-D Military is a 10-shot, .22-caliber Long Rifle, semiautomatic pistol with a visible hammer, automatic slide lock, and an adjustable rear sight. It is available with either a 6¾-inch barrel or a 4½-inch barrel, and weighs about 41 ounces. The regular model has walnut grips, but thumb-rest grips are available at a slightly higher price. This gun does not have the take-down feature of the G-series guns described below.

## The High Standard G Series

The G series of semiautomatic pistols made by High Standard have a take-down feature that makes it possible to take the pistol apart easily and quickly for cleaning or for changing barrels.

The Model G, caliber .380, 6 shot, is chambered for the caliber .380 Automatic Cartridge (abbreviated Auto. Ctg.), has a 5-inch barrel, a visible hammer, plastic grips, and a weight of about 40 ounces.

The Model G-B, caliber .22 Long Rifle, 10 shot, is a hammerless pistol with special diamond-checkered plastic grips. With a 6¾-inch barrel it weighs about 36 ounces, and with a 4½-inch barrel it weighs about 34 ounces.

The Model G-D, caliber .22 Long Rifle, is a 10-shot, hammerless model with an automatic slide lock and an adjustable rear sight, and available with either a 6¾-inch barrel or a 4½-inch barrel. It weighs about 41 ounces with the 6¾-inch barrel and about 36 ounces with the 4½-inch barrel. The grips are checkered walnut.

The Model G-E is similar to the G-D but heavier. With the 6¾-inch barrel it weighs about 44 ounces; it weighs about 39 ounces with the 4½-inch barrel. It is sold equipped with walnut thumb-rest grips, whereas the Model G-D is not equipped with such grips except on special request.

High Standard emphasizes the desirability of buying two barrels of different lengths when the gun is ordered, because this gives the shooter the advantage of having whichever barrel length he needs for the particular type of shooting he is doing.

## Advantages of Semiautomatic Pistols

The following are the advantages of a semiautomatic pistol in comparison with a revolver:

(1) It is easier to load.

(2) It is easier to clean.

(3) It provides more shots at one loading.

(4) The barrel can be replaced without sending the gun back to the factory.

(5) Usually, but not always, the stocks fit the hand better and point more naturally.

(6) It can be fired faster and more easily.

(7) The bullets are not shaved when they jump from the cylinder into the barrel.

(8) There is no leakage of the gases of combustion.

## Disadvantages of Semiautomatic Pistols

The following are the disadvantages of a semiautomatic pistol in comparison with a revolver:

(1) It is more dangerous for untrained people because after the first shot it is always loaded and cocked.

(2) The ammunition must be practically perfect or the gun will jam, and misfires may occur that will stop the gun from functioning.

(3) Reduced loads and blanks cannot be used.

(4) The jacket bullet customarily fired in a semiautomatic pistol is not as good for some purposes as a plain lead bullet.

(5) The empty cartridge cases are ejected as fast as the gun is fired, making it more difficult to recover cases for reloading. Some semiautomatic pistols tend to eject the empty case toward the face, causing flinching.

(6) In some visible-hammer models, the hammer may gouge the hand, or the slide may hit the hand and cause a minor injury.

(7) The trigger pull is often not as good on the semiautomatic, although this is by no means a general statement.

(8) The spring in the magazine is under tension while it is loaded. If kept loaded for a long time, the spring deteriorates and various malfunctions may occur. This can be remedied by not keeping the same magazine loaded at all times.

# Chapter 5

## CARTRIDGES AND
## ELEMENTARY BALLISTICS

### The Cartridge and Its Parts

A cartridge consists of the cartridge case, the primer, the powder, and the bullet. One cartridge is sometimes referred to as a round; two cartridges are described as two rounds, and so forth.

The word *ball* is sometimes used to mean a bullet. This is a holdover from the early days of firearms when a round lead ball was the only available projectile. Today, ball ammunition is any ammunition loaded as a single projectile, regardless of its shape. Small-arms ammunition includes cartridges fired in rifles, semiautomatic rifles, automatic rifles, pistols, revolvers, shotguns, and machine guns up to caliber .60.

The word *shell*, in referring to small-arms ammunition, may mean: (1) a loaded shotgun cartridge; (2) an empty metallic cartridge case; or (3) a loaded metallic cartridge, although this last use is not to be recommended.

The cartridge case is a brass (or copper) case in which the primer, powder, and bullet are assembled.

The primer is the compound in the base of the cartridge case that explodes when crushed by the firing pin and sends a hot flame into the powder charge. In rimfire cartridges, such as the ordinary .22-caliber cartridges, the primer composition is inserted from the inside and placed in a tiny gutter around the rim of the case. The case must be crushed easily by the firing pin in order to explode the primer, hence the case is made of a soft metal that will not withstand high pressures.

The primer for a centerfire cartridge is a separate unit contained in a soft brass cup and inserted into a primer pocket in the base of the cartridge case from the outside. Since the firing pin is not required to crush the case in order to crush the primer, the case may be made of a stronger metal than that used in rimfire cases. High-power cartridges are always of the centerfire type because they develop high pressures that the soft case of the rimfire type could not withstand.

The powder is the compound in the body of the cartridge which, when set afire by the primer, burns and produces rapidly expanding gases that force the bullet from the barrel. The powder in a modern cartridge is called *smokeless* powder, but it is not entirely smokeless, and it is by no means in powder form. In general, smokeless powder is made in the form of cylindrical grains, flakes, strips, or pellets, depending on the size and type of cartridge and the purpose for which it is intended. The powder used in cartridges fired in revolvers and semiautomatic pistols does not have tubular form. Instead, pistol powder is in the form of very fine thin flakes or wafers. Its shape causes it to burn very fast in order to be consumed rapidly in the short barrel of the hand gun.

Smokeless powder is not a high explosive. It is not sensitive to shock and must be ignited by a spark or a flame. When the flash from the primer sets it afire, it burns and generates gas so rapidly that in a fraction of a second it produces a pressure of several thousand pounds per square inch.

The bullet is the projectile fired from the gun. It is a lead or alloy or metal-jacketed missile seated securely at the front of the cartridge case. Since the base of the cartridge case is opposed by a portion of the gun and the bore (inside of the barrel) surrounds the sides of the case, the expanding gases generated by the burning powder cannot escape unless they drive the bullet through the bore and out the muzzle.

## Bullet Types

There are various types of bullets. Figure 1 shows an ordinary lead bullet, a general-purpose or service load. This is a .38 Special revolver bullet weighing 158 grains and made with a lubricating knurl, also known as a lubricating groove, or a cannelure, around the circumference of the base.

A metal-point bullet gives better penetration than the regular lead bullet because it has a nonfouling gilding-metal jacket over the nose. The one illustrated in Figure 2 is a .38 Special 158-grain bullet with a lead core, lubricating knurl, and metal point.

Fig. 1. An ordinary lead bullet. (*Courtesy Peters Cartridge Division, Remington Arms Co.*)

Fig. 2. A metal-point bullet. (*Courtesy Peters Cartridge Division, Remington Arms Co.*)

Fig. 3. A wadcutter bullet. (*Courtesy Peters Cartridge Division, Remington Arms Co.*)

Fig. 4. A metal penetrating bullet. (*Courtesy Peters Cartridge Division, Remington Arms Co.*)

Fig. 5. A metal-case hollow-point bullet. (*Courtesy Peters Cartridge Division, Remington Arms Co.*)

A wadcutter bullet is one with a sharp shoulder on the forward end. It is usually cylindrical in shape although some bullets have a short rounded teat on the forward end. A semiwadcutter bullet has a short nose with the forward shoulder made sharp. The purpose of wadcutter bullets is to leave clean round holes about the same size as the bullet when fired through a paper target. Figure 3 shows a .38 Special 146-grain wadcutter bullet having three knurls or cannelures.

A metal penetrating bullet is especially designed for the use of law-enforcement agents who must shoot at criminals in automobiles, behind barricades, etc. The one illustrated in Figure 4 is a .38 Special 110-grain bullet made of special metal.

A metal-case, hollow-point bullet is one designed to give both penetration and expansion for big-game hunting. The one illustrated in Figure 5 is a .32–20 80-grain bullet, showing the lead core and the gilding-metal jacket.

## Cartridge Designation

The designation of cartridges is often confusing because it is not based on any system. Years ago, a certain center-fire cartridge was known as the .45–70–500, which meant that it was caliber .45, loaded with 70 grains of black powder, and had a 500-grain bullet. When smokeless powder came into use, the new powder weighed less than black powder but occupied the same space in the cartridge case, even though it could do more work for the same quantity. This threw the designation system out because the weight of the powder now had less meaning.

Under the old system several cartridges were known by the caliber and the weight of the powder charge, such as the .25–20, .30–30, .32–40, etc. Thus, the .25–20 had a caliber .25 bullet and 20 grains of black powder. Bullet weights for these cartridges were not given in the name because a variety of bullet weights were available for each. When smokeless powder came into use, the weight of the powder charge also became meaningless, but several cartridges are still given these old names even though they are modern loads and have little in common with their predecessors of the same designation.

Although the above discussion of designation pertains principally to rifle cartridges, the same principle applies to hand-gun loads, but here we encounter a special kind of confusion. For example, the .38 Special cartridge is not caliber .38 at all. Instead, it is about caliber .359 and hence should be called caliber .36. However, experienced shooters understand this and accept it without argument.

Cartridges designated Hi Speed, High Velocity, and by similar trade terms are intended for rifles only and must not be used in hand guns.

The caliber of any rifled firearm, as explained elsewhere in this text, is the diameter of the bore measured between the lands. Also, the caliber of the bullet is its diameter. However, we must not confuse the caliber designation with the actual caliber. For example, the Smith and Wesson .375 Magnum revolver has the same bore diameter as the .38 Special revolver and can fire the same cartridges in spite of the apparent difference in designations of caliber.

Just to make things more confusing, some firearms and ammunition are designated according to the groove diameter, that is, the distance between the grooves in the bore rather than the distance between the lands.

Turning to another confusing method of cartridge designation, we find that some manufacturers indicate high-velocity cartridges by giving the theoretical velocity figure after the caliber. An example is the .250–300. Savage rifle cartridge. The 3,000 means that the maximum velocity is supposed to be 3,000 feet per second. You will observe that the caliber is given as .250, but this merely means caliber .25. Designating the caliber in thousandths of an inch means nothing because all measurements are carried further than that in cartridge and firearm design. It is merely another means of impressing the customer.

Fig. 6. A .22 short cartridge, a .22 long cartridge, and a .22 long rifle cartridge.

## .22-Caliber Cartridges

Figure 6 shows a .22 Short cartridge, a .22 Long cartridge, and a .22 Long Rifle cartridge. Never fire anything but the .22 Long Rifle cartridge in a firearm chambered for this cartridge. When a manufacturer says that one of his guns is "chambered for .22 Short, Long, or Long Rifle," he means that it is chambered for the .22 Long Rifle cartridge but will take either of the other two if necessary.

The .22 Short cartridge is the oldest of this family. It is well balanced from the viewpoint of the cartridge designer, is of low power, and is reasonably accurate at ranges up to fifty feet and, in weapons chambered and rifled exclusively for this short cartridge, give fair accuracy under favorable conditions up to about fifty yards.

The manufacturers later brought out the .22 Long cartridge, using the same bullet as that in the .22 Short. The result was an unbalanced cartridge. Even up to fifty feet it is less accurate than the .22 Short, and it becomes progressively less accurate as the range increases. Never use the .22 Long cartridge for any purpose! It is a waste of time and money.

The .22 Long Rifle cartridge was the last to be developed. It has the same length case as the .22 Long cartridge, but the bullet is heavier and it is known as a "ballistically balanced" cartridge among experts. It is one of the most accurate of all cartridges at all ranges up to 100 yards, and it will shoot more accurately than many high-power centerfire cartridges at ranges up to 200 yards unless there is a strong, gusty, or shifting wind to deflect it from its course.

## Cartridge Rims

Cartridges may be classified according to their rims as rimless, rimmed, semirimmed, and belted. A *rimless cartridge* has an extractor groove cut around its head. This type is generally used with semiautomatic pistols and with rifles of military caliber.

A *rimmed cartridge* may be used in all types of weapons from the revolver to sporting and military rifles. It has an external rim around the head that prevents the cartridge from entering the chamber too far.

A *semirimmed cartridge* closely resembles the rimless type and can be distinguished from the rimless type only by laying it on a flat surface and examining it against a strong light.

A *belted cartridge* also resembles the rimless type, except that the head of the case is very slightly larger than the head of a true rimless case.

Regardless of the type of construction, the purpose of the rim is to provide a projecting edge that the extractor can grasp to withdraw the empty case after discharge.

## Military Cartridges

There is a cartridge known as the .45 Army, which was originally used in the Colt Single-Action Army Revolver, originally known as the New Model Army Metallic Cartridge Revolving Pistol, and also called the Colt Army Revolver, Model 1872, the Peacemaker, and the Frontier Model. This cartridge has a rimmed case and a lead bullet and is not used in the U.S. Revolver, Model 1917, or the Colt semiautomatic pistols, Models 1911 and 1911-A-1.

The ammunition for the U.S. Revolver, Model 1917, and the semiautomatic pistols, Model 1911 and Model 1911-A-1, is designated by the armed services as Ball Cartridge, caliber .45, Model 1911. The word *ball* shows that it is not a blank, dummy, shot, or tracer cartridge, but is one loaded with a bullet. Figure 7 consists of two sectionalized drawings, one of the .45-caliber, Model 1911 cartridge on the left and one of a .22 Long Rifle cartridge on the right, to show their interior construction and relative sizes.

Fig. 7. Two sectionalized drawings of cartridges. The one on the left is the .45-caliber Model 1911 cartridge, and the one on the right is a .22 long rifle cartridge.

Figure 8 is a sectionalized drawing of the caliber .45, Model 1911 cartridge showing design features. The letters refer to the parts, as follows: *A*, cannelure; *B*, extracting groove; *C*, head; *D*, mouth; *E*, neck; *F*, primer pocket; *G*, shoulder, and *H*, vent. The upper view shows how the base of this cartridge is marked when made by the Frankford Arsenal. The letters "F A" represent Frankford Arsenal and "41" shows that the cartridge was made in 1941.

Figure 9 is a sectionalized drawing of the primer of the 1911 cartridge, marked as follows: *1*, brass anvil; *2*, brass cup; *3*, gilding metal cup; *4*, paper disk; and *5*, primer pellet. The anvil is the metal dome inside the primer against which the priming pellet is crushed by the impact of the firing pin (or the hammer when the hammer and firing pin are integral), causing the explosion that sets fire to the powder charge.

It should be understood that this 1911 cartridge cannot be loaded into the U.S. Revolver, Model 1917, made by both Colt and Smith and Wesson, without the use of metal clips shaped like a half moon. If you wish to avoid the use of clips in these 1917 revolvers, you must obtain a .45 Auto Rim cartridge, but this particular cartridge is not used in the .45-caliber semiautomatic pistols made by Colt.

(*Left*) Fig. 8. A sectionalized drawing of the caliber .45 Model 1911 cartridge.

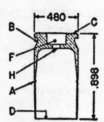

(*Right*) Fig. 9. A sectionalized drawing of the primer of the caliber .45 Model 1911 cartridge.

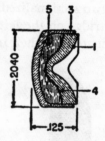

## Simplified Ballistics

Ballistics is the science of projectiles in motion and of the action of their propelling agents. Interior ballistics includes the explosion of the primer, the ignition and burning of the powder, the internal pressures and stresses caused by the combustion of the powder, and all the various motions, stresses, torques, etc., caused by the bullet being forced through the bore by the gases resulting from the combustion of the powder. Exterior ballistics includes everything that happens to a projectile in flight from the time it leaves the muzzle of the gun until it strikes its target.

## Rifling

We have previously explained that rifling is a system of spiral grooves cut into the bore of a firearm to give a spin to the bullet that will cause it to fly steadily, nose forward, to the target. The lands are the portions of the bore left after the grooves have been cut. Figure 10 shows the stages in the development of a rifled barrel. A

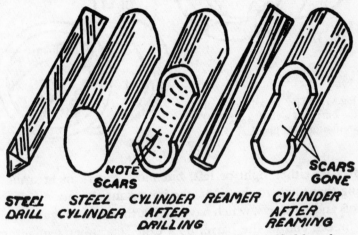

NOTE SCARS     SCARS GONE

STEEL DRILL   STEEL CYLINDER   CYLINDER AFTER DRILLING   REAMER   CYLINDER AFTER REAMING

Fig. 10. The stages in the development of a rifled barrel.

steel drill is used to cut a hole through a steel cylinder. A reamer is used to remove the scars left by the drilling operation.

After reaming the hole, its diameter is the bore diameter or caliber. Grooves are cut, leaving raised portions that are known as the lands. The distance from the top of one land to the top of the opposite land is the same as the diameter of the bore before the rifling was cut, and is measured in decimal fractions of an inch to designate the caliber. Thus, a .45-caliber weapon has a bore diameter of .45 inch. We have deliberately repeated these ideas for purposes of emphasis.

The twist is the inclination of the rifling grooves to the axis of the bore, that is, the angle the grooves make with the long dimension of the bore. The direction of the twist is the direction that the grooves turn. You can see it by looking through the bore from the breech.

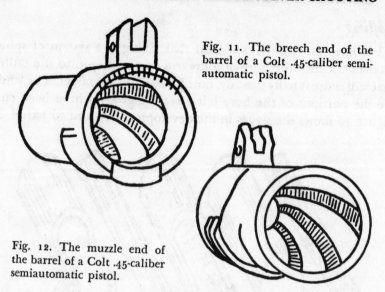

Fig. 11. The breech end of the barrel of a Colt .45-caliber semi-automatic pistol.

Fig. 12. The muzzle end of the barrel of a Colt .45-caliber semiautomatic pistol.

It may be either right or left, but most American firearms have rifling that twists to the right, the important exception being Colt pistols and revolvers, which have a twist to the left. Figure 11 shows the breech end of the barrel of a Colt .45-caliber semiautomatic pistol and Figure 12 shows the muzzle end.

The pitch is the distance that the rifling advances for each complete turn. For example, the rifling of the Colt semiautomatic pistols, Models 1911 and 1911-A-1, makes one turn in 16 inches, but the barrel is only 5.03 inches long, hence the rifling makes less than one third of a complete turn. Pitch and twist are related, but there is a distinct difference, and they should not be confused.

If a bullet is long in proportion to its diameter, the rifling should have a quicker twist, that is, it should make a complete turn in a shorter distance in order to give the bullet a faster spin. On the other hand, if the bullet is short in proportion to its diameter, a fast spin is not required and the rifling may have a slower twist. These are problems met by the designer, but as a shooter you should understand something about the design and construction of your arms.

## Pressure

When a cartridge is fired, the burning powder gases develop pressure in the chamber of the revolver and exert a thrust against the cartridge case, the chamber of the revolver, the bullet, and the bore of the revolver. Similar forces are exerted in the semiautomatic pistol. The gases find it easier to escape by driving the bullet through the bore under ordinary conditions, hence the bullet leaves the muzzle and travels toward the target.

If the pressure is too great, the gun may blow up, but it must be sufficient to drive the bullet through the bore and toward the target, hence the control of gas pressure is a matter of great importance. The pressure must be kept within the desired limits, and it must be maintained reasonably uniform or the performance of the cartridges will not be consistent. Various methods are used to test pressure in the laboratories of the manufacturers, but all of them are devised to improve the accuracy and reliability of ammunition.

## Velocity

The muzzle velocity, also called initial velocity, is the speed at which the bullet travels when it leaves the muzzle, usually given in feet per second (f.s.). As soon as the bullet leaves the muzzle it begins to lose velocity, hence the velocity it has when it hits the target is always less than the muzzle velocity.

## Point-blank Range

When people use the expression point-blank range, they usually mean the distance from the muzzle at which the bullet will strike the target when the rear sight of the gun is in its lowest position. However, this is a loose and inaccurate expression that should be avoided by anyone who makes any pretense of understanding firearms.

## Trajectory

The shooter's line of sight is a straight line from his eye through both the rear and front sights of the gun to the target. The line of sight is higher than the bore because the sights are above the bore. When the gun is fired, the trajectory (flight path of the bullet) rises from the muzzle to the line of sight, crosses above the line of sight, curves over the line of sight, and finally drops to the line of sight at the target. At short ranges the curved line followed by the flight of the bullet is almost flat, but at longer ranges it is a pronounced curve or arc because it is then necessary to raise the sights and fire at an angle farther above the ordinary line of sight in order to counteract the force of gravity, which pulls the bullet downward.

## Bullet Upset

The upset of a bullet is its expansion caused by the force of the powder gases at the discharge of the cartridge. When the gun is fired, the powder gases expand and push against the base of the bullet, but the point of the bullet does not move as soon as the base, hence the base expands or upsets. This upsetting is desirable because it causes the bullet to fill the grooves of the barrel (rifling) completely and prevents the powder gases from sneaking forward around the sides of the bullet. Thus, the bullet is forced through the bore at great speed.

## Keyholing

Keyholing is the tumbling of the bullet in flight. It may be caused by some defect in the bullet that destroys its balance, or it may be caused by the failure of the twist in the rifling to give it the correct spin. If a bullet has been keyholing, it almost never strikes the target point first, but leaves an elongated hole when it hits. Obviously, there is a great loss of accuracy and energy from keyholing.

## Sectional Density

The sectional density of a bullet is its weight in pounds divided by the cross-sectional area in square inches. If one bullet has a greater weight than another bullet of the same diameter, the first has a greater sectional density. If both have the same weight, the one with the smaller diameter has more sectional density. Other factors remaining the same, the bullet with the greater sectional density has more range and penetrating power because it has a smaller area exposed to the resistance of the air while in flight.

## Misfires and Hangfires

A misfire is an absolute failure of a cartridge to fire after the primer has been struck by the firing pin (or the hammer when the firing pin and hammer are integral).

A hangfire occurs when there is a delayed ignition of the powder charge in the cartridge. In a misfire, the cartridge is not fired at all, but in a hangfire ignition takes place eventually, often many seconds after the primer has been struck by the firing pin. It is impossible to predict when a hangfire may occur, and it is often impossible to discover the cause.

## Cartridge Deterioration

Weather affects ammunition. Extreme changes of temperature have an unfavorable effect on the powder in cartridges. If cartridges are corroded, even slightly, or if they are very old, dispose of them by throwing them in a river or burying them.

# Chapter 6

## SAFETY FIRST!

You must learn safety precautions before you fire your first shot. The .22-caliber hand gun has furnished more real sport and valuable marksmanship training to more people than any other firearm except the .22-caliber rifle, but .22-caliber firearms are not toys. They are real guns.

Primarily the .22-caliber pistol or revolver is for sport, and its greatest sporting use is not for hunting or self-protection but for shooting at targets. It is true that it is used by the armed services of the United States in training men and women in marksmanship, but it is not essentially a military device any more than an automobile or a motorboat is.

No one is born with a knowledge of firearms. The new shooter must learn a few simple safety rules, not only for his own protection, but also to safeguard the lives and property of others. The .22-caliber pistols and revolvers are small, but they have a comparatively long danger range and a surprisingly great depth of penetration. The following simple safety rules should be thoroughly learned, kept in mind, and always applied while handling pistols and revolvers.

(1) *Unload the weapon every time it is picked up for any purpose.* Never trust your memory. Consider every gun as loaded until you have proven otherwise. This first safety rule is the cardinal rule upon which all other safety rules are based. Having made certain that a gun is empty, do not hesitate to look again. Continue to assume that it is loaded even if you, yourself, have unloaded it. If you do this, you will never have an accident and you will automatically obey all other safety rules.

(2) *Always unload the gun if it is to be left where someone else may handle it.* This is especially important if there is any possibility that it might be picked up by children or by adults who are not trained to handle firearms properly.

(3) *Always point the gun up when snapping it after examination. Keep the hammer fully down when the gun is not loaded.* If the gun is pointed up and a shot is accidentally fired, there is less probability of hurting anyone. It is practically impossible to discharge most firearms when the hammer is fully down, even if they are loaded. In addition, keeping the hammer down relieves the spring from tension and prolongs the life of that part.

(4) *Never place the finger within the trigger guard until you intend to fire or to snap for practice.* This reduces the possibility of an accidental discharge.

(5) *Never point the gun at anyone you do not intend to shoot, or in a direction where an accidental discharge may do harm.* On the range, do not snap for practice while standing back of the firing line. You may know that your weapon is unloaded, but bystanders do not.

(6) a. *Before loading a revolver, open the cylinder and look through the bore to see that it is free from obstruction.*

b. *Before loading a semiautomatic pistol, draw back the slide and look through the bore to see that it is free from obstruction.*

(7) a. *On the range do not load the revolver until the time for firing.*

b. *On the range do not insert a loaded magazine in a semiautomatic pistol until the time for firing.*

(8) *Never turn around at the firing point while you hold a loaded pistol or revolver in your hand, because by so doing you may point it at the man firing alongside of you.*

(9) a. *On the range do not cock the revolver until immediate use is anticipated. If there is any delay, lower the hammer and recock it only when ready to fire.*

b. *On the range do not load the semiautomatic pistol with a cartridge in the chamber until immediate use is anticipated. If there is any delay, lock the pistol and only unlock it while extending the arm to fire. Do not lower the hammer on a loaded cartridge; the pistol is much safer cocked and locked.*

(10) a. *If the revolver fails to fire, open the cylinder and unload if the hammer is down. If the hammer is cocked or partly cocked, a break has occurred. In this case, hold the revolver at the position of raise pistol and announce the fact to the person in charge of the firing line.*

b. *If a semiautomatic pistol is jammed, first remove the magazine.* Further instruction on this difficulty is given in the rule below.

(11) a. *To remove a cartridge not fired from a revolver, open the cylinder and eject the cartridge, first lowering the hammer if it is cocked.*

b. *To remove the cartridge not fired from a semiautomatic pistol, first remove the magazine and then extract the cartridge from the chamber by drawing back the slide.*

(12) a. *While hunting, or in a military campaign, the revolver is carried in the holster fully loaded with the hammer down. The cocked revolver should never be put in the holster whether or not it is loaded.*

b. *While hunting, or in a military campaign, when the early use of the semiautomatic pistol is not foreseen, it should be carried with a fully loaded magazine in the socket, chamber empty, hammer down. When early use of the pistol is probable, it should be carried loaded and locked in the holster or hand. In a military campaign, extra magazines should be carried fully loaded.*

c. *When the semiautomatic pistol is carried in the holster loaded, cocked, and locked, the butt should be rotated away from the body when drawing the pistol in order to avoid displacing the safety lock.*

(13) *Safety devices on both revolvers and semiautomatic pistols should be tested frequently.* A safety device is a dangerous device if it does not work properly.

The above safety rules are given in almost the exact language used by the armed services of the United States in the instruction of all personnel armed with revolvers or semiautomatic pistols. The same rules apply to sheriffs, policemen, industrial-plant guards, home-defense units, and all individuals who are worthy of being entrusted with responsibility for the defense of life and property. In addition to the above formal rules, there are some common-sense precautions that should be understood by everyone, especially civilians who learn to shoot without the strict supervision given in the armed services. These are as follows:

(1) *Know the range and penetrating power of the cartridge you are using and shoot only where the bullet will not hit anything except the target.* For example, the bullet from a .22 Long Rifle cartridge can go through two ordinary doors or the side of an ordinary frame house and still have enough velocity to kill a man. For this reason, it is wrong to hang a target on a door or the side of a house where people whom you cannot see might be hurt or even killed.

(2) *Be sure you have a proper target and backstop.* Do not shoot at rocks, bottles, chunks of ice, or other hard-surfaced objects, because the bullets will ricochet (glance off) and may injure or even kill someone you cannot see.

(3) *In case of a misfire, which occurs when a cartridge does not fire after being struck by the firing pin, leave the gun closed and*

*keep it pointed down the range toward the target for at least 30 seconds.* It may be a case of a *hangfire,* which occurs when a cartridge does not fire at the instant of being struck by the firing pin, but fires later, hence extreme care is necessary.

(4) *At a shooting match always carry a revolver with the cylinder swung out and carry a semiautomatic pistol with the slide locked back.*

That covers safety with the hand gun. The rules can be learned in a few minutes. There are no dangerous firearms. There are only dangerous people who do not know how to handle firearms safely. In the next chapter we shall make further progress toward success in marksmanship.

# Chapter 7

## HOW TO SELECT YOUR
## FIRST HAND GUN

### The Beginner's Gun

Your first gun should be .22 caliber because the ammunition is inexpensive, the recoil is not apparent, and the noise is not disturbing. As a beginner, you are not interested in how far the bullets will fly so long as they are accurate up to the usual target distances. You are not concerned with the shocking or killing power of the gun because it is for marksmanship and not for self-defense, although you should remember that the .22-caliber gun is deadly if you hit vital spots in the body of a person or an animal.

Your second choice is between a single-shot and a repeater. You are not going to limit yourself to slow-fire shooting, hence you do not want a single-shot pistol. Instead, you need either a revolver or a semiautomatic pistol.

There are several objections to a semiautomatic pistol that are given in detail in another chapter, but the most important to a beginner is safety. You may forget after firing a shot with a semiautomatic pistol that you can fire again by pressing the trigger, hence you may fire a shot accidentally. Second, you will fire too fast with a semiautomatic. Third, in order to get the best results from the semiautomatic you should have a skilled gunsmith work on the trigger and stock and perhaps add a weight to give it proper balance. Not knowing what changes will help to raise your scores, you may waste money on alterations that may be of little or no benefit.

With the elimination of the semiautomatic pistol and the single-shot pistol, all that is left is the revolver. You must decide between a single-action and a double-action gun. The difference lies in the method of cocking the hammer. As explained before, you can cock a double-action revolver by pulling back either the hammer or the trigger. You can cock a single-action revolver only by pulling the hammer back. You will learn to fire more slowly with a single-action revolver, and you also will learn to cock it easily and quickly. During your shooting career you will eventually fire both single-action and double-action revolvers, but now is the time to learn the correct use of the single-action.

## The Harrington and Richardson Sportsman Model 199 Revolver

One of the best revolvers for the beginner is the *Sportsman Model 199,* illustrated in Figure 1, made by the Harrington and Richardson Arms Company, Worcester, Massachusetts. It is a caliber .22, 9-shot, single-action revolver sold at a reasonable price. It has a 6-inch barrel, weighs 30 ounces, and has super-speed short-action locks, the latter meaning that there is a short interval of time between pulling the trigger and the discharge of the cartridge.

The stocks were designed by Walter F. Roper, one of America's leading authorities on pistol stocks. They are full sized, well rounded, and very comfortable in the average hand. They are made of walnut and hand checkered.

### SELECTING YOUR FIRST HAND GUN

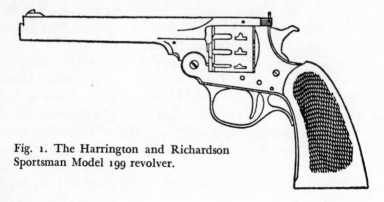

Fig. 1. The Harrington and Richardson Sportsman Model 199 revolver.

The tang (projecting rear portion) of the trigger guard extends to the rear to fill the space between the back of the trigger guard and the front of the stock, permitting the second finger of the shooter's hand to aid in holding the gun without the use of a grip adapter, plastic wood, or other filling material or device intended to fill this space on revolvers that are not properly designed to fit the hand.

The Patridge-type sights are 7.3 inches apart and are adjustable, the front sight for range and the rear sight for windage. The front sight adjusting screw moves by half turns and locks in position by means of spring pressure. If you move the front-sight adjusting screw one half turn, the shot group on the target will move about $\frac{1}{2}$ inch at 20 yards and $1\frac{1}{4}$ inches at 50 yards.

Two screws are used for the windage adjustment. Each of the screws pushes one side of the rear-sight leaf. If you give the rear sight a quarter-turn adjustment either right or left, the shot group on the target is moved $\frac{1}{2}$ inch right or left at 20 yards and $1\frac{1}{4}$ inches right or left at 50 yards.

The revolver has a safety cylinder made of heat-treated steel and designed for the use of high-speed ammunition. The cylinder is positively locked by an independent cylinder latch. The cartridge head is enclosed in a recess affording the protection of a solid ring of steel against defective ammunition. The cylinder has a raised ring around its outside circumference to prevent metal particles from being thrown out when the rim of a cartridge head bursts.

All metal parts are finished in a crown-luster blue and the barrel has a non-glare upper surface. Coil springs are used throughout. The parts are all hand fitted.

This is a "top-breaking" and automatic-injection type of revolver. After shooting nine shots, you break the gun open, the empty cartridge cases pop out, and the gun is ready to reload.

The Pope-type rifling makes one turn in 16 inches, that is, the rifling in this revolver makes about .375 of a complete turn in the 6-inch barrel. The rifling is cut at the factory with a broaching tool that cuts all six rifling grooves in one operation instead of cutting each groove separately, thus assuring no deviation between grooves and greater accuracy.

It is perfectly safe to use high-speed ammunition in this revolver, but it operates better with ammunition of ordinary speed. This statement also applies to any .22-caliber rimfire revolver. When high-speed ammunition is used, the cartridge head exerts pressure against the recoil plate, causing drag and making the revolver difficult to cock. You will find that using cartridges of ordinary speed will cause the gun to function more easily, fire more accurately, and produce higher scores.

The model of this revolver made before World War II had a longer hammer fall. Also, the firing pin and the hammer were separate parts. The post-World War II model has a shorter hammer fall, and the hammer and firing pin are made integral, forming one part, as shown in Figure 2.

This revolver, Sportsman Model 199, must not be confused with Sportsman Model 999, also made by Harrington and Richardson, which is the same except that it is made for both single action and double action. For precision shooting, especially for learning marksmanship, we prefer the Model 199, single action only.

Fig. 2. The firing pin and hammer are made integral in the post-World War II Harrington and Richardson Sportsman Model 199 revolver.

## Other Target Revolvers for the Beginner

Other target revolvers suitable for the beginner are the Colt Officers' Model Target Revolver and the Smith and Wesson New

K-22 Masterpiece Target Revolver. Both are chambered for .22 Long Rifle cartridges, are built on the same frames as large-caliber target revolvers of the same makes, and are comparatively heavy. If you intend eventually to adopt a large-caliber revolver, you may prefer to start with one of these models, but they are both comparatively expensive, and it is believed that you will be better satisfied if you start with the Harrington and Richardson Model 199, which is both cheaper and lighter in weight.

## How to Choose Between Similar Revolvers

If you wish to choose between two revolvers of similar size, weight, construction, and type, such as the Colt and Smith and Wesson target revolvers previously mentioned, assume a firing position with each gun and select the one that fits your hand better. The fit of the stock is the determining factor when other things are equal. If possible, fire several shots with each gun.

## Trigger Test Weights

In order to enter certain National Rifle Association matches and tournaments, you must comply with the requirements for trigger pull, that is, your trigger pull must not be too light. Figure 3 shows the correct method of weighing triggers. As an individual shooter you are not required to own these weights, but you should understand their use.

Under National Rifle Association rules for matches and tournaments, triggers may be weighed with official N.R.A. test weights, at the discretion of the N.R.A. official referee or executive officer before the firing of any match. The failure of any trigger to meet the trigger pull requirements may disqualify in matches previously fired, unless the trigger pull has been previously officially weighed and found satisfactory.

During the time that the trigger is being weighed, the gun must be held with the barrel perpendicular to the horizontal surface on which the test weight is supported. The rod or hook of the test weight must rest on the lowest point of the curve in curved trig-

### SELECTING YOUR FIRST HAND GUN

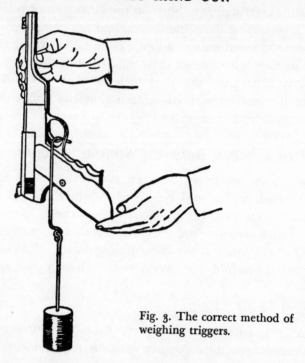

Fig. 3. The correct method of weighing triggers.

gers, or on a point about one quarter inch from the lower end of straight triggers.

In order to pass the weight test, a gun must lift a weight of the correct number of pounds from the horizontal surface on which it is resting. The magazine must be removed from an automatic pistol while the trigger is being weighed. In guns equipped with a device to prevent firing while the magazine is out, the magazine and chamber must be closely inspected to see that no cartridges are contained in either. The magazine is then inserted and the trigger pull weighed.

Competitors are permitted to adjust triggers that have failed to pass the weight test if they do so without delaying the firing of a match. However, failure to pass the weight test is the responsibility of the competitor, and no delay in firing is permitted because of required adjustments.

## Classification of Hand Guns for N.R.A. Matches and Tournaments

All hand guns are classified according to construction in order that you may compete on equal terms with others having the same type of weapon. The following classes of guns are recognized:

SERVICE PISTOL. Colt semiautomatic, caliber .45, Model 1911 or Model 1911-A-1, having not less than a 4-pound trigger pull, issued by the Army Ordnance Department, or the same type and caliber of pistol as manufactured by Colt's Manufacturing Company, privately owned, which must be equipped with fixed sights, the front sight blade type (not undercut) and the rear sight an open U-shaped or rectangular notch, and issue or Colt-factory standard stocks. Except as above, the parts may be specially fitted and include alterations that will improve the functioning and accuracy of the arm provided that such alterations do not interfere with the proper functioning of the safety devices as manufactured.

CALIBER .45 SEMIAUTOMATIC PISTOL. Any .45-caliber semiautomatic pistol. The trigger pull must not be less than 4 pounds; the sights may be adjustable but must be strictly open, not more than 7 inches apart and in front of the hammer when the hammer is in the forward position. All standard features of the weapon must operate properly. Muzzle brakes and similar barrel extensions are not permitted. A muzzle brake is defined as a device mounted at the muzzle of the gun to deflect the escaping powder gases to the side or rear and thus reduce recoil.

SERVICE REVOLVER. The U.S. Revolver, Model 1917, caliber .45, with stocks and sights as issued, or of identical dimensions and design, except that stocks and backstrap may be checkered. Trigger pull must not be less than 2½ pounds.

ANY CENTERFIRE PISTOL OR REVOLVER. This class includes centerfire pistols or revolvers of .32 caliber or larger, barrel length, including cylinder, not more than 10 inches, trigger pull not less than 2½ pounds. Sights may be adjustable but must be strictly open and in front of the hammer when the hammer is in the forward position and not more than 10 inches apart. Programs may specify particular calibers or types of centerfire weapons that will be permitted or not permitted in stated events.

FREE PISTOL. This class includes pistols of any caliber, any barrel length, no restriction as to trigger pull, any type of grip except that no attachments may be used that extend along the forearm and serve as an aid in support of the gun.

.22 PISTOL OR REVOLVER. Any pistol (single shot or semiautomatic) or revolver using a .22 rimfire cartridge having an over-all length of not more than 1.1 inches and with a lead or alloy bullet not greater than .23 inch in diameter and weighing not more than 40 grains; barrel length, including cylinder, not more than 10 inches; strictly open sights, which may be adjustable but not more than 10 inches apart. Trigger pull not less than 2 pounds. Programs may limit competition to particular types of .22 pistols or revolvers.

SIGHTS. All rear sights must be strictly open, which means that they must not have hoods or other covers. The notch must be as wide at the top as at any other part. Aperture or peep sights or any covered, shaded, or telescopic sights are not permitted. Unless specified in the conditions of the match, both front and rear sights may be adjustable laterally and vertically and may include light reflecting substances.

## Concentrate on One Gun

While you are learning to shoot, use only one weapon, but learn that one gun thoroughly. Each pistol is like a person. It has its good and bad points, but you will delay your progress if you switch from one gun to another during your preliminary practice. Later, when you have acquired skill, you may want a battery of pistols and revolvers to meet various special purposes.

# Chapter 8

---

## HOW TO GRIP PISTOLS
## AND REVOLVERS

---

### Mental Preparation for Good Shooting

The mind must be trained before the body is trained. Three things are essential to good shooting. First, you must form the habit of constantly applying the correct methods. Second, you must remain relaxed in mind and body while shooting. Third, you must think of nothing except the shot you are about to fire.

In order to acquire correct habits of shooting you must learn the proper procedures at the beginning and follow these throughout your shooting career. Constant practice is essential but it must be practice in correct procedures. If you repeat good shooting methods over and over again, it will be extremely difficult for you to miss the target. As a beginner, you may find that you must consciously think of each separate step, but through correct practice you will gradually learn to shoot accurately with no more effort than you use in driving an automobile.

You can relax while shooting if you assume the correct firing position and do not worry about anything. Stand comfortably, hold your head erect but not stiff, grip your pistol loosely, and extend your shooting arm straight but not stiffly. Do not worry about your score.

You must concentrate on what you are doing. If the previous shots were poor, forget about them. Think only of the shot you are about to fire. If the noise on the firing line bothers you, stuff cotton in your ears. Do not listen to the other shooters or watch their targets. Tend to your own business!

## The Correct Grip

Before you can take a correct firing position, you must learn how to grip the pistol or revolver. Hold the gun in your left hand and stand on the firing line with your left side toward the target so that the barrel will point toward the target. This is a safety precaution. When you assume a firing position, you will stand with your right side toward the target.

Make sure that the gun is empty. Then cock it. The correct grip can be taken only when the trigger is back in the firing position. Having cocked the gun and while you are taking a grip, hold the gun in your left hand with your thumb between the hammer and the frame, as illustrated in Figure 1. This position of the thumb makes an accidental discharge impossible.

Figure 2 shows the location of the thumb and fingers. A very light grip on the handle is sufficient. Do not try to press the palm of your hand against the right stock. Do not exert any pressure with your finger tips. They are not intended to come into contact with the handle.

Figure 3 illustrates the correct grip as it is seen from above. The spur of the hammer barely clears the web of your hand between the thumb and the trigger finger. This is called "the high hold." Also, the gun is held with the thumb straight along the left side of the frame.

The purpose of holding the hand high on the gun is to bring the axis of the gun barrel approximately in line with the arm to reduce the effect of recoil (kick). There is no noticeable recoil in firing .22-caliber cartridges, but recoil is very apparent when the larger calibers are fired.

Recoil disturbs the aim. This is not important in slow fire because the shooter can correct his aim at his leisure, but it becomes very important in timed and rapid-fire shooting. Since the successful shooter must learn correct methods in the beginning and make them fixed habits, you should learn this high hold and use it for slow fire as well as timed and rapid-fire shooting. Likewise, you should hold the gun the same whether you are firing .22-caliber or .45-caliber cartridges.

Fig. 1. Having cocked the gun, and while you are taking a grip, hold the gun in your left hand with your thumb between the hammer and the frame.

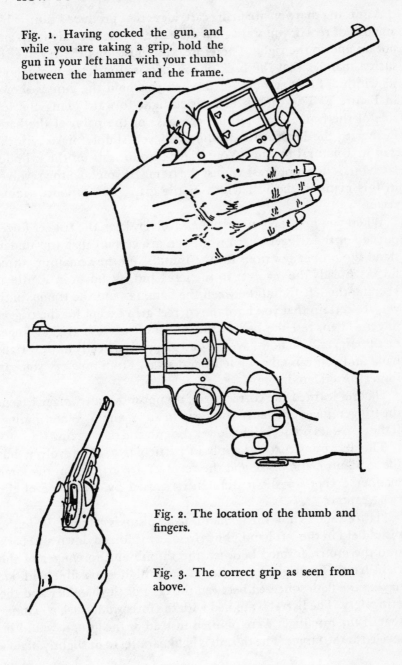

Fig. 2. The location of the thumb and fingers.

Fig. 3. The correct grip as seen from above.

Assuming that you are firing cartridges that produce a noticeable amount of recoil, you want the gun barrel to move straight up and not up and to the right. Therefore, you must hold the revolver in such a manner that the back of the grip is supported throughout its width. This is accomplished when you hold the gun as shown in Figure 2. The thumb extends straight forward along the left side of the frame, thus pulling the base of the palm of the hand farther to the left than it would be if you simply picked up the gun in a natural manner. Your right thumb rests on the cylinder latch but it does not press against the frame. If you hold the revolver in this manner, the full width of the grip gives support against recoil.

When you first learn to grip the revolver, keep the trigger finger outside of the trigger guard until you are certain that you understand the proper positions for the thumb and the remaining three fingers. Steady the revolver in the left hand, as shown in Figure 1, keeping the left thumb between the hammer and the frame, until you are certain that you have the correct grip except for the trigger finger. Then, rest the ball of the end joint of your trigger finger on the trigger. You now have the gun gripped correctly in your right hand and you can take the left hand away. From now on, you can forget the left hand.

Having learned the correct grip, do not move any finger except the trigger finger or change your grip in any manner. When aiming, if the grip does not feel right, lower the gun and start again.

The above instructions apply in particular to the revolver, but the semiautomatic pistol and the revolver are gripped in the same manner except for slight differences caused by the shape of the two weapons.

Figure 4 shows how the semiautomatic pistol is gripped. With the pistol held in the left hand, the grip safety is forced down and back into the crotch formed between the thumb and forefinger of the right hand. The right hand should be as high as possible without having the flesh squeezed between the tang of the hammer and the grip safety. The barrel is aligned with the forearm in such a manner that, if the forefinger were pointed instead of the gun, it would be leveled at the target. The thumb is held parallel to or slightly higher

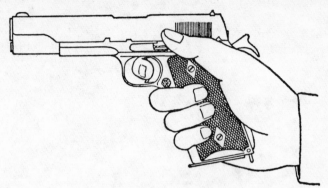

Fig. 4. How the semiautomatic pistol is gripped.

than the forefinger, but it should never be lower. The lower three fingers grasp the stock firmly to prevent the recoil from twisting the weapon in the hand and causing the next shot to go wild.

Notice that in gripping the semiautomatic pistol the frame is squeezed by the thumb and base of the forefinger, but the ball of the thumb may or may not be in contact with the frame, depending upon the shape of the hand. By means of the pressure exerted upon the frame by the thumb and the base of the forefinger, the movement of the gun to the right or left is controlled and the application of trigger squeeze is more effectively co-ordinated with other details.

The muscles of the arm are firm without being rigid in holding either the revolver or the semiautomatic pistol. The barrel is a direct prolongation of the pistol arm and the wrist is locked so that the weapon cannot weave up or down. The elbow is straight and locked. The only pivot is at the shoulder joint. After recoil, when you are firing correctly, the pistol arm should automatically carry the pistol back to the original position in approximate alignment with the bull's-eye.

# Chapter 9

## THE CORRECT FIRING
## POSITION

### Basic Requirements

When you are ready to take a correct firing position, you should know how to grip the pistol or revolver as explained in the previous chapter, the proper position of your body with relation to the target, how to hold your breath, and how to aim. In this chapter, we shall explain the position of the body and the breathing technique used by successful shooters.

### Body Position

In order to assume a correct body position, stand on a line perpendicular to the face of the target with your right side toward the target and your body faced slightly more than 45 degrees to the left of a line to the target. Stand flat on both feet, with the heels from 12 to 18 inches apart, hold your head erect, and keep your body in balance when the pistol is held in the firing position. Figure 1 shows the raise-pistol position. This is the same with both the revolver and the semiautomatic pistol. In this position, the shooter is ready to extend his arm.

The position varies slightly according to the size and shape of the shooter, but the shooter must be relaxed and comfortable. The pistol in the firing position should point naturally and without special effort at the center of the target. If the body, the pistol, and the target are not in correct alignment, the muscles of the body will be under tension while aiming and firing each shot. This will cause the body to tremble, and you will tire easily. When this

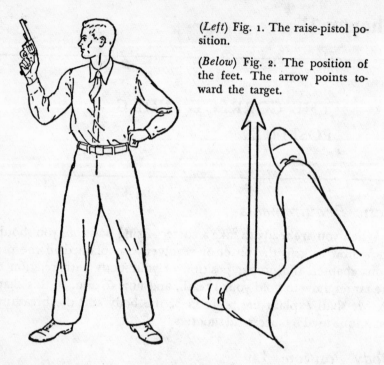

(*Left*) Fig. 1. The raise-pistol position.

(*Below*) Fig. 2. The position of the feet. The arrow points toward the target.

occurs, shift the entire body until the pistol, held in a position to fire, points directly at the center of the target.

## Spreading Your Feet Apart

There is no set distance for spreading the feet apart. A general rule is to separate your heels about one half of your normal stride. For example, if you take a 30-inch step, then your heels should be 15 inches apart. Figure 2 shows the position of the feet with relation to the line of sight for a man who normally takes a 30-inch step. The arrow points toward the target. Regardless of the general rule, the feet should be spread apart just enough to prevent your body from swaying to the front or rear. Stand flat on both feet. Distribute your weight evenly on both feet and stand with your legs straight but without having your knees stiff. Do not lock your knees. Avoid anything that will make your muscles tense.

## Facing the Target

Although the general rule is to face the body slightly more than 45 degress to the left of a line to the target, you must find your own correct position. If you face too far to the left, your shots on the target will be strung out horizontally. If you face the target too directly, the shots will be strung out vertically. In both cases, the trouble is caused by your body's swaying and the cure is the correction of your position.

## What to Do with the Left Arm

You can let your left arm hang idly at your side, put your left thumb in your left-side trouser pocket, or put your entire left hand in your trouser pocket. Regardless of what you do with your left arm, hold your left shoulder slightly lower than the right or your pistol will tend to drop.

## Breathing

Correct breathing is important. Just before you extend your arm to the aiming position, take a fairly deep breath and exhale normally. Then take a second breath normally, exhale some of it (about one third), and hold the rest by closing the throat until you fire a shot. Do not hold the breath by constricting your diaphragm. If you do, you will place a strain on your muscles, your body will tremble, and you will undo all the good you are trying to accomplish by holding your breath.

## Details of the Raise-Pistol Position

When on the firing line, pistol and revolver shooters do not keep their arms extended in the firing position. Instead, they often assume the raise-pistol position before and after firing each shot in slow fire. The thumb and last three fingers hold the stock; the forefinger is extended outside the trigger guard; the barrel is to the rear and inclined to the front at an angle of 30 degrees; the hand is as high as the point of the right shoulder and is 6 inches in front of the point of the right shoulder, as illustrated in Figure 1.

## Assuming the Firing Position

Before moving the pistol from the raise-pistol position to the actual firing position, focus your eyes on the target and be sure that you are firing at your own target. Stand with your head erect. Do not lean your head over until it almost touches your right shoulder. This will strain your muscles and lower your score.

When you are ready to aim, extend the pistol straight out and upward at an angle of about 10 degrees above the horizontal. Do not stretch the arm enough to strain the elbow muscles but extend the arm until the elbow is straight without discomfort. Then lower the arm slowly without bending the elbow until your pistol comes to rest just below the bull's-eye with the top of the front sight barely touching the bottom of the bull's-eye. This is known as the six o'clock aiming point and is illustrated in Figure 3.

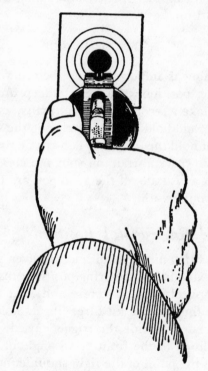

Fig. 3. The six-o'clock aiming point.

Constantly maintain the same loose grip on your pistol. While you are lowering your arm from the raise-pistol position, the weight of the pistol tends to exert pressure upon the base of the palm of your hand and also upon the second finger between the trigger guard and the handle. This pressure may tempt you to grip the pistol tighter with your finger tips, but you must resist this temptation and keep your relaxed easy grip.

Keep your eyes on the target. While your arm carries the pistol downward into the six-o'clock aiming position, concentrate upon the bull's-eye. Think of nothing except aiming your pistol. Forget your past shots. Ignore any conversation you hear. Stay relaxed.

As your sights come into your field of vision, you may find that they are not correctly aligned with the bull's-eye. The front sight may be to the right or left of the center of the rear notch. You can

Fig. 4. The correct standing position.

correct this with a slight movement of the wrist, but do not let anything change your loose grip.

Figure 4 shows a shooter just behind the firing line, standing at his firing point, which is that part of the pistol range provided for the competitor immediately in the rear of the firing line. Each firing point should have a minimum width of 4 feet, and it should be numbered to correspond with the frame of the target at which the man at that point is firing.

The firing line is immediately in front of several firing points. In this case it is marked by a small board on the ground. All ranges are measured from the firing line to the face of the targets when the targets are hung in their proper position in front of the backstop.

The man in this illustration is in the correct firing position. His shooting kit or case is on the stand to his left and is open for access to blackening equipment, replacement parts, and other accessories.

# Chapter 10

## AIMING AND TRIGGER SQUEEZE

### *Blackening Sights*

In all pistol and revolver firing, except combat firing, both sights of the gun, if not already sufficiently black, should be blackened to eliminate glare and to show the sights as distinct silhouettes. Before blackening the sights, clean them and remove all oil. You can blacken them by holding each sight for a few seconds in the point of a small flame, which will deposit a uniform coating of lampblack on the metal. Carbide gas from a lamp is considered the most satisfactory by experts, but a kerosene lamp, a candle, a small pine stock, a piece of camphor, or shoe polish can be used for this purpose.

### *How to Aim*

Figure 1 represents the front sight of a revolver or semiautomatic pistol. Figure 2 represents an open rear sight. Figure 3 represents the correct alignment of the front sight with the rear sight. Figure 4 represents the correct method of aligning the sights with the bull's-eye in aiming. These drawings are correct except that the width of the rear sight is exaggerated for purposes of instruction. Actually, the alignment of the sights with the bull's-eye more closely resembles Figure 5.

In Figures 4 and 5, you will observe that the top of the front sight is level with the top of the rear sight and exactly in the center of the notch. The vertical center of the bull's-eye is in line with the vertical center of the front sight, hence it is also in line with the

AIMING AND TRIGGER SQUEEZE

Fig. 1.                Fig. 2.                        Fig. 3.

Fig. 1. The front sight. Fig. 2. An open rear sight. Fig. 3. The correct
alignment of the front sight with the rear sight.

vertical center of the rear sight. The bull's-eye sets on top of the
front sight.

Notice that there is no line of white between the top of the
front sight and the bottom of the bull's-eye. Also observe that the
front sight does not extend up into the bull's-eye but barely

Fig. 4. The correct method of
aligning the sights with the
bull's-eye.

Fig. 5. Another view showing
the correct alignment of the
sights with the bull's-eye.

touches the bottom. If you allow a small amount of white to appear
between the sight and the bull's-eye, or if you hold the front sight
above the bottom edge of the bull's-eye, your shots will be scattered up and down the target because you cannot accurately judge
how much white you are allowing or how far into the black you
are aiming for each shot.

## The Master Eye

You should shoot with both eyes open. Naturally, if you shoot
with your right arm, it is better if the right eye is the master eye,

that is, the right eye takes charge and controls the alignment of the gun on the target. It is easy to determine which eye is the master eye. Keep both eyes open. Aim your finger at some object. Close the left eye. If the finger remains pointed at the object, the right eye is the master eye. If the finger seems to move out of alignment with the object, the left eye is the master eye. Next, point your finger at the object with both eyes open and close the right eye. If the left eye is the master, the finger will remain pointed at the object.

One test for shooting vision is to close the master eye, point the finger at some object with the weaker eye, and then open the master eye. If the finger does not seem to jump positively and immediately out of line with the object, your vision is defective and an oculist should be consulted. However, remember that this is only one test and not a final determination of the condition of your eyes.

## The Reasons for Keeping Both Eyes Open

Years ago, almost everyone believed that it was correct to aim pistols, revolvers, rifles, and shotguns with one eye closed. We now know that this is wrong. The human eyes are intended to be used together. Closing one eye in aiming lowers the efficiency of the other. Beginners should learn to shoot with both eyes open at all times.

Many people advise a shooter whose left eye is his master eye to learn to shoot right-handed, but during World War II the instructors for the armed services learned that it is better to let the man whose left eye is the master eye learn to shoot left-handed. Also, they learned that when we tell the shooter to keep both eyes open, we do not mean that both eyes are wide open. The master eye is wide open, but the other eye is only partly open.

Experienced shooters who have always closed one eye while aiming can improve their scores by training themselves to aim with both eyes open. This may be difficult at first because long years of aiming with one eye have lowered the power of the eyes to accommodate in changing from the use of one eye to the use of two. The master eye fails to take charge promptly, and the two eyes do not work well together. This may cause lower scores temporarily but as soon as the eyes become accustomed to being used together, the scores will start rising.

The use of two eyes in aiming is important in firing at moving targets, especially if the targets appear unexpectedly at different places, as in hunting or under combat conditions. This applies not only to pistol and revolver shooting, but also to rifle, trap, and skeet shooting.

In all kinds of shooting it is advisable to wear shooting glasses as a protection from imperfect ammunition, glancing bullets, or flying fragments from targets. Glasses also afford protection against glare and dust.

## Gun Sway

You will discover that no shooter can hold any firearm absolutely still. There is always a certain amount of sway up and down or right and left. If you do not worry about this, you will find that you are swaying into the bull's-eye as much as you are swaying out of it. If you practice correct methods of assuming a firing position, gripping the gun, breathing, and trigger squeeze, you will gradually reduce the amount of sway. In addition, you will learn how to fire when the sights are correctly aligned with the bull's-eye.

You will find that after holding the pistol in an aiming position for a few seconds it will begin to tremble and your front sight will dance around the bull's-eye. The probable cause of this condition is tightening the muscles of the entire hand while squeezing the trigger to fire a shot. The remedy is to loosen your hand and use only the muscles of the trigger finger, keeping a loose grip as we previously recommended. If your knuckles are white, your grip is too tight.

## Trigger Squeeze

A good pistol shot never tries to fire his gun as soon as he aligns his sights on the bull's-eye. He holds his aim as accurately as possible and keeps a steady increasing pressure upon the trigger until the shot is fired. The correct method of squeezing the trigger may be described as the independent movement of the forefinger straight to the rear, with a uniformly increasing pressure that the shooter does not know the instant when the pistol will be discharged.

You can easily learn to aim and hold the aim either on the bull's-eye or very close to it for at least ten seconds. When you have learned to squeeze the trigger in such a manner as not to spoil your aim you have become a good shot.

A person who tries to teach himself how to shoot often gives a wild yank on the trigger as soon as the sights are aligned with the bull's-eye. The sights and the bull's-eye may have the correct relationship when he starts the yank, but something happens. Instead of scoring a ten, as the sight alignment indicated, the shot may be a three, or even a complete miss.

## Flinching

All men flinch in firing the pistol if they know the exact instant at which the discharge is to take place. This is an involuntary action. Flinching is usually defined as a movement of the body made when the shooter knows in advance when the recoil will come. A sudden pressure of the trigger may derange the aim slightly, but the extreme inaccuracy of the shot fired under these conditions is caused principally by thrusting forward the hand to meet the shock of recoil. However, pistol shooters frequently flinch when shooting a .22-caliber pistol that has no noticeable recoil. When the pistol is fired unexpectedly and unknowingly, the same shooter does not flinch. Therefore, it may be concluded that flinching is nothing but a wild jerk at the trigger made by the shooter in an effort to fire at a particular moment.

The logic of this reasoning may be tested by handing an empty pistol to a shooter, or one loaded with an empty cartridge case. When he jerks the trigger, he will flinch because he thinks that he knows when the gun will discharge. The cure is to train this kind of shooter to apply a steady pressure to the trigger while aiming so that the pistol fires suddenly and unexpectedly. Not knowing exactly when the pistol will fire, the shooter has no reason to flinch.

If you hold the sights of the pistol as nearly on the bull's-eye as possible and continue to squeeze the trigger with a uniformly increasing pressure until it goes off, you are a good shot. If you have learned to increase the pressure on the trigger only when the sights are in alignment with the bull's-eye, holding the pressure when the muzzle moves and continuing with the pressure when the sights are again in line with the bull's-eye, you are an excellent shot. If you try to "catch the sights" as they touch the bull's-eye and attempt to fire the pistol at that instant, you are a very bad shot.

We have said before that you should not worry about the sway of the pistol in aiming, although you should try to reduce it. The apparent unsteadiness of the pistol while aiming does not cause much variation in the location of the bullet on the target because the sway is caused by the movement of the whole extended arm and pistol, not the pistol alone. However, the sudden pressure of the trigger that always comes with flinching moves the muzzle of the pistol and causes the bullet to strike far from the bull's-eye.

In squeezing the trigger, exert pressure straight to the rear. Do not press the trigger to the left while squeezing to the rear. Start the squeeze as soon as the sights are in line with the bull's-eye, and continue your steady increase of pressure until the pistol fires. Disregard any trembling or wavering of the sights or sway of the arm. Increase the pressure at such a rate that the hammer will fall four or five seconds after the sights have come into alignment with the bull's-eye.

## Dry Practice

The correct trigger squeeze may be developed by "dry practice" at home without ammunition. Knowing that the gun is empty, you will not jerk the trigger. You know that there will be no recoil and no noise. You do not try too hard. You remain relaxed, and you do not tire easily, although you should limit your dry practice to a daily session of ten or fifteen minutes at first. Pin a small bull's-eye to the wall of your room. It should be of a size which, at the short distance, appears to you to be the same size as the regular bull's-eye at the standard distance at which you customarily fire.

In dry practice, apply correct trigger squeeze until it becomes a habit with you and seems more natural than jerking the trigger. When you have reached this stage, pretend that you are firing with a loaded gun and concentrate on the correct squeeze even though you pretend to expect a recoil and a noise. When you are absolutely convinced that you have mastered trigger squeeze in dry practice, go to the range and apply it with a loaded pistol.

In dry practice, which is also called "dry snapping," you concentrate on correct trigger squeeze and may not notice that your arm is swaying. This is a good thing because forgetting the sway helps you to concentrate on the trigger squeeze, but if you do pay any attention to the sway you will find that it is having little effect on the scores you would receive if your pistol were loaded.

On the range, continue this attitude. Disregard the arm sway and start the trigger squeeze when the sights are at six o'clock on the bull's-eye. Continue the squeeze until the pistol fires, paying no attention to whether the sights move a little to one side or the other. If you do this, you should do as well on the range as you did in dry snapping.

## Rest between Shots

Lower the pistol after each shot. Lay it on a shooting stand or some other clean, dry object. Let your shooting arm rest at your side to allow the blood to resume its free circulation. Also, close and open your fist to keep your finger muscles limber. When you are ready to fire again, fit your pistol into your hand as explained in a previous chapter, using the left hand to place the pistol into the right hand to obtain a correct grip.

## Increase Trigger Pressure Wisely

Having perfected your trigger squeeze by means of dry snapping followed by actual practice on the range, train yourself to increase the pressure on the trigger only when the sights are in the proper alignment with the bull's-eye. This will give you smaller shot groups and higher scores. If any of the shots are wild, that is, outside your usual shot group, you may be squeezing incorrectly. Remember that each shot should be a surprise. The shot that you expect is usually always a poor shot caused by flinching.

## Canting

Canting is the act of rolling or twisting the pistol right or left. If the pistol is canted to the right, the shot goes low to the right, as shown in Figure 6. If it is canted to the left, the shot goes low to the left, as shown in Figure 7.

## Common Errors in Aiming

In addition to canting, which is a frequent error, there are other mistakes commonly made by beginners. Figure 8 shows that if the front sight is to the right in the notch of the rear sight, the shot goes to the right. Figure 9 shows that if the front sight is to the left in the notch, the shot goes to the left. Figure 10 shows that if the front sight is high in the notch, the shot goes high. Figure 11 shows that if the front sight is low in the notch, the shot goes low.

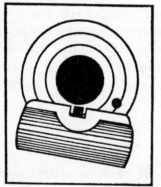 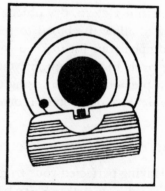

Fig. 6. If the pistol is canted to the right, the shot goes low to the right.

Fig. 7. If the pistol is canted to the left, the shot goes low to the left.

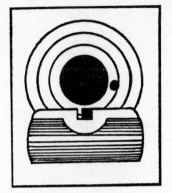

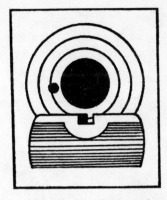

Fig. 8. If the front sight is to the right in the notch in the rear sight, the shot goes to the right.

Fig. 9. If the front sight is to the left in the notch, the shot goes to the left.

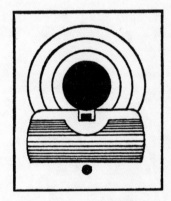

Fig. 10. If the front sight is high in the notch, the shot goes high.

Fig. 11. If the front sight is low in the notch, the shot goes low.

# Chapter 11

## FINAL INSTRUCTIONS BEFORE ACTUAL FIRING

### Calling the Shot

Calling the shot is announcing where the sights were pointed at the instant the hammer fell. For example, a simple method of calling the shot is to say that the shot is "high," "a little low," "to the left," "slightly to the right," or "bull's-eye." If you cannot call your shot correctly in range practice, you have not pressed the trigger properly and therefore you do not know where the sights were pointed when the hammer fell.

If you squeeze the trigger properly, so that the pistol is fired unexpectedly, your aiming eye will be open and looking through the sights at the target when the shot is fired. Even the champion pistol shooters cannot hold the pistol so perfectly that the sight picture is always perfect. The bull's-eye appears slightly low, high or to one side. Obviously, the better the shooter the less this error amounts to, but because it is almost always present, it is possible for you to call your shot. In other words, you simply say where the shot struck as shown by the error in the sight picture at the instant the bullet started toward the target.

A good instructor will always insist that you call your shots aloud, especially during your apprenticeship period. By doing this you will correct your errors, and if you still shoot poorly, your instructor can determine whether or not the fault lies in your trigger squeeze. If you do not squeeze the trigger, the jerk is so sudden that it is difficult for you to call the shot. If you habitually fail to call your shots with a reasonable degree of accuracy, the instructor is certain that you are either careless in aiming or you are flinching. When you flinch, you close your aiming eye and simply jerk the trigger, thus obtaining a poor score.

## The Vertical Clock System

Both rifle and pistol shooters have a definite system for calling shots accurately. Imagine the face of the target as the face of a clock. A shot directly under the bull's-eye is at six o'clock, a shot directly to the left is at nine o'clock, and a shot low and to the right is at five o'clock. Figure 1 shows clock numerals drawn on a target.

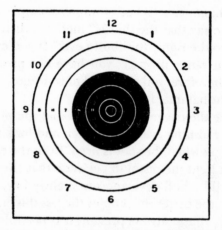

Fig. 1. The vertical clock used in calling the shot.

In calling your shot you should give the amount of your error. For example, you may call "very high at one o'clock," or "a little to the left at eight o'clock." When you become an experienced shooter, you will be able to give both the location and the value of your shot. For example, you will be able to say, "The shot was an eight at one o'clock" or "I just fired a nine at five o'clock." All of this shot calling is done aloud to your coach or instructor except when you are firing under circumstances that require quiet, such as individual pistol matches.

## Analyzing Your Mistakes

Learning to call your shots accurately will raise your scores and increase your confidence. Remember that an "accident" is merely an occurrence for which we have no explanation. There is always some reason for everything that happens. If we can learn the cause, we may be able to prevent the repetition of unfavorable events.

For example, you may call "bull's-eye," "a high nine at six o'clock," or some other value and location that is almost in the bull's-eye and then find that you have received a low-value shot at one or perhaps two o'clock. If you are working with an instructor, he will have you fire another shot while he concentrates on watching the manner in which you hold your pistol. He will observe your grip to see if you have the base of the palm of your hand far enough to the left to support the pistol handle against the recoil of the pistol straight to the rear. If the base of your palm is not supporting the handle at the moment of firing, the recoil will tend to raise the muzzle high and to the right.

The instructor does not overlook the possibility that you may be jerking the trigger. For example, if you call your shot in or near the bull's-eye and then find that it is a low-value shot in one of the outer rings of the target, low to the left, at seven or perhaps eight o'clock, the cause may be jerking the trigger. You *thought* that you fired a good shot, you had the sights aligned with the bull's-eye, and you intended to squeeze the trigger properly, but something caused you to jerk the trigger just as you fired. The recoil distracted your attention so that you did not realize that your sights were not correctly aligned with the bull's-eye at the exact instant of firing. This is a common error.

## The Horizontal Clock System

Wind and light directions on the pistol range can be given according to the horizontal clock system illustrated in Figure 2. The target is always at twelve o'clock. The firing point is always at six o'clock. Your right is three o'clock and your left is nine o'clock.

If a wind is blowing from the target toward the firing line at a velocity of 20 miles an hour, you can describe it as a "twenty-mile, twelve-o'clock wind." If the wind is blowing from behind the firing point toward the target at a velocity of 10 miles an hour, you can describe it as a "ten-mile, six-o'clock wind." If the wind is blowing from left to right across the range, at a velocity of 15 miles an hour, it is a "fifteen-mile, nine-o'clock wind." If it is blowing from right to left across the range, at a velocity of 5 miles an hour, it is a "five-mile, three-o'clock wind."

In the late afternoon, if the sun is sending low slanting rays of

Fig. 2. The horizontal clock used in describing the direction of wind and light.

light across the range from right to left, you would say, "All the light is coming from three o'clock."

This horizontal clock system is rarely used in pistol shooting at ordinary ranges because wind and light are relatively unimportant under normal conditions. However, in long-range pistol shooting wind and light become important factors, which must be considered if you expect high scores.

## Testing Your Trigger Squeeze

At this stage of your progress you should learn how an instructor can test your trigger squeeze. If you are firing a revolver on the range, he can load it, leaving one or more chambers empty, and then close the cylinder before handing the revolver back to you. Do not watch him while he is loading, and do not examine the cylinder to see which chambers are empty.

Fire the revolver as if all chambers were loaded. Take your position and grip in the usual manner. Aim correctly, and squeeze the trigger when the sights are aligned with the bull's-eye. If the hammer of the revolver falls on an empty chamber and you still hold the sights in line with the bull's-eye, you have squeezed the trigger properly. On the other hand, if you have not held the revolver correctly, or if you have jerked the trigger, you will find that the sights are knocked out of alignment with the bull's-eye at the fall of the hammer.

If you are firing a semiautomatic pistol on the range, your instructor can test your grip and trigger squeeze by unloading the pistol, inserting an empty magazine, and handing you the pistol with the slide back and the hammer in the cocked position. Fire without glancing at the chamber. Naturally, you may suspect what he is doing, but if you play fairly with him and do not look at the chamber, he will repeat this test several times, occasionally handing you the pistol with a cartridge in the chamber. When conscientiously performed, this test will reveal your faults.

## Follow Through

The phrase *follow through* is used extensively in all sports. In pistol and revolver shooting it means that you must keep your eyes on the target and keep the weapon fully extended in the aiming position for several seconds after you have fired a shot. It is essential that you keep your arm extended long enough to call the location and value of the shot you have just fired.

## Continue Dry Snapping

If you lower the pistol or revolver as soon as the hammer falls, you will develop a tendency to let the gun drop just as you are about to fire. The cause is your anxiety to see where the shot hit the target. This is a good example of the importance of forming correct habits early in your shooting career. The habit of lowering the gun on firing is easy to form and difficult to cure.

As you progress in pistol marksmanship, you will begin to think that you are becoming an expert and do not need to practice the exercises learned at the beginning of your training, but this is a wrong assumption. Continue dry snapping with the same care as before. Do not take a careless position, grip the gun in a haphazard manner, or jerk the trigger just because the gun is not loaded. Inaccurate dry practice is worse than no practice. Simulate the firing of each shot in dry snapping with all the thought and care that you would give to firing a loaded gun.

## Correct Thinking

Good pistol and revolver marksmanship begins in your mind. Form correct habits, learn to relax, and concentrate only on the thing you are doing. Forget the past, and let the future take care of itself. In the next chapter we shall learn how to load, and then we can put into practice all that we have already learned.

# Chapter 12

## HOW TO LOAD, COCK, AND FIRE A REVOLVER

### How to Load the U.S. Revolvers, Model *1917*

The word *pistol* is used in all commands for firing either a semi-automatic pistol or a revolver. In order to explain the proper loading and unloading of a revolver, we must assume that an instructor, coach, or range officer is standing near you giving the necessary commands, just as though you were on the range firing with other shooters present.

Being at the raise-pistol position previously explained, at the command "load," raise the left hand to the front until the forearm is horizontal, palm up. Place the revolver at the cylinder in the left hand, latch up, barrel inclined to the left front and downward at an angle of about 30 degrees. Press the latch with the right thumb, push the cylinder out with the second finger of the left hand and, if necessary, eject the empty shells by pressing the ejector rod head with the left thumb, right hand steadying the revolver at the stock. Take cartridges either singly or in clips from the belt with the right hand and insert one in each chamber to be loaded. Close the cylinder with the left thumb and resume the position of raise pistol.

This describes the loading of either the Colt revolver, caliber .45, Model 1917, or the Smith and Wesson revolver, caliber .45, Model 1917. If cartridge clips are not used, empty shells must be removed from the chambers with the fingernails.

### How to Unload the U.S. Revolvers, Model *1917*

Being at the position of raise pistol, at the command "unload," lower the revolver to the left hand, latch up, barrel inclined to the left front and downward at an angle of about 30 degrees. Press the latch with the right thumb, push the cylinder out with the second finger of the left hand and eject the empty shells by pressing the ejector rod head with the left thumb, right hand steadying the revolver at the stock. Return unfired cartridges to the belt, or to the loading block if the latter is being used at the range.

## General Instructions for Loading a Revolver

Regardless of the make, model, or caliber of revolver used, the instructions previously given for the U.S. Revolvers, Model 1917, should be followed in general. However, the U.S. Revolvers, Model 1917, may be loaded with six cartridges in two clips holding three rounds each, or they may be loaded without clips by placing cartridges individually in the chambers. Clips are not used with the other revolvers described in this book.

## How to Fire the First Shot with a Revolver

When you are ready to fire the first shot with a revolver at a range, first cock the revolver by pulling back the hammer with the thumb of the right hand. Then, take the revolver in the left hand, with the left thumb between the frame and hammer, and place it in the right hand, with the muzzle pointing toward the target. Keeping the trigger finger outside the trigger guard, place the right thumb on the cylinder latch and wrap the three lower fingers around the handle. Do not exert any pressure on the stock with the tips of your fingers.

Taking the standing position previously explained, holding the revolver in one hand only, the other hand and arm being used in no way to assist your shooting. All portions of your clothing, body, and gun must be clear of artificial support. Take your position immediately to the right of your numbered firing-point marker. No portion of your body should rest upon or touch the ground in advance of the firing point. Any artifical support, such as any supporting surface other than the ground or some such flat, firm surface, is forbidden.

Having taken the correct standing position, assume the raise-pistol position. Your right hand should hold the stock with the thumb and last three fingers, trigger finger extended outside the trigger guard, arm bent and revolver inclined forward at an angle of about 30 degrees, your hand about 6 inches in front of the point of the shoulder. Your left hand should be in some comfortable position.

Take one reasonably deep breath and then expel it. Take another breath, exhale part of it, and hold the remainder with your throat. Extend your right arm and allow your arm and hand to come down, pivoting from the shoulder but not from the elbow, until the sights are aligned at six o'clock on the bull's-eye of your own target. Remember that the target frames are numbered to correspond with the firing-point numbers. The target numerals are usually painted above the targets. Be sure to fire on your own target.

Now that your sights are aligned with the bull's-eye, start to squeeze the trigger, slowly and with a uniformly increasing pressure. If your sights appear to be out of line with the bull's-eye, hold the pressure you have on the trigger and do not take any more until your sights are once more aligned with the bull's-eye. With the sights back on, squeeze the trigger some more. If the sights are off again, hold your pressure, align the sights again, and squeeze some more, exerting pressure with the trigger finger only, being careful not to exert any pressure with the tips of the other fingers. Concentrate on the bull's-eye and a steady squeeze—*bang!* You fired a shot before you expected the revolver to discharge. It should be in the center of the bull's-eye. You have scored ten on your first shot and feel that you are on your way to the world's championship. Do not get cocky. There is much more to learn.

## The Two Methods of Cocking the Revolver for Succeeding Shots

There are two methods of cocking the revolver for the succeeding shots. These are the side or rolling method and the straight-back method. Both methods of cocking are good. Each requires practice before enough skill is acquired to cock the hammer without changing the position of the stock in the hand. The method you will finally adopt depends upon the size, shape, and muscular development of your hand. Therefore, you should learn and practice both methods until you have acquired enough skill with each to choose the one which is more satisfactory. Thereafter, use only that one method in all firing and dry snapping.

## The Side or Rolling Method of Cocking

The side or rolling method of cocking is the older method. The recoil of the revolver causes it to rise about 4 to 6 inches above the point of aim. As it reaches the top of its upward path, relax your grip slightly, place the ball of your thumb on the spur of the hammer, exert a downward pressure with your thumb, and at the same time move the muzzle to the right about 4 inches with a rolling wrist motion, being sure to use only the wrist for this motion. Figure 1 shows the positions of the thumb and fingers.

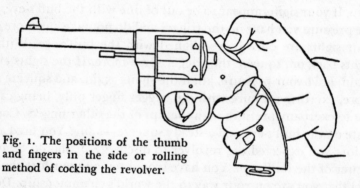

Fig. 1. The positions of the thumb and fingers in the side or rolling method of cocking the revolver.

During the movement, the thumb exerts pressure to the left as well as downward. In spite of the fact that the palm of the hand is not in contact with the stock, the slight pressure against the fingers on the left of the stock helps in the control of the revolver, but the fingers on the left must be kept in place throughout the movement.

As soon as the revolver has reached its farthest right position in rolling, snap the hammer back to the full-cock position with the thumb, and then roll the revolver back into the aiming position and replace the thumb along the side of the frame.

During the operation of cocking and bringing the revolver back to the aiming position, keep the muzzle elevated so that the front sight is visible and can be easily aligned in the rear-sight notch. If you allow the muzzle to sag, you will have to hunt for the front sight and lose time in aligning it in the rear-sight notch.

## Little Finger under the Bottom of the Butt

During the firing of a string of shots, you may find it difficult to keep your grip in the same position on the revolver. Your hand may tend to work higher on the stock, thus restricting the action of your thumb in cocking and making it necessary for you to re-grip the revolver in the middle of the string. You can overcome this difficulty by gripping the revolver in such a manner that your little finger is under the bottom of the butt of the stock.

## The Straight-back Method of Cocking

In the straight-back method the grip is not loosened nor is the revolver shifted from its line of recoil. As soon as you have fired a shot and while the revolver is still recoiling, place your thumb on the hammer spur and draw the hammer straight back to the full-cock position, using your thumb only, as shown in Figure 2. During the time that you are drawing the hammer back, lower the revolver from its highest recoil position to the aiming position so

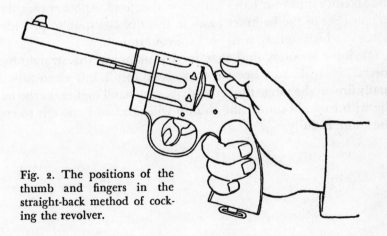

Fig. 2. The positions of the thumb and fingers in the straight-back method of cocking the revolver.

that you will be ready to align the sights with the bull's-eye as soon as the hammer reaches the full-cock position. In other words, if you have held the revolver correctly, it recoils straight up and then you merely lower it to bring the front sight into the rear-sight notch. As soon as the hammer is cocked, replace your thumb alongside the frame.

The advantages of the straight-back method are:

(1) You can maintain a more uniform grip throughout the firing of a string of shots when you wish to keep the revolver pointed at the target.

(2) The sights can be more easily realigned and brought back to the point of aim because there is no side movement of the revolver during the process of cocking.

(3) You can keep your trigger finger in the same position on the trigger, hence your trigger pull remains uniform.

The disadvantages of the straight-back method are:

(1) Some shooters cannot bend their thumbs enough to draw the hammer all the way back. If your thumb is too long or if you cannot bend it just right, your thumb will become cramped when the hammer is about two thirds of the way back to the full-cock position. This, in turn, makes it necessary for you to take a new grip on the revolver to complete the cocking. Time is wasted and the rhythm of firing during a string is destroyed. One remedy is to lower your grip slightly, but if you take a grip that is too low, the stock will slide farther into your hand with each shot fired. Another remedy is to cut some of the hammer away in front of the spur to provide a notch in which you can rest the tip of your thumb.

(2) Some shooters find that in dry snapping the straight-back method is satisfactory because there is no recoil, but when they actually fire on the range the recoil drives the hand higher on the handle with each shot until the thumb will not bend enough to cock the hammer fully.

# Chapter 13

## HOW TO LOAD AND UNLOAD
## THE AUTOMATIC PISTOL

### How to Test Safety Devices

This chapter describes the loading and firing of the Colt automatic pistols, caliber .45, Model 1911 and 1911-A-1, but the instructions are generally applicable to other automatic pistols of similar construction.

Safety devices should be examined frequently because they are sources of danger if they do not work when needed.

SAFETY LOCK. Cock the hammer and then press the safety lock upward into the safe position. Grasp the stock so that the grip safety is depressed, and squeeze the trigger three or four times. If the hammer falls, the safety lock is not safe and must be repaired.

GRIP SAFETY. Cock the hammer and, being careful not to depress the grip safety, point the pistol downward and squeeze the trigger three or four times. If the hammer falls or the grip safely is depressed by its own weight, the grip safety is not safe and must be repaired.

HALF-COCK NOTCH. Draw back the hammer until the sear engages the half-cock notch and squeeze the trigger. If the hammer falls, the hammer or sear must be replaced or repaired. Draw the hammer back nearly to full cock and then let it slip. It should fall only to full cock.

DISCONNECTOR. Cock the hammer. Shove the slide one quarter inch to the rear; hold the slide in that position and squeeze the trigger. Let the slide go forward, maintaining the pressure on the trigger. If the hammer falls, the disconnector is worn on top and must be replaced. Pull the slide all the way to the rear and engage the slide stop. Squeeze the trigger and at the same time release the slide. The hammer should not fall. Release the pressure on the trigger and then squeeze it. The hammer should then fall. The disconnector prevents the release of the hammer unless the slide and barrel are in the forward position safely interlocked. It also prevents more than one shot following each squeeze of the trigger.

## Manual of the Pistol

In the armed services of the United States, the movements described in this chapter differ in purpose from the manual of arms for the rifle in that they are not intended to be executed in exact unison, there being, with only a few exceptions, no real necessity for their simultaneous execution. They are not therefore planned as a disciplinary drill to be executed in cadence with the snap and precision, but merely as simple, quick, and safe methods of handling the pistol.

Law-enforcement bodies usually execute the movements of the manual of the pistol in the same manner as the armed services. Civilian pistol instructors generally teach the manual of the pistol in order to exercise control over their students during instruction and also because the commands for executing the manual of the pistol, with a few exceptions, are used in firing for record and in marksmanship competitions.

In general, movements begin and end at the position of raise pistol. Commands for firing, when required, are limited to "commence firing" and "cease firing."

Officers and enlisted men of the armed services when armed with the pistol remain at the position of attention during the manual of arms, but render the hand salute at the command "present arms," holding the salute until the command "order arms."

When a lanyard (a cord hooked to the pistol at one end and to the shooter's belt at the other end) is used, it should be long enough so that the arm may be fully extended without difficulty.

## Raise Pistol

The command is given as two distinctly separate words, with the emphasis on the second, thus: (1) "raise," (2) *"pistol."* At the command "pistol," unbutton the flap of the holster with the right hand and grasp the stock, back of the hand outward. Draw the pistol from the holster; reverse it, muzzle up, and assume the position of raise pistol as explained before in this text, and illustrated in Figure 1.

## Withdraw Magazine

At the command "withdraw magazine" (equal emphasis on both words), without lowering the right hand, turn the barrel slightly to the right, press the magazine catch with the right thumb, and with the left hand remove the magazine as illustrated in Figure 2. Place the magazine between the belt and the outer garment.

## Open Chamber

At the command "open chamber," withdraw the magazine if not already withdrawn and resume the position of raise pistol. Without lowering the right hand, grasp the slide with the thumb and the first two fingers of the left hand (thumb on left side of slide and pointing downward). Keeping the muzzle elevated, shift the grip of the right hand so that the right thumb engages the slide stop. Push

Fig. 1. The raise-pistol position.

Fig. 2. Withdrawing the magazine.

Fig. 3. Opening the chamber.

the slide downward to its full extent and force the slide stop into its notch with the right thumb without lowering the muzzle of the pistol, as illustrated in Figure 3.

## Close Chamber

At the command "close chamber," with the right thumb press down the slide stop and let the slide go forward. Squeeze the trigger, being sure that the muzzle is still elevated.

## Insert Magazine

At the command "insert magazine," without lowering the right hand, turn the barrel to the right. Grasp a magazine with the first two fingers and thumb of the left hand; withdraw it from the belt and insert it in the pistol. Press it fully home.

## Load

At the command "load," if a loaded magazine is not already in the pistol, insert one. Without lowering the right hand, turn the barrel slightly to the left. Grasp the slide with the thumb and fingers of the left hand (thumb on right side of slide and pointing upward). Pull the slide downward to its full extent, as illustrated in Figure 4. Release the slide and engage the safety lock.

## Unload

At the command "unload," withdraw the magazine. Open the chamber as explained before. Glance at the chamber to verify that it is empty. Close the chamber. Take the position of raise pistol and squeeze the trigger. Then insert an empty magazine.

## Inspection Arms

The command is given with emphasis on the second word, thus: (1) "inspection," (2) "*arms*." At the command "arms" withdraw the magazine. Open the chamber as explained before. Take the position of raise pistol. The withdrawn magazine is held in the open left hand at the height of the belt as illustrated in Figure 5. After the

Fig. 4. Pulling the
slide downward to
load.

Fig. 5. The position
of "inspection arms."

pistol has been inspected, or at the command (1) "return," (2) "*pistol*," close the chamber, take the position of raise pistol, and squeeze the trigger, being sure that the muzzle is still elevated. Insert an empty magazine and execute return pistol.

## Return Pistol

The command is given with the emphasis on the second word, thus: (1) "return," (2) "*pistol*." At the command "pistol," lower the pistol to the holster, reverse it, muzzle down, back of the hand to the right; raise the flap of the holster with the right thumb; insert the pistol in the holster and thrust it home; button the flap of the holster with the right hand.

# Chapter 14

## HOW TO IMPROVE
## YOUR SCORES

### *The Center Hold*

The usual, normal method of aiming is to align the sights so that the top of the front sight exactly touches the bottom of the bull's-eye. The reason for using this alignment is that it presents a good silhouette of front and rear sights against the solid-white paper target. Everyone agrees that it is the only correct method of aiming for slow fire, but a substantial number of good shooters use the center hold during timed, sustained, rapid, and quick fire.

If you adopt the center hold, aim exactly as you would for a six-o'clock hold, except that you must align your sights so that the top of the front sight touches an imaginary horizontal line running through the center of the bull's-eye. This is illustrated in Figure 1.

Fig. 1. In the center hold, the top of the front sight touches an imaginary horizontal line running through the center of the bull's-eye.

Those who prefer the center hold argue that with this hold during timed, sustained, rapid, and quick fire, they find it impossible to see the sights well enough against the black bull's-eye to know when they are *slightly* out of alignment. In other words, they feel more confident if they do not see their sight alignment too clearly at the faster rates of fire!

When the center hold is used, you can see when the sights are badly out of line, but a *slight* deviation from the correct alignment is not apparent, hence you will continue to exert a steadily increasing pressure on your trigger and you should obtain a good score. This assumes that you have learned how to aim properly in preliminary practice. Most of your aiming will be very good, and your sights will seldom be out of alignment enough to produce a bad score if you hold your gun properly, have a good standing position, breath correctly, and squeeze the trigger.

Assuming that you are obtaining very good scores during slow fire and want to improve your standing, you should experiment with the center hold at timed, sustained, rapid, and quick fire. A slight misalignment of sights is difficult to see when you are using a center hold because the black sights of your gun are not silhouetted against the black bull's-eye. You will continue your trigger squeeze and fire shots that you would not fire with the six-o'clock hold.

Using a six-o'clock hold, you will always remember your basic marksmanship training, hold your squeeze when the sights are even slightly out of alignment, and continue your squeeze only when they are once more in correct alignment. This is proper for slow fire, but during the higher rates of fire you may develop a mental attitude that leads to jerking the trigger in an effort to get off all your shots during the time limit. Obviously, one jerked shot usually lowers your total score so badly that it can be offset only by several very good shots. Therefore, give the center hold a fair trial. If it raises your scores, use it for everything except slow fire. If your scores remain the same or drop after a reasonable amount of practice with the center hold, return to the six-o'clock hold. After all, it is the standard, regular, generally approved method of aiming.

## Aiming Point at 25 and 50 Yards

We have previously told you to use a six-o'clock aiming point because this is a uniform, standard method of aiming that avoids the commission of errors, but among the outstanding pistol and revolver experts this rule is often violated. At a range of 25 yards, most men hold at six o'clock, but a number of the great shooters use the center hold. At a range of 50 yards, a little less than half of the experts use a six-o'clock hold, about the same number use the center hold under all conditions, and a minority vary their hold according to the caliber of the weapon they are firing.

## Changing Sight Settings According to the Range

In moving from 25 to 50 yards, the range is increased, hence it would seem logical to raise the rear sight slightly when the weapon is equipped with an adjustable rear sight. Rifle shooters always raise their rear sight as the range increases and pistol shooters should do the same thing, but less than half of the great pistol shooters do this. Those that do not raise the rear sight compensate for the increase of distance by changing their aiming point, that is, they raise the front sight into the bull's-eye, usually aiming at its center.

## The Thin-Line-of-White Method of Aiming

Some shooters use the six-o'clock hold except that they do not align their sights so that the bull's-eye seems to set on the front sight. Instead, they leave a thin line of white between the top of the front sight and the bottom of the bull's-eye, as illustrated in Figure 2. This is wrong because they cannot estimate how thin the thin line of white is for each shot. During one shot the thin line may be twice as thick as it is during another shot. On the other hand, if you do not leave a thin line of white, but have the top of the front sight

Fig. 2. A thin line of white between the top of the front sight and the bottom of the bull's-eye is not recommended.

touch the exact bottom of the bull's-eye during the six-o'clock hold, you have a definite and standard method of aiming for all shots.

## Do Not Aim Too Long

As soon as you have learned to aim correctly at slow fire, watch yourself to be sure that you do not form the unfortunate habit of aiming too long. If you do, your gun will begin to wave up and down and right and left across the target, and you find yourself jerking the trigger. Even during slow fire, you should be able to fire each shot in less than 6 seconds and not more than 10 seconds without sacrificing correct marksmanship principles. A good way to speed up your aiming is to fire a few shots in timed fire at 50 yards every time you go to the range, even if your principal interest happens to be slow-fire practice.

## How to Verify Your Grip and Standing Position

Let us assume that you have learned the fundamentals of good pistol marksmanship. You know how to stand, grip your gun, aim, breathe, and squeeze the trigger. Your mental attitude is calm and confident. You know how to call your shots, and you are calling them correctly, but unfortunately all your shots are going to the right or left, very high or very low at two, five, or ten o'clock on the imaginary vertical clock face. An experienced shooter, acting as your coach, can soon tell you your trouble. He may diagnose your problem as either a poor grip or a faulty standing position, but you can do the same thing for yourself.

Fire a few shots at slow fire, using your regular grip and standing position. Sit down and rest a few minutes. Then get up and aim your pistol in your regular manner at any object. Do this without looking at the target. Simply extend your arm and pistol toward anything that takes your fancy while you are looking at something else. As soon as you have fully extended your arm, glance at the sights and see if the front sight is correctly aligned with the rear sight. You are not concerned with alignment of the sights with a bull's-eye. You are only interested in their alignment with one another.

If the front sight is not in the center of the rear-sight notch, or if it is too high or too low in the notch, those poor scores you have been worrying about have been caused by a poor grip. The trouble is that you have been tensing your wrist muscles in aligning your sights. The remedy is to lay your gun down, pick it up with a proper grip, and repeat the test we have just described. Do this until you can align the sights properly every time you extend your arm, without looking at them, and without using your wrist muscles to make a final correction of the alignment.

Having checked on your grip, you should now review your standing position to be sure that it is correct. Take your normal firing position, fire a few shots, sit down and rest a few minutes, take a standing position again and extend your arm this time toward a target but without looking at the target. As soon as your arm is fully extended, look at your alignment of the sights and the bull's-eye. If your pistol is not pointing very close to the bull's-eye, change your standing position, particularly the position of your feet, until you can aim at the bull's-eye without looking at it and still find your sights lined up with it well enough to be in the black. This exercise may seem difficult, or even foolish at first, but if you will give it a fair trial you can raise your scores easily and quickly, assuming that you are not violating any other principles of good marksmanship.

In correcting your grip, we explained that a poor grip was often caused by tensing the muscles of the wrist. In a similar manner, a poor standing position is usually one that requires tension in the muscles of the neck and shoulder to bring the sights into alignment with the bull's-eye. In a good standing position and with a good grip your muscles are relaxed during aiming and firing. The object is to make your muscles work with you and not against you. A good shooter is always relaxed during firing. He may be nervous before and after firing, but while he is squeezing the shots into the black he is as relaxed as a wet dishrag hanging from a hook in the kitchen.

## How to Hit the Bull's-eye without Seeing It

Here is another method that may improve your scores. Reverse a target in its frame so that its back is toward you. Guess at the location of the bottom of the bull's-eye if you use the six-o'clock hold or the center of the bull's-eye if you use the center hold. Align your sights on that portion of the target where you estimate your normal aiming point to be and then fire. Do this several times, and you may find that your score is better than it is when you see the bull's-eye. Many men have used this method successfully. It works because you concentrate on the alignment of the sights with each other and on the trigger squeeze. You do not worry about the bull's-eye, hence you fire before you become tired.

## The Swinging Aim

Still another method is to align your sights with each other to one side of the bull's-eye, swing the gun slowly toward the bull's-eye, and fire when you have your usual six-o'clock or center hold, whichever you prefer. Do not attempt to get a perfect alignment of the sights with the bull's-eye. Start squeezing the trigger before you come to the bull's-eye, and time your squeeze so that you fire just about the instant that your sights are aligned with the bull's-eye.

## The Blurred Bull

A rather drastic way to achieve a result similar to firing at the back of the target is to have an oculist fit you with glasses that show everything clearly except the bull's-eye, which is blurred. If you normally wear glasses to see the bull's-eye clearly, shoot without them. Since it is impossible for you to obtain a sharp alignment of the bull's-eye with your sights, you will concentrate on aligning the sights with each other and on the trigger squeeze. The results will be good.

## The Effect of the Wind

On a windy day shooting outdoors, if the wind is blowing from either six or twelve o'clock, that is, from either the targets or the firing line, you can have a steadier standing position if you face at a greater angle away from the target and stand with your feet farther apart.

If the wind is blowing across the range from either three o'clock or nine o'clock, that is, from either the right or left, face your target more fully, at a smaller angle to the target than usual, and stand with your feet farther apart.

The usual procedure in slow fire is to rest after each shot, but if there is a wind blowing in spurts, some of your shots will be fired during gusts that sway your body and also have some effect on the flight of the bullet. Under such conditions it is better to rest during gusts and then fire as many shots as possible during the lulls between gusts. Your total score may not be as good as it would be if there were no wind, but it should be better than it would be if you fired in the normal manner with rests between shots.

The wind, depending upon its force and direction, may deflect the bullet from its straight course between the muzzle and the target. It may move the bullet up or down, or to either side. Thus, a wind from the left will carry a bullet to the right, causing it to strike to the right of where it would hit if there were no wind. Wind blowing toward the shooter may very slightly increase the resistance offered by the air to the flight of the bullet, causing it to strike slightly lower on the target. Wind blowing toward the target may very slightly decrease the air resistance, causing a bullet to strike slightly higher on the target. However, the effect of the wind is extremely slight under the usual conditions of pistol firing because of the short ranges involved. Do not blame the wind for poor scores unless you are absolutely certain that there can be no other cause.

## Adjusting the Sights to Correct for Wind

When you have fired your pistol at a known distance on a calm day, you know the settings of the rear sight, both vertically and horizontally, that you must have to hit the center of the bull's-eye with a normal firing technique. This is the *zero* of the pistol for that particular range.

Assuming that you know your zero and that you have an adjustable rear sight on your pistol, you can correct for the effect of the wind by moving your right sight up or down and right or left. Any correction you make will be based on your estimate of the force and direction of the wind, but this cannot be absolutely accurate, and the wind may change every few seconds even at the same firing point. Furthermore, the wind may have a different force and direction between the firing point and the target than it has at the firing point. Because of all these reasons, it is not recommended that you make any attempt to adjust your sights for wind unless you are convinced beyond a reasonable doubt that such adjustment is necessary.

## The Effect of Light

Most people tend to aim a little lower in a poor light than in a good light, and therefore it would appear that the rear sight should be raised slightly when the light is poor. However, at the short ranges used in pistol target shooting, changes in light do not have enough effect on accuracy to warrant adjusting the rear sight.

Light from one side and not from the other has much the same effect with the average shooter as wind from that side. This is because the side of the front sight toward the light is more clearly defined and is unconsciously held under the center of the bull's-eye. This kind of holding places the bullet toward the opposite side of the bull's-eye from the main source of light. If any adjustment is made, the rear sight is moved toward the main source of light, that is, right or left. However, there is no need to change the sight setting for the effect of light from one side or the other under normal shooting conditions.

## Mirage

A mirage, in the ordinary sense of the term, is an optical effect, such as that sometimes seen on the ocean or on plains and deserts, caused by the total reflection of light at the surface common to two differently heated layers of air. The reflected image is seen commonly inverted, although the real object may or may not be in sight.

In shooting, the word *mirage* refers to heat waves and their effect. On a hot day the heat waves between the firing point and the target seem to bend or lean in the direction in which the wind is blowing. The shooter then beholds an optical illusion in which the bull's-eye is not perfectly round but elongated and slanting in the direction of the mirage. He may unconsciously center his sight under the *apparent* center of the bull's-eye instead of aiming it under the true center, hence he places his shots to the right or left of where he wants them to go.

## Conclusions Regarding Wind, Light, and Mirage

The greatest distance at which targets are fired for record is 50 yards. The wind affects the shooter more than it does the flight of his bullet at that range. We have already told you what to do about your standing position in a wind and have recommended firing between gusts during slow-fire shooting.

The effects of light and mirage are not very noticeable at 50 yards or under, hence it is not recommended that you make any change in your sight adjustment for target shooting on account of wind, light, or mirage. However, if you fire a pistol in hunting or in combat, you will find these weather conditions do have a noticeable effect at 100 yards and become more important as the range increases.

Instead of changing your sight setting, you may find that by aiming slightly higher, lower, or slightly to the right or left, as the case may be, you can compensate for unfavorable weather conditions, but you must exercise great care to be sure that you are not basing your aiming on wild guesses. Any method of aiming that deviates from the standard six-o'clock hold previously explained is dangerous because it does not permit you to know exactly where you are holding on the bull's-eye.

## Shooting Uphill or Downhill

In shooting uphill or downhill, less elevation is required than when shooting on level ground. The steeper the hill, the less elevation is required, hence no elevation is required in firing vertically up or down, regardless of the distance to the target. The very slight slopes found on target ranges have no appreciable effect upon the elevation and do not require any correction of the sight setting. Therefore, these comments apply only to hunting or combat firing at a distance greater than 50 yards.

## More Dry Practice

We have previously urged you to engage in dry or snapping practice to improve your scores at slow fire. The same exercise will improve your scores at sustained, timed, quick, and rapid fire.

If you are armed with the revolver, be sure that you have learned how to cock it while your arm is extended toward the target. Regardless of whether you are firing the revolver or the automatic pistol, remember that you must not bend your elbow. Keep your arms straight but without stiffness or any tendency to lock the elbow.

Try to induce some friend to time you during dry practice so that you can keep within the limits prescribed for the various rates of fire. If you do not have a companion with you, carry a stop watch in your left hand and time yourself. Try to start the watch three seconds after you begin to extend your arm and before snapping the first shot in simulated fire. This will reproduce the usual range conditions.

Learn to simulate the firing of only five shots, because this is the number in each string fired under the usual conditions of pistol competition. If you always practice dry firing in strings of five simulated shots, you will soon form a fixed habit that will save you trouble during actual firing. Otherwise, you may find yourself firing too few or too many shots during a match, either of which will penalize your standing.

An electric clock with a large second hand is an excellent timing device for dry practice. Mount an aiming bull's-eye over the clock, or, better yet, paste a bull's-eye of the appropriate size on the center of the glass covering the clock dial. Assume the proper standing position, start aiming three seconds before the second hand reaches the twelve-o'clock mark, start squeezing when it reaches twelve o'clock, and pretend to fire five shots. When you have snapped the fifth shot, look at the clock and then record your elapsed time.

Some shooters find that it bothers them to watch the hand of the clock until it reaches the twelve-o'clock mark. Instead, they start aiming three seconds before the hand reaches twelve o'clock, and then count to themselves "one hundred and one," "one hundred and two," and "one hundred and three." This gives them the three-second interval, and they start the trigger squeeze as soon as they have said "one hundred and three."

## Correcting Faults during Dry Practice

Your mental attitude is important during dry practice. If you are overly optimistic, you may think you are doing better than you are. If you are a pessimist, you may imagine that you are doing poorly. One method of checking on yourself if you are armed with a revolver is to have a friend load one or more cartridges in the cylinder without letting you know which cylinders are loaded. Then, just as you think you are firing another simulated shot, the revolver goes *bang*, and the location of the bullet on the target tells you whether or not you are applying correct principles in your snapping practice. If you are armed with an automatic pistol, you can have a friend substitute a loaded magazine for your usual empty magazine from time to time, but be sure you do not peek.

Dry practice reveals many faults, especially if you fire live rounds without expecting them. This keeps you on your toes and tends to make you fire each imaginary shot as carefully as though it were a live cartridge. For example, if you snap the hammer on an empty revolver chamber, any trigger jerk becomes more noticeable than it would be with an actual shot. Perhaps you jerk the trigger and cause the barrel to point downward simply because you tighten your fingers at the instant you expect the hammer to fall.

Perhaps you anticipate the fall of the hammer and push your arm out when you expect the gun to fire, pointing the muzzle right or left or up or down. Maybe you are afraid of the loud report and shut your eyes when you expect the discharge. You may be doing all these things plus a few more that we have not mentioned. It costs money to find and cure faults during actual practice. It is cheaper and often easier to locate and remedy bad habits in dry practice.

## Practice before Matches and Tournaments

Do not postpone either dry practice or the firing of live rounds until just before a match or tournament and expect to make up in a few days for weeks of idleness. That is like a student who neglects his studies until the night before the examination and then tries to cram enough to pass the course.

If you have achieved some local fame as a marksman, try to avoid having people watch you practice during the week before a match. If they are following your success, you will try to live up to their expectations and will think about your scores too much to relax. Then, on the day of the match or tournament, fire a few sighting shots at slow, timed, and rapid fire to accustom yourself to the local conditions and to adjust your sights. When you are satisfied with your sights, stop firing and rest until your relay goes on the line.

## Scorebook

Rifle shooters keep careful records of each shot fired. They write down such details as the name and location of the range, the day of the month and the hour, the force and direction of the wind, the intensity and direction of the light, the temperature, the make and type of ammunition used, and sometimes even the humidity.

It is not necessary for you, as a pistol shooter, to keep such elaborate records. The distances at which you fire at targets are much shorter than those used by riflemen. The wind and temperature will affect you far more than they will the flight of the bullet. Nevertheless, you should keep records of your pistol firing in a scorebook, especially when you compete in matches and tournaments conducted by the National Rifle Association or other organizations. Keep a separate scorebook for each gun. Record the score for each stage of firing, showing the ammunition used, the light conditions, and any other facts that will help you in the future.

Paying attention to the ammunition will enable you to know the make and type that gives the best average score under any set of conditions. Information about light conditions will help you to set your sights correctly if they are adjustable or tell you where to aim if you have fixed sights or do not care to move adjustable sights.

Do not fall into the unfortunate habit of recording only good scores. Information about the conditions that produced low scores is far more valuable because it makes it possible to improve your shooting and get into the expert class more quickly. Even if you are an experienced and skillful shooter, a scorebook is a valuable guide to better marksmanship.

# Chapter 15

## STOCKS AND ACTIONS

### Butt, Grip, Handle, or Stock

There are two pieces of wood, hard rubber, or composition attached to the steel frame of the hand gun, one on each side, to give you a better hold on the gun and to prevent slipping. The one on the right side is called the right stock and the one on the left is called the left stock. Or, if you prefer, you may refer to them as the right grip and the left grip. Figure 1 shows a variety of stocks for pistols and revolvers.

In addition to this use of the words *stock* and *grip*, we have a broader meaning. Thus, when you pick up your pistol or revolver, you may say that you take hold of the grip, stock, butt, or handle, and you mean the same thing in each case. Generally, the way that one of these words is used in a sentence makes its meaning perfectly clear, but we have discussed this subject here to point out the possibility of confusion. In this chapter we shall use the word *stock* in its singular meaning, that is, to refer to one of the pieces fastened to the side of the gun.

### Fit Your Gun to Your Hand

The stocks on a hand gun are designed to fit the hand of the average man, an imaginary person who elects presidents and wins wars. Unfortunately, you may not be average. Your hands may be bigger or smaller than those of the average shooter. Your gun stocks

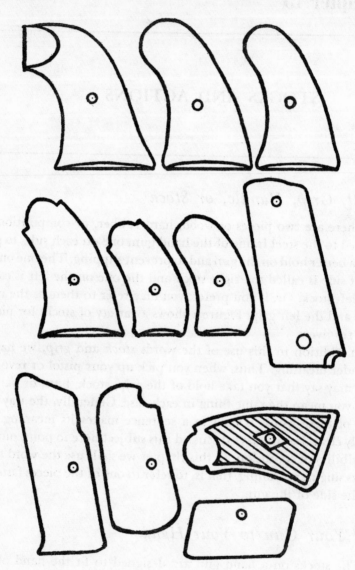

Fig. 1. A variety of stocks for pistols and revolvers.

must fit your hand for any kind of shooting, but they must fit better for sustained, timed, quick, and rapid fire than for slow fire.

In slow fire, if your gun slips down in your hand after recoil, you have time to adjust it again before firing the next shot. When firing against a time limit, you have only a few seconds for firing each shot. You cannot afford to readjust the gun in your hand when it is knocked out of the correct position by recoil or by the motion of pulling the hammer back to the full-cock.

You may receive low scores in shooting simply because your stocks do not fit your hand. For example, during a time-limit match, if you bend your elbow between shots, shake your gun to make it fit your hand, or awkwardly fumble the hammer in drawing it back, it is probable that you need special stocks.

## The Grip Adapter

The average revolver stock is designed so that your trigger finger is placed too high above the line of your trigger squeeze. If the stocks were properly designed, you could hold the butt of the gun in the crotch of your hand, your trigger finger would fit the trigger comfortably, and the heel of your hand would overlap the center line of the back strap at least a half inch, thus preventing the gun from slipping outward and permitting you to hold the gun correctly during either single-action or double-action shooting and at sustained, timed, or rapid fire.

Many experts tell you that you should squeeze the trigger with the second joint of your first or index finger. This is not necessarily true. Some of the regional and national pistol champions use the first joint of the trigger finger and others use the second joint, depending upon the size and shape of the hand.

Regardless of which joint of the trigger finger you use to squeeze the trigger, your grip on the gun often can be improved by using a grip adapter, which is a filler that fits back of the trigger guard of a revolver to lower the point of contact between your hand and the revolver. Figure 2 illustrates three sizes of grip adapters made by the Pachmayr Gun Works, Los Angeles. The arrow in the illustration shows that the grip adapter is fastened between the rear of the trigger guard and the front strap of the butt. The three sizes, large, medium, and small, can be used on all Colt and Smith and Wesson revolvers and single-shot pistols except the Smith and Wesson Hammerless and the .22 Smith and Wesson Single-Shot "Straight Line." Usually, a man with a large hand requires the small size and a man with a small hand needs the large size. This device can be installed or removed in a few seconds by loosening the screw that holds the standard wooden or hard rubber stocks (grips) on the frame.

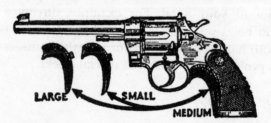

Fig. 2. Three sizes of grip adapters. (*Courtesy Pachmayr Gun Works*)

Instead of buying a commercial adapter, you can improvise one of your own. For example, you can whittle a block of wood that will serve the purpose if you are handy with a knife.

A better method is to make the filler of plastic wood by forming a ball of it about the size of a small egg and placing it between the rear of the trigger guard and the front strap, squeezing the plastic wood until it fills the space usually left vacant above the finger of your shooting hand. Trim off any excess plastic wood and place the revolver to one side, upside down, for about twenty-four hours, until the plastic wood hardens. If you did not trim away too much in shaping the wood, the filler block should be wide at the top and extend beyond the frame of the revolver about a quarter inch on each side.

Try to make the filler block exactly the size you need. If it is large, it will be helpful in slow-fire shooting. In sustained, timed, or rapid fire the stock should be smaller for good scores. You must grip the revolver firmly enough with the fingers to control it when you cock the hammer, but if the stock is too large for your hand this is impossible. Of course, if your fingers are long, you can fire well with a large stock, but in case of doubt, it is better to use a stock that is too small than one too large.

The most successful shooters seldom make their own stocks, use grip adapters, or make plastic-wood filler blocks. Instead, they put their hand on a sheet of paper, draw its outline with a pencil, indicate the measurements, and send this pattern to a specialist in the manufacture of stocks, telling him the make, model, caliber, and other details of the gun for which the stocks are to be made.

## The Trigger Stop

Some shooters use a trigger stop to limit the movement of the trigger after it has been squeezed enough to fire the gun. If the trigger moves far after the gun fires, the resulting motion of the trigger finger may be transmitted to the main portion of the hand enough to move the gun slightly and change the aim.

One remedy is to wrap adhesive tape around the trigger guard behind the trigger, applying enough layers so that the trigger will strike the tape before it travels far enough to knock the hand out of position.

Another method is to drill a hole in the rear of the trigger guard and tap it for a small machine screw, which is adjusted to stop the travel of the trigger after the shot is fired.

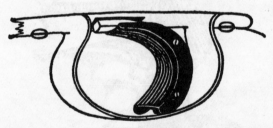

Fig. 3. A trigger shoe. (*Courtesy Harvey E. Henshaw*)

## The Trigger Shoe

Shooters who find that their trigger finger tends to slip off the trigger sometimes use a trigger shoe, such as the one illustrated in

Figure 3, which was designed by Harvey E. Henshaw, of Pittsburgh, Pennsylvania. It is made for most rifle and revolver triggers, and for the Colt .45-caliber semiautomatic pistol. It is attached by means of two screws. The width of the shoe and its corrugated surface give the shooter a better grip on the trigger and hence may raise his score.

## The Free-Pistol Stock

In a free-pistol match, the pistol may be of any caliber, any barrel length, any trigger pull, and any type stock except that no attachment may be used that extends along the forearm and serves as an aid in supporting the gun. This classification makes it possible for the stock to have a shelf for the thumb on the left side, and a ledge or projecting shelf in the lower portion to support the bottom of the hand, as illustrated in Figure 4, which is a right-side view. Generally, the stock is made especially for the shooter so that when he extends his arm the pistol seems to hold itself correctly in his hand and point naturally toward the bull's-eye.

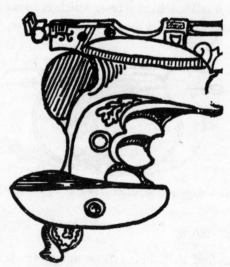

Fig. 4. A stock for a free pistol.

## Checkering the Stock

Checkering, also called checking, is the cutting of squares and diamonds for decoration and to prevent slipping. The checkering tools are of various sizes and shapes. Most of then are wood-cutting tools but the checkering file is used for checkering metal. On a factory-made stock it is advisable to have a competent gunsmith continue the checkering across the borders of the stock at the rear of the revolver and then checker the back strap to prevent the stock from changing its position in the hand when the gun recoils. When this work is done, the gunsmith should shape the diamonds so that they have their long axes pointing vertically, that is, the diamonds point up and down but not horizontally.

At the same time, the gunsmith should use his checkering file to deepen the checkering on the hammer spur, shaping the diamonds so that they have their points horizontal to prevent slipping. If the hammer spur is not checkered, it is more difficult to obtain a firm grip on the hammer with the thumb during cocking.

## Weights

Some experienced shooters like to improve the balance of their guns by the use of weights. One method is to attach a lead weight on the bottom of the stock; another is to fill the inside with lead. Those who are troubled by the swaying of the gun while shooting in the wind sometimes fasten steel rods, such as lengths of ordinary drill rod, on each side of the top rib of a target pistol with friction tape. Among the regional and national champions, very few use weights, and these are usually located under the barrel near the muzzle, averaging about 2½ ounces for each gun.

## Speed Locks and Short Actions

When a shooter says that he has a speed lock or a short action, he means that the lock has been altered to decrease the time that elapses between the squeezing of the trigger and the ignition of the powder in the cartridge case. This lock time may be shortened in various ways. The weight of the moving parts may be decreased by cutting lightening holes, such as those illustrated in Figure 5, cutting away nonessential portions of parts, or by using metal of the same strength but lighter weight. Another method is to strengthen the hammer spring or firing-pin spring. Also, the throw of the hammer of a revolver may be shortened. Generally, the lock time is reduced by a combination of such alterations.

Fig. 5. The weight of moving parts may be decreased by cutting lightening holes.

The greatest advantage of a speed lock is found during rapid fire with a revolver because the shortened action enables the shooter to recock his gun without disturbing the alignment of his sights with the bull's-eye.

Figure 6 shows how the hammer of an Officer's Model .38-caliber revolver can be altered. The three views show the notch in the hammer before alteration; dotted lines indicate the parts cut away,

## STOCKS AND ACTIONS

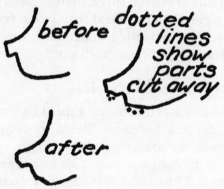

Fig. 6. Alterations to a revolver hammer.

and the shape after the work is completed. When performed by an expert, this alteration produces a clean, smooth pull, but when done by an amateur, the result is usually a ruined hammer.

In most alterations to the action, the gunsmith must be both an expert welder and an expert in hand filing. Skilled welders are fairly common, but hand filing is almost a lost art outside of the firearm factories and a few other industries requiring this type of work. Filing looks easy, but success comes only with long years of experience, and it requires a vast amount of patience.

Unless you are confident that the gunsmith who shortens your action knows his business, be sure that he hardens and retempers any parts that have been welded, because welding, in itself, is one form of heat treatment.

Further details regarding the construction and alteration of wood and metal parts of firearms can be found in the author's earlier text, *Gun Care and Repair, a Manual of Gunsmithing.*

# Chapter 16

## SLOW, TIMED, SUSTAINED, RAPID, AND QUICK FIRE

### Slow Fire

In the armed services of the United States, unlimited time is permitted for slow fire in order to permit the instructors to have sufficient time for explaining the causes of errors and the appropriate remedies. It is intended to be the elementary phase of instruction in the proper operation of pistols and revolvers and for determining and correcting personal errors of the shooters. Slow fire is not used in firing for military record.

Under the rules of the National Rifle Association of America, the time limit for slow fire is 5 minutes per 5-shot string at 50 yards, 20 yards, 50 feet, and at 25 yards when the reduced 50-yard target is used. In all open matches (generally open to all comers), where the timed- and rapid-fire 25-yard target is used for slow fire at 25 yards, the time limit is 2½ minutes per 5-shot string, but 5 minutes per 5-shot string may be allowed in restricted and special class matches if the program so specifies.

### Timed Fire

In timed fire under the rules of the National Rifle Association of America, the time limit is 20 seconds for each string of 5 shots. Time is taken for the period during which the target is fully exposed. The range is 25 yards.

In the armed services of the United States, the range for record firing is also 25 yards, although practice firing is at ranges of 15 and 25 yards. Training for timed fire is begun after the fundamentals of slow fire, particularly the trigger squeeze, are thoroughly understood and some skill in applying them has been gained. The trigger squeeze in slow fire, however, should be continued during the entire period of training because it is the basis of good pistol and revolver marksmanship.

Timed fire in the armed services is the same as slow fire except that the time between shots is limited. The restriction placed upon the time makes the progress from slow fire, without any time limit, to sustained fire, with only a few seconds allowance, a fairly easy step. Two minutes and 10 seconds are allowed for firing 5 shots for record, which is an allowance of 26 seconds per shot, a greater time than permitted by the National Rifle Association.

The first shot in timed fire should be fired without too much delay. The following shots should be approximately evenly spaced so that the last shot will be fired just before the expiration of the time limit. Although the grasp on the weapon may be relaxed after each shot, the correct position and grasp should be taken for each shot. Also, the breath should be held, the sights correctly aligned, and the trigger properly squeezed for each shot. The trigger squeeze is the same in timed fire as in slow fire. When the shooter is armed with a revolver, it should be recocked immediately after each shot.

If you have been getting a good score in slow fire, you may think that it will be lowered in timed fire. This is not true. The principles of slow-fire shooting apply without change to timed fire. If you jerk the trigger in timed fire, you will receive a poor score the same as in slow fire. Actually, speeding up your rate of fire slightly may improve your score in both slow and timed fire because you learn to avoid wasting time in squeezing the trigger. It is a common fault to aim longer than necessary before firing the gun. The arm becomes tired, your weapon wobbles, and you may be tempted to fire when the sights are not properly aligned on the bull's-eye.

Do not let time restrictions of timed fire cause you to jerk the trigger. If you begin to flinch, forget the time limit until you have eliminated any tendency to jerk the trigger. When you disregard time, you know that you have plenty of time to correct a tendency to flinch by lowering the gun, resting a few seconds, and aiming again. When firing against time, however long the period may be, you may imagine that you lack time to correct your faults, you hurry your shots, and if you are not very careful, you may build up a flinching habit that will be difficult to overcome.

When you first change from slow to timed fire, your shots may not be evenly spaced as to time. You will allow three seconds between some shots and six seconds between others. The cause of this irregular timing is usually a poor trigger squeeze and can be corrected only by practicing trigger squeeze very slowly and correctly when you are not on the firing line.

In firing the revolver, you must practice cocking it so that you can do it smoothly. When you have attained some skill in cocking, you should find that after each shot your revolver comes back on the target with the bull's-eye and that you can immediately begin to squeeze the trigger.

Practice your trigger squeeze now for timing, allowing the same number of seconds between shots. If you squeeze the trigger too slowly for one shot, you may become conscious of the passing time, hurry the next squeeze, and jerk the trigger so badly that you miss the target. Aside from the necessity of avoiding a trigger jerk, you must be careful that you do not tighten your fingers on the gun just as the hammer falls, because this too will ruin your scores.

Try to use as much of your time allowance as possible. Most shooters finish two or three seconds ahead of time, but do not try to finish in any shorter period. Endeavor to judge the amount of time already spent and the amount left for your remaining shots, and space the last shots accordingly. If you are short on time, you must hurry up, but do not try to hasten one shot more than the others.

Long experience has shown that the first and last shots are the ones that are most often fired without squeezing the trigger properly. The cause is usually psychological, and the remedy is correct thinking.

When the targets first appear or when the command to commence firing is given, most shooters open fire. The noise disturbs you in itself, and it suggests that you had better get busy and do what everyone else is doing. You forget to squeeze the trigger, you give a jerk, and you miss or receive a poor score. This is a bad start. You worry about that first bad shot and try too hard the second time. Again you get a poor score or a miss, and unless you suddenly wake up to the fact that you are defeating yourself, you are headed for a very poor total score.

Let us imagine that your first shot is poor, but your second is fairly good. The first blast of firing is over, and the men on the line have settled down to a reasonably even rhythm, but there is still noise. You are firing according to your basic instruction, your nerves have recovered from the original shock, and you hope to make a good showing. Unfortunately, you begin to wonder about the time. As you continue to fire, the fear of time grows until you finally decide that little time is left. You are afraid that you may be caught with one or two rounds left in your gun. You hurry these last shots, jerk the trigger, and once more curse yourself for being a poor shot.

Returning to the first appearance of the targets or the command to commence firing, if you do not start your trigger squeeze until you have heard the first big blast of firing on the line, you will complete your squeeze during the quiet period when the others have already fired their first shot and are waiting to fire their second shot. Of course, the fallacy of this advice is that if everyone did this, no one would start. We are assuming that you are a beginner or possibly an experienced shooter who is trying to improve his scores.

Eliminating the trigger jerk on the last shot depends upon your ability to estimate time. You may find that everyone else has completed firing, but do not let this disturb you. It does not necessarily mean that the period is about to end. Remember, we told you before that most shooters finish several seconds before the limit. Fire the last shot just as carefully, with just as much attention to trigger squeeze, as you did the early shots.

Although it is best to space your shots evenly, one remedy for a bad last shot is to allow yourself more time for the last shot than you do for the others. Knowing that you have provided ample time, you can concentrate on your squeeze. Say to yourself, "Squeeze with a gradually increasing pressure. Do not jerk. Squeeze."

## Sustained Fire

Sustained fire is the same as slow fire and timed fire except that the weapon remains pointed at the target for five consecutive shots, and there is no pause or delay between the discharge of one shot and the application of the operations to fire the next shot. Sustained fire is not part of the civilian program of the National Rifle Association of America, but it is an integral part of the program of the armed services of the United States.

Training for sustained fire is begun after the principles of slow fire and timed fire are thoroughly understood and some skill in applying them has been acquired.

## Sustained Fire for the Automatic Pistol

In firing the automatic pistol, the time consumed in squeezing the trigger must be shorter in sustained fire than in slow or timed fire, but the process is the same.

To fire the first shot, the pistol is brought by the shortest route from raise pistol to the aiming position, and the sights are aligned on the bull's-eye. This is done by smoothly and rapidly extending the right arm straight from the shoulder, inserting the right forefinger in the trigger guard during the movement, and holding the breath. To bring a pistol through the arc of a circle to the aiming position is a loss of time.

For succeeding shots, the sights should be held as nearly on the bull's-eye (in the regular manner) as possible and the breath held throughout the firing of the string. The recoil after each shot will throw the sights out of alignment, but they must be brought back immediately to the bull's-eye by the shortest route.

An upward movement of the arm, also caused by recoil, moves the hand from six to eight inches. The wrist and elbow must not be bent. The sights will then come back on the bull's-eye automatically after each shot. It is a waste of time to flourish the pistol between shots.

In order to simulate the self-loading action of the automatic pistol, you can tie the end of a strong cord about four feet long to the thumbpiece of the hammer, with a knot on top. Take a few turns of the other end of the cord around the thumb or fingers of your left hand. The cord should be long enough to permit your left hand to hang naturally at your side while aiming the pistol with your hand, your right arm being fully extended.

Each time that the hammer falls, a quick backward jerk of your left hand will recock the pistol and, at the same time, jerk the sights out of alignment with the bull's-eye. This derangement of the alignment of the sights represents very closely the jump of the pistol when it is actually fired.

Be sure to keep the knot of the cord on top. If it is underneath the hammer or if the cord is too thick, the hammer will not remain cocked when you jerk it back.

## Sustained Fire for the Revolver

In order to attain the degree of accuracy required for proficiency in sustained fire with the revolver, it must be cocked by the use of the thumb and not by using double action.

The grip on the stock is the same as for slow fire and timed fire except that you will experience a slightly tighter feel and your finger tips will contact the stock. The position of the arm and the position of the body are the same as for slow and timed fire.

Keep the grip the same throughout the firing of each string. If you shift the position of the revolver in your hand or vary the pressure of your hand and fingers during the firing you will lower your score. Skill is developed only through dry shooting.

To fire the first shot, bring the revolver from the position of raise pistol by the shortest route to the firing position with the sights properly aligned on the aiming point. Do this by smoothly but deliberately and rapidly extending your right arm straight from your shoulder, cocking your revolver, inserting the forefinger in the trigger guard during the movement, and holding your breath.

In sustained firing, you can gain time by: (1) taking position accurately, (2) applying a heavy initial pressure on the trigger as soon as the sights are aligned and then maintaining a continuously increasing pressure until the shot is fired, (3) cocking your revolver rapidly and smoothly, (4) keeping the focus of your eye on the front sight during the firing of the entire string, and (5) absorbing the shock of recoil at the shoulder, not at the wrist or elbow, thus reducing the movement of the revolver to a minimum.

Remember, you must not try to save time by pulling the trigger quickly when your aim is perfect.

## Range and Time for Sustained Fire

During practice, 5 shots of sustained fire are fired at a range of 15 yards with the automatic pistol in 12 seconds, and with the revolver in 15 seconds. Five shots are fired at a range of 25 yards with the automatic pistol in 15 seconds, and with the revolver in 18 seconds. In firing for record, the ranges and time are the same except that 20 seconds are allowed for the revolver at 25 yards. However, in firing for record, twice as many shots are fired, that is, 10 shots are fired at 15 yards and 10 at 25 yards.

## Rapid Fire

Rapid fire is a National Rifle Association term that is not used by the armed services. In most N.R.A. matches, the following courses of fire are used to make up the tournament program: 20 shots slow fire, 20 shots timed fire, 20 shots rapid fire, and in the National Match Course, 10 shots slow, 10 shots timed, and 10 shots rapid. In the larger tournaments this entire course of fire is repeated once for the .22-, .38-, and .45-caliber arms.

Under the N.R.A. rules, the time limit for rapid fire is 10 seconds for each string of 5 shots. Time is taken for the period during which the target is fully exposed. Rapid fire, like timed fire, is fired at a range of 25 yards.

A shooter who first learns the time limit for rapid fire is usually worried because he thinks that it is almost impossible to hit the target with each shot at that rate of fire, but he soon discovers that it is common for experienced shooters to make a score of 95 out of a possible 100 at rapid fire.

You should not expect to do as well at rapid fire as you did at slow and timed fire when you begin, but gradually you can raise your scores if you review the fundamentals of marksmanship and apply them carefully. When properly approached, rapid fire is a gradual step from timed fire and not a sudden change to something entirely new.

In preparing for rapid fire, gradually cut down your interval between shots at timed fire. Do not reduce this interval too fast or you may sacrifice your hard-earned trigger squeeze. If your score starts to fall, go back to the longer interval until you have regained your confidence. It is foolish to take up rapid fire if you are still doing poorly at timed fire.

## Special Instructions for Rapid Fire

In rapid fire, the stock is held very slightly tighter than in slow fire. The finger tips come into contact with the stock, but you must not exert any noticeable pressure with them or you will tighten them just as you are about to fire, and this form of flinching will throw your shots low and to the left if you shoot with your right hand, or low and to the right if you shoot with your left hand.

In firing the revolver, the high grasp, with the base of the hand supporting the entire rear portion of the revolver stock and the thumb extending straight forward along the frame, is correct for rapid as well as for timed fire.

Stand in the same position for rapid and timed fire as you did for slow fire. Relax. Do not worry. Try to get on the firing line early enough to lay out your equipment and prepare yourself mentally and physically for firing. Remember all that you have learned in slow and timed fire but do not worry.

Under N.R.A. rules, the shooters may point their guns toward the target after the command "ready on the firing line" has been given. As soon as you come to the raise pistol position, forget every shot previously fired, your business worries, and your family problems. Concentrate on the next five shots. Keep your eyes on the bull's-eye until you have fired your last shot. Think about hitting the center of the bull's-eye and avoid any negative thoughts about missing or getting one low to the right or left.

Three seconds after the range officer commands "ready on the firing line," you can start firing. Extend your arm straight out and upward at an angle of about 20 degrees. While you are extending your arm, take a reasonably deep breath. As soon as the arm is fully extended (but without strain), lower your gun into the aiming position by dropping your whole arm from the shoulder.

While you are lowering your arm into the aiming position, breathe out about one third of the air you took into your lungs and then, just as the sights come into the aiming position, hold your breath (but without strain). Remember to breathe in while extending the arm and to breathe out while lowering it into position for aiming. If you practice this a few times it will become a natural procedure and will require no conscious thought.

Most men take about two seconds for extending the arm and lowering it into position and about one second for lining up the front and rear sights. Therefore, if you start to lower your shooting arm at the command "ready on the firing line," you are ready to line up the sights with the bull's-eye and start squeezing when the targets appear.

## Military Targets

In the armed services of the United States, Pistol Target L, usually referred to as the L target, is used for slow, timed, and sustained fire. This target, illustrated in Figure 1, is a rectangle 6 feet high

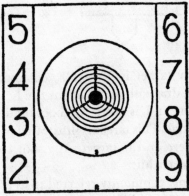

Fig. 1. The L Target

and 4 feet wide, with a black bull's-eye 5 inches in diameter and 7 outer rings. The value of hits in the bull's-eye is 10. The diameter of each ring and the value of hits in that ring are as follows:

| DIAMETER | VALUE OF HIT |
|---|---|
| 8½ inches | 9 |
| 12 " | 8 |
| 15½ " | 7 |
| 19 " | 6 |
| 22½ " | 5 |
| 26 " | 4 |
| 46 " | 3 |
| Outer, remainder of target | 2 |

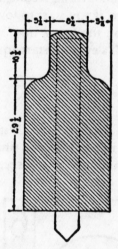

Fig. 2. The E Target.

Another military target is Target E, commonly referred to as the E target. It is a drab silhouette about the height of a soldier in a kneeling position and is made of bookbinder's board or any other similar material. This target is illustrated in Figure 2. Hits are valued at 1 anywhere on the target. Any shot cutting the edge of the target is counted as a hit.

Target E, bobbing, commonly referred to as a bobbing target, is illustrated in Figure 3, which shows the construction and method of mounting. The upper drawing is a top view to show the angles of rotation. This target is so arranged as to be fully exposed to the firer for a limited time. The edge of the target is toward the firer when the target is not exposed.

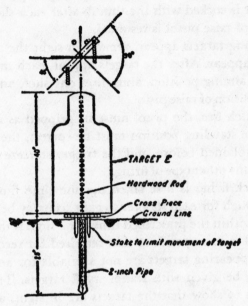

*TARGET E*

*Hardwood Rod*

*Cross Piece*
*Ground Line*

*Stake to limit movement of target*

*2-inch Pipe*

Fig. 3. The bobbing target.

In the armed services, no specific targets are prescribed for small-bore practice with the pistol and revolver. Any suitable target may be used.

## Quick Fire

In quick fire for instruction purposes, 5 shots are fired at Target E, bobbing, at 15 yards, at the rate of 3 seconds per shot; and 5 shots are fired at 25 yards at the same rate. In quick fire for record, 5 shots are fired at the rate of 3 seconds per shot at 25 yards and then this is repeated to obtain one score, that is, 10 shots are fired in all.

Training in quick fire is taken up after the sustained-fire instruction has been satisfactorily conducted. For each shot, the pistol is brought from the position of raise pistol to the aiming position by the shortest route after the target appears.

The automatic pistol may be cocked between shots by means of a cord (as in sustained-fire instructions) or by using the left hand to pull the hammer back after the position of raise pistol is resumed. The revolver is cocked with the thumb after each shot but before the position of raise pistol is resumed.

The bobbing targets appear, remain in sight the allotted time, and then disappear. After the targets appear, each man brings his pistol to the aiming position, aims, fires one shot, and returns his gun to the position of raise pistol.

During quick fire, the pistol must be gripped as in timed and rapid fire, the standing position must be correct, the breath must be held as explained before, and the trigger squeeze is just as important as in any other type of firing.

When quick firing is first taken up, the time limit should be extended enough for each shooter to gain accuracy before attempting to shoot within the prescribed time. The time is then gradually reduced until it corresponds to that required for record purposes.

When disappearing targets are not available for any reason, instruction can be given with stationary E targets. The command "up" is given to show that the targets are in sight, and the command "down" is given to signify that they have been withdrawn.

## Civilian Targets

Targets approved by the National Rifle Association for civilian shooting are discussed in another chapter. It must be remembered that the selection of targets, the range, the rate of fire, and many other details of pistol marksmanship are subject to change. In this chapter we have emphasized fundamental training methods, which can be applied in any marksmanship program regardless of the details of execution.

# Chapter 17

## THE FAST DRAW FOR
## SELF-DEFENSE AND COMBAT

### Pocket and Home-Defense Hand Guns

It is very difficult to segregate any particular group of revolvers and semiautomatic pistols as being distinctly home-defense hand guns. For example, the long-barrel target arms as well as the large military weapons, may be used for home defense. Also, we think of pocket-type hand guns as being small weapons that can be carried in the pocket, yet there are many men who carry large semiautomatic pistols in their pockets. Therefore, in this chapter we shall disregard any grouping of guns and concentrate on the technique of the fast draw from holsters.

### Drawing from the Shoulder Holster

In order to make a fast draw from any type of holster, you must grip the gun while it is still in the holster, in such a manner that when it comes out of the holster it lies in the hand in approximately the same position that you would have if you were assuming an ordinary firing position. In other words, you must hold the gun in your hand with a practically correct shooting grip both before and after it is drawn.

Figure 1 shows the first step in drawing a revolver from a spring-clip shoulder holster on the left side when the revolver is carried with the butt to the front and the barrel to the rear, which is normal for a left-shoulder holster. Notice that the holster is open to the front so that the gun can be drawn straight forward and it is not necessary to lift it out of the top of the holster.

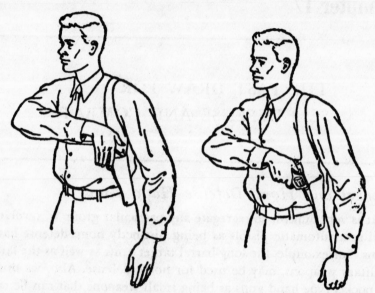

Fig. 1. The first movement in the shoulder holster draw.

Fig. 2. The second movement in the shoulder holster draw.

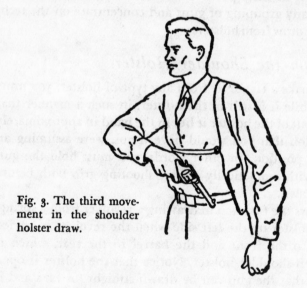

Fig. 3. The third movement in the shoulder holster draw.

In Figure 2, the gun is freed from the spring clip in the holster. The hand is moved downward a short distance and also away from the holster, but the gun is not yet entirely free from the holster.

In Figure 3, the gun is entirely free from the holster. The shooter can now move his wrist slightly and go into any shooting position appropriate to the occasion. For example, he may have his right forearm horizontal, with his right elbow against the right side of his body, or he may raise his arm to a regular shooting position with the arm fully extended to the front, as previously explained in this book.

## The Cross Draw with One Gun

Figure 4 shows the first step in the cross draw with one gun. The shooter twists his hips slightly to his left as he begins the draw by placing his right hand on the gun and starts to pull it from the top of the holster. Notice that this holster is not open toward the front, and therefore the gun is lifted out of it.

In Figure 5, the twisting motion of the hips is continued as the shooter continues to draw the gun from the holster. The purpose of the twisting motion is to carry the holster away from the hip into a position for a straight-out movement of the shooter's hand.

In Figure 6, the gun has been turned away from the body and is just above the belt buckle, ready to fire. If the gun is fired now, the elapsed time should be less than a second for a man who has practiced the draw, and it may be as short as three fifths of a second if he is an expert.

## Holster Location for the One-Gun Cross Draw

For a one-gun cross draw, the holster may be worn left of the belt buckle with the top of the holster about even with the top of the belt. In this location, the gun barrel points downward and to the left, and the butt is to the right.

## Body Position in Fast Drawing

The unnatural but dramatic body positions assumed by characters in motion pictures or Western fiction are usually wrong from the viewpoint of efficient fast-draw shooting. It is not necessary to spread the legs apart, crouch, lean forward, or otherwise assume awkward, tense positions. In fact, such theatrical posing announces to your opponent your intention to draw and fire and may cost your life.

There is one exception to these statements. Law-enforcement officers are often taught a standing-crouch position because it presents less of their bodies as a target for opponents directly in front of them. However, a criminal expects a policeman or sheriff to fire at him if he resists or attempts to flee, hence the crouched position does not telegraph any intentions not already understood by the criminal.

## Other Fast-Draw Methods

There are many types of holsters especially designed for fast-draw shooting and numerous methods of quick drawing. A complete discussion of the subject is beyond the scope of this text. The outstanding reference is *Ed McGiven's Book on Fast and Fancy Revolver Shooting and Police Training,* by Ed McGiven, of Lewistown, Montana.

(Left) Fig. 4. The first movement in the one-gun cross
draw.

(Above) Fig. 5. The second
movement in the one-gun
cross draw.

(Left) Fig. 6. The third movement in the one-gun cross
draw.

# Chapter 18

## HAND GUNS FOR POLICE AND SHERIFFS

### Advantages of a Good Training Program

A good training program conducted for law-enforcement officers by a city, county, or state government has three advantages. First, it may save the life of an officer. Second, it inspires confidence on the part of the law-abiding public. Third, it reduces crime by causing potential criminals to think twice before committing an offense. Unfortunately, some governmental bodies have no training program, and most of the courses in existence are inadequate.

### The Revolver for Officers of the Law

Earlier chapters of this text have explained why a revolver is superior to a semiautomatic pistol for many purposes. This is especially true of police work. The majority of all law-enforcement bodies in the United States have adopted a revolver as the principal weapon.

It is generally accepted that the revolver for police should not be less than .38 Special in caliber and that the make should be either Colt or Smith and Wesson. City police departments often adopt a revolver with a 4-inch barrel and a light or medium frame. Sheriffs and state police usually favor a 6-inch barrel with a medium or heavy frame, and they often prefer the .357 Magnum Smith and Wesson revolver, although some departments use a .45-caliber weapon. Mounted officers, both horse and motorcycle, usually wear a lanyard over the shoulder with one end attached to a lanyard loop on the gun. Some dismounted officers wear the gun at the end of the lanyard for the same reason, that is, to avoid losing the gun or dropping it, especially if the shooting-arm is shot in combat.

## Colt Revolvers for Police

Modern Colt revolvers suitable for police use are the Official Police Revolver, the Police Positive Special Revolver, and the Detective Special Revolver, all caliber .38 Special. The Officers' Model Target Revolver, caliber .38 Special, is a target arm as its name indicates and is not regarded as a duty weapon.

The Official Police Revolver is made in calibers .22 Long Rifle and .38 Special, the former being for practice only. The .38 Special is available with a 4-, 5-, or 6-inch barrel. With the 6-inch barrel the total length is 11¼ inches and the weight is 36 ounces. The trigger is grooved, and the hammer spur is checkered. The stock are made of a plastic substance and checkered.

The Police Positive Special Revolver is made in calibers .32 Police Positive, .38 Police Positive, and .38 Special, the latter being the one suitable for a duty sidearm. The barrel is 4 inches long, the total length is 8¾ inches, and the weight is 22 ounces. This is a medium-weight revolver used by some departments but not as extensively as the Official Police Revolver described above.

The Detective Special Revolver is made in calibers .32 Police Positive, .38 Police Positive, and .38 Special, the latter being the one selected for duty weapons. The barrel is 2 inches long, the total length is 6¾ inches, and the weight is 21 ounces. Except for the short barrel and the specially rounded stocks, this is a powerful compact version of the Police Positive Special. It is preferred by many detectives, pay-roll clerks, and others who wish to carry a weapon in the pocket or a shoulder holster.

The Colt 1917 revolver, often called the U.S. Revolver, Model 1917, has been discussed elsewhere in this text. It is adopted by some police departments as a duty weapon.

## Smith and Wesson Revolvers for Police

The most powerful revolver made by Smith and Wesson is the .357 Magnum, which is discussed in detail in the chapter on hunting with hand guns and mentioned in other chapters of this text. It is a 6-shot revolver made in a variety of barrel lengths, ranging from 3½ to 8⅜ inches. With an 8⅜-inch barrel, it weighs 47 ounces; with a 6½-inch barrel, it weighs 44½ ounces; with a 6-inch barrel, 44 ounces; with a 5-inch barrel, 42½ ounces; with a 3½-inch barrel, 41 ounces. The total length is 11⅜ inches with a 6-inch barrel.

The .38/44 Heavy Duty revolver is caliber .38, Smith and Wesson Special and is available with a 4-, 5-, or 6½-inch barrel. With a 5-inch barrel, it is only 10⅜ inches long and weighs 40 ounces.

The New .38 Military and Police is caliber .38, Smith and Wesson Special, and is available with a 2-, 4-, 5-, or 6-inch barrel. With the 6-inch barrel it is 11⅛ inches long and weighs 31 ounces. This model has a square butt and a short action. The same revolver with a round butt and a short action is available with the same barrel lengths. With a 2-inch barrel it is 6⅞ inches long and weighs 6⅞ ounces. This latter model is often carried by detectives, pay-roll messengers, and others who wish to carry the gun concealed in a pocket or a shoulder holster.

All of the above models are suitable for general police duty. These, and all other Smith and Wesson revolvers, are 6-shot arms. We shall now turn to some models that are sometimes used by police and sheriffs but that are not generally adopted. One of these is the 1926 Model .44 Military revolver, caliber .44 Smith and Wesson Special, available with a 4-, 5-, or 6½-inch barrel. With a 6½-inch barrel, it is 11¾ inches long and weighs 39½ ounces. An accompanying model for target practice is the 1926 Model .44 Target revolver, which has a 6½-inch barrel, is 11¾ inches long, and weighs 39½ ounces. The 1917 Army revolver, caliber .45, has a 5½-inch barrel, is 10¾ inches long, and weighs 36¼ ounces. It is sometimes called the U.S. Revolver, Model 1917 and is discussed elsewhere in this text. Colt makes a similar model.

There are two other revolvers that should be considered because they are of police caliber, but both are in the target class. One is the .38/44 Outdoorsman, caliber .38, Smith and Wesson Special, with a 6½-inch barrel, a total length of 11¾ inches, and a weight of 41¾ ounces. The other is the New K-38 Masterpiece, also caliber

.38, Smith and Wesson Special, with a 6-inch barrel, a total length of 11⅛ inches, and a weight of 36 ounces when loaded.

## Duty Models Distinguished from Target Revolvers

It should be understood that in distinguishing between target revolvers and duty models of the same caliber, the barrel length and the type of sights are critical features. Thus, the target model usually has a Patridge-type front sight and a square-notch rear sight and a barrel that is generally available in one length only. On the other hand, the duty model usually has service-type sights and a variety of barrel lengths.

## Combat Firing Conditions

Firing in combat is vastly different from shooting on a well-constructed range at a fixed target, which cannot return the fire. Within the limits of safety and common sense, combat firing should represent the difficulties to be encountered when firing at an armed enemy. It is obviously impracticable to attempt to reproduce exactly combat conditions on any revolver range, particularly the mental and physical tension and reactions of the man under fire. However, thorough instruction and properly supervised combat training will develop the ability to fire instinctively, accurately, and quickly.

## Two-Hand Grip

The two-hand grip enables the shooter to support the ordinary one-hand grip previously described in this text, thereby increasing accuracy. The weapon is first grasped in the right hand in the usual manner. The butt (stock or handle), still grasped in the right hand, is then seated firmly in the palm of the left hand. The fingers and thumb of the left hand are then closed over the right hand in a manner that will provide maximum support as shown in Figure 1, which illustrates the two-hand grip for the .45-caliber semiautomatic pistol. The two-hand grip should duplicate as closely as possible the support that is provided when a barricade, automo-

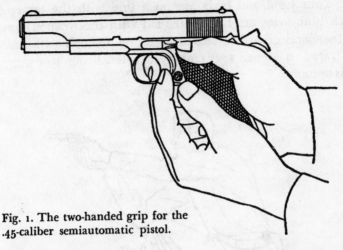

Fig. 1. The two-handed grip for the
.45-caliber semiautomatic pistol.

bile hood, fence post, or other object is used as a rest during combat. This two-hand grip can be applied to either revolver or a semiautomatic pistol.

Fig. 2. The two-handed prone position with a revolver.

## Prone Position

Lie as flat as possible on the ground with your legs apart and heels down in the same manner as the prone position used when firing the rifle. Your head and body are on a line with the target toward which both arms are fully extended with the weapon grasped in the two-hand grip. The two-hand prone position with a revolver, illustrated in Figure 2, is employed when firing at a range of 50 yards or more.

Fig. 3. The two-handed kneeling position with a revolver.

## Kneeling Position

The kneeling position is best employed at ranges of 25 to 50 yards. It is similar to the kneeling position used when firing the rifle. Kneel on your right knee and rest your left upper arm on your raised left knee with your elbow projecting beyond your knee. The butt of the weapon, grasped in your right hand, is then seated in the palm of your hand and the two-hand grip assumed, as illustrated in Figure 3, which shows this position with a revolver.

## Crouch-standing Position

In the crouch-standing position, your body is in a forward crouch with your knees flexed and your trunk bent forward from the hips as shown in Figure 4. Your feet are placed naturally in a position

that will allow you to take another step toward the target. Keep
your body in a comfortably balanced position at all times in order
to move easily in any direction. This position is used when engaging targets at ranges of about 15 yards, particularly surprise targets.

Fig. 4. The crouch-standing position with a revolver.

## Combat-ready Position

In the combat-ready position, grasp the gun in your right hand
in the usual manner. Flex your gun arm with the forearm in a horizontal position, and hold the upper arm close to your body with your
elbow resting comfortably against your hipbone.

## Co-ordinating Movements

In combat firing you must co-ordinate your eyes, ears, brain, and
muscles. As soon as you see a target or even suspect its presence in

the vicinity, assume the best position indicated by the situation, and aim and fire or prepare to fire. You must shoot quickly and instinctively without deliberately using your sights, except that at ranges of 25 to 50 yards you should use your sights if time permits.

## Firing in the Prone and Kneeling Positions

When you are in the ready position previously described in this chapter and a target appears at ranges greater than 25 yards, assume the prone or kneeling position in the same manner as you would if armed with a rifle. At ranges of 50 yards or more, you can fire accurately by using the prone position and the two-hand grip to facilitate regular sighting and aiming. At ranges of 25 to 50 yards, the kneeling position may give you the additional support required to fire rapidly and accurately.

## Firing in the Crouch-standing Position

You should give the greatest amount of practice to the crouch-standing position because it is the one you will use most often in combat. When standing or walking with the gun held in the ready position, take an additional step toward a target appearing at a range of less than 25 yards. At the same time, thrust your gun toward the target as if you were pointing your finger at it. Your first shot may be fired as you extend the gun. The second shot is fired with your arm fully extended and the wrist and elbow locked, with the only pivot point being your shoulder. Although you fire almost instinctively, without careful aiming, if you practice carefully for a reasonable period of time, you will develop a surprisingly high degree of accuracy in this method of engaging targets at short ranges.

In order to practice firing in the crouch-standing position, thrust your revolver at various targets at short ranges. Keep your eyes on the target only. Do not align the sights. Then, holding the revolver in the same position without the slightest change, drop your eyes and determine how closely the sights are aligned with the target. Then squeeze the trigger with a steadily increasing pressure and see if your trigger squeeze moves the revolver out of alignment.

## Sitting Position

The F.B.I. in their practice pistol course have a sitting position that is especially helpful in firing heavy revolvers such as the .357 Magnum. The feet are together, the lower legs form an angle of about 90 degrees with the upper leg. Both arms are straight without stiffness and are braced between the knees, which are held quite close together. In this position, you can align the sights with the target.

## Hip Shooting

In hip shooting, you should draw and fire your revolver from about the level of your belt, not necessarily from your hip. Keep the forearm of your gun arm parallel with the ground or floor. If you hold it at about belt level, you will hit your enemy at about the same elevation, preferably in the belly.

Hold your revolver in the same alignment with relation to your body each time you fire. Some experts recommend holding your revolver directly under and in front of your nose, which means moving your gun from over the holster to the center of your body. Your left foot is forward and your body crouched. Your knees are bent slightly, and your weight is evenly distributed on both feet. Keep your elbow in alignment with the revolver so that the recoil will not push the gun backward and send the shots low and to the left. If you are using a one-hand grip, it will keep your shoulders square with the target if you hold the left hand in the same relative position as the right hand, assuming that you are firing with the right hand. This also puts the left hand in a position to catch the revolver if you are shot in the right hand during combat.

## Combat Courses

Various combat courses which embody the positions previously described are used by law-enforcement officers. The targets may be silhouette targets rotated like the bobbing targets of a military course, they may be moving targets that run on wires toward and away from the shooters, or the targets may be arranged in a "Hogan's

Alley" or "house of horrors" system whereby dummies representing enemies spring up, shots are fired, and there is a background of disturbing noise played on a phonograph. In addition, some departments have their men shoot at moving pictures displayed on revolving paper screens, so that they can be examined and scored.

All such combat courses are of value but they should be preceeded by thorough training in the basic principles of marksmanship. It is a waste of time and money to permit a man to fire a combat course without adequate preparatory instruction. Worst of all, it may form bad habits that will prevent him from ever becoming an accurate shot.

## The F.B.I. Practical Pistol Course

Members of the F.B.I. are given detailed instruction in the mechanical operation of firearms, including nomenclature, assembly and disassembly, functioning, etc., in order that each officer may have respect for his gun and its danger, thus avoiding accidents to himself and others.

Before an agent of the F.B.I. is permitted to shoot on the range he is given a thorough preparatory course in safety precautions, gripping the gun, the correct firing positions, sight alignment, aiming, trigger squeeze, breathing, and dry firing.

The practical pistol course consists of 50 shots, and is intended to cover as many combat situations as possible under which an agent may have to shoot. For this course, the regular Colt Official Police revolver, caliber .38 Special, is fired at the Colt silhouette target.

The first 10 shots are fired at a distance of 7 yards, from hip level. At the first command given by the range officer, the revolver is loaded with 5 cartridges and placed in the holster. At the second command, the revolvers are drawn and fired from hip level without aiming. When 5 shots have been fired, the fired cartridge cases are removed, and five live cartridges are loaded and fired at the target. Twenty-five seconds are allowed for these 10 shots, including loading and unloading.

Five shots are fired from a prone position at a range of 60 yards. The shooter then moves to the 50-yard line, where he fires 5 shots sitting, 5 shots prone, 5 shots from behind a barricade with his left hand, and 5 shots from behind a barricade with his right hand.

The shooter then moves rapidly to the 25-yard line, where he fires 5 shots sitting, 5 with his right hand behind a barricade, and 5 with his left hand behind a barricade. The score is obtained by adding the K values on the target and multiplying by .4. The whole course, from start to finish, is accomplished in 6 minutes and 10 seconds of firing time.

## The F.B.I. Hip-shooting Course

The F.B.I. agents also fire 50 shots in a course of hip shooting based upon the first 10 shots of the practical pistol course, firing on command at a silhouette target, with a value of 2 for each shot in the black.

The hip-shooting course starts with 12 shots fired singly, followed by 12 shots fired in succession, 6 shots in groups of 3, 6 shots singly, 4 shots in groups of 2, and finally 10 shots in groups of 5.

## The F.B.I. Care and Safety Rules

During training, safety is emphasized. An agent must determine whether or not a revolver is loaded every time he picks it up or puts it down. He must load only on the range at the firing line with the muzzle either raised to an angle of 45 degrees or pointed toward the targets. He must keep his revolver in his holster unless he is on the firing line, and then he may draw and load only on the command of the range officer.

While on the firing line, the shooter may speak to his own coach or to the range officer, but he is not permitted to talk to the other shooters. If he must go to the targets for any reason, he can do so only when he receives permission from the range officer, who first has all shooters unload and either put down their revolvers or return them to their holsters.

After firing, each weapon is cleaned and oiled. The tension on the firing mechanism, recoil springs, and hammer is released before any gun is put in a locker or vault. Dust, rust, and corrosion are removed from the barrel and the exterior surfaces.

## Other F.B.I. Weapons

Field officers of the F.B.I. keep on hand .357 Magnum revolvers for emergency use where the maximum fire power is required. Since this revolver has an effective range of 200 yards and a maximum range of 2,700 yards, it is regarded as too dangerous for ordinary use. For example, in one case a shot from a .357 Magnum fired at a fleeing automobile penetrated the trunk compartment, back seat, front seat, driver, and steering wheel, killing the driver and wrecking the car.

A caliber .30 autoloading rifle with an effective range of about 300 yards and a muzzle velocity, with an appropriate load, of 2,250 feet per second is used in open country. A 12-guage, cylinder-bore, repeating shotgun is available. Another F.B.I. weapon is the Thompson sub-machine gun equipped with a box-type clip. It has an effective range of 100 yards and will shoot at the rate of 600 shots per minute when on full automatic fire.

# Chapter 19

## CARE AND CLEANING

### Removing Rust Spots

If a rust spot appears in the bore, use a brass-bristle brush on the end of a cleaning rod, stroke it back and forth through the full length of the bore several times, and then run several cloth patches dipped in a light oil through the bore.

### Removing Lead

When little lumps of lead appear in the bore, use a brass-bristle brush in the manner explained for removing rust spots, except that it should be dipped in kerosene before running it through the bore.

If the bore is moderately rusted or leaded, remove all oil and grease from the bore and then pour mercury into the bore and wait until it forms an amalgam with the lead, after which the amalgam can be poured out. Some shooters prefer to use "blue ointment," a mercury preparation obtainable at any drugstore, to loosen the fouling, but the former method is more effective.

If the previous methods fail, especially if the bore of a revolver is badly rusted or leaded, take the revolver to a gunsmith and have him put on a new barrel. This is necessary if the outlines of the rifling do not appear distinct when viewed with a strong light. It is dangerous to fire any gun if the barrel is in this condition because a bullet may become stuck in the bore, causing the gun to rupture. The best cure is prevention. A barrel that is properly used and cleaned will not rust or lead. If the barrel of a semiautomatic pistol is to be replaced, you can do this job yourself.

## Cleaning Patches

Cleaning patches can be bought from any sporting-goods dealer or made at home. They should be of medium weight Canton flannel, previously moistened throughly with water and wrung out several times to make it more absorbent. The flannel is then cut into squares. The correct size for a .22-caliber gun is from three-fourths to one and one-half inches square. Other patches are cut in sizes appropriate to the caliber.

## Do Not Use Antirust Ropes

An antirust rope is a rope saturated in oil. In theory, the oil or grease excludes air and moisture, thus reducing rusting. In practice, the owner trusts the antirust rope, fails to inspect the bore, and finds that he has a badly rusted barrel when it comes time to fire. Do not use this device under any condition.

## Storage Cases and Covers

An airtight wooden cabinet is a good storage medium for the average gun owner, but a steel cabinet provides protection against fire and theft to some extent and is best if it can be made airtight. Do not store firearms in canvas, leather, sheepskin, or wooden gun cases, covers, holsters, or scabbards because they absorb moisture and cause rusting. Avoid all muzzle covers, gun covers, rack covers, and plugs. These are merely catch-penny devices promoted for the profit of the sellers to the detriment of the gun owners. Finally, store your guns in a horizontal position if you must, but it is better to store them with the muzzle down so that any moisture can drain out.

## Corrosion and Erosion

Two words that are often confused by beginners are *corrosion,* which is the eating away of the bore from rusting or the action of salts deposited from the primer or powder, and *erosion,* which is the wearing away of the bore from the friction of bullets passing through or from powder gasses.

## Powder Solvents

Powder solvents are obsolete. They were developed during the period when the gun experts believed that "after corrosion" was due to the fact that chemical products from the burning powder were driven into the pores of the steel barrel and that powder residue after the barrel had been swabbed out was the primary cause of corrosion. The only real value possessed by powder solvents lies in the limited amount of emulsified oil that they contain. However, many of the older shooters will argue in favor of powder solvents. Listen politely, do not argue with them, and avoid wasting money on powder solvents.

## Metal-fouling Solvents

Metal-fouling solvents are almost obsolete. They were developed during the period of cupronickel-jacketed bullets for the purpose of dissolving the lumpy metal fouling from bullets of that type. With modern gilding-metal jackets, the old metal-fouling solvents are scarcely ever required. If you use a metal-fouling solution after firing bullets with gilding-metal jackets, you can get color for quite a long time on your cleaning patches, but you are more likely to cause corrosion than you are to obtain any benefit from the removal of the thin even plating of gilding metal that has been deposited in the bore.

## General Rules for the Care of Hand Guns

(1) After firing, never leave a gun uncleaned overnight. The damage done may be irreparable.

(2) Keep the gun clean and lightly lubricated, but do not let it become gummy with oil.

(3) Do not place the gun on the ground, where sand or dirt may enter the bore or mechanism.

(4) Do not plug the muzzle with a patch or plug. You may forget to remove it before firing, in which case the discharge may bulge or burst the barrel at the muzzle.

(5) Do not keep a hand gun in a leather holster indefinitely because the gun may rust due to moisture absorbed by the leather from the atmosphere, even though the holster may appear to be

perfectly dry. If the holster is wet and the gun must be carried in it, cover the gun with a thick coat of oil.

(6) Do not snap the hammer when the gun is partially disassembled.

(7) The semiautomatic pistol should be squeezed with the forefinger. If the trigger is squeezed with the second finger, the forefinger extending along the side of the receiver is apt to press against the projecting pin of the slide stop and cause a malfunction when the slide recoils.

(8) In firing the semiautomatic pistol, pressure on the trigger must be released enough after each shot to permit the trigger to re-engage the sear. In firing a revolver, pressure on the trigger must be released enough after each shot to permit the trigger to re-engage the hammer strut in single-action firing and to permit the trigger to engage the hammer strut in double-action firing.

(9) In using the semiautomatic pistol, to remove cartridges not fired, disengage the magazine slightly and then extract the cartridge in the barrel by drawing back the slide.

(10) Care should be taken to see that the magazine of a semiautomatic pistol is not dented or otherwise damaged. Care must be exercised in inserting the magazine to insure its engaging with the magazine catch. Never insert the magazine and strike it smartly with the hand to force it home, as this may spring the base or the inturning lips at the top. The magazine should be inserted by a quick continuous movement.

(11) The slide plate of the revolver should not be removed except by a gunsmith or someone who is familiar with revolver disassembly. Do not try to remove the side plate by prying it out of place.

(12) The crane and cylinder of the Colt Model 1917 revolver and the crane and cylinder of similarly constructed revolvers should not be removed except by someone familiar with revolver diassembly.

(13) Never attempt to open the cylinder of a revolver when the hammer is cocked or partly cocked.

(14) Never attempt to cock the hammer of a revolver until the cylinder is fully closed and locked in the frame.

## Clean from the Breech When Possible

Solid-frame revolvers must be cleaned from the muzzle. Hinge-frame (tipup, etc.) revolvers, semiautomatic pistols from which the slide can be removed, and certain solid-frame pistols such as "free pistols," are cleaned from the breech. The general rule is to clean from the breech whenever possible, even though the slide of a semi-automatic pistol should be removed. In some cases the stocks over-lap the takedown mechanism of a semiautomatic and must be taken off before the slide is removed.

In cleaning from the muzzle, guide the cleaning rod with the finger and thumb of the left hand to avoid friction between the rod and the rifling. Also, hold the rod close to the muzzle, not back at the handle.

## Cleaning Equipment

The metal of which the cleaning rod should be made is a subject of debate among experienced shooters. Most men seem to prefer a steel rod, although brass, aluminum, and wooden rods have their champions. For wooden rods, hickory is preferred, although a few experts like birch or maple.

The tip of the cleaning rod should be shaped like a button. A tip with jagged projections, called the jag-type tip, is difficult to start into the chamber from the breech or into the muzzle from the front. A ball-bearing handle for the cleaning rod permits the rod to turn in the handle and follow the rifling as the patch is pushed through the bore.

## Cleaning Procedure

Push the cleaning rod with a brush or patch on it all the way through the bore. If you are using the modern non-corrosive cartridges, as you should, they will not leave a corrosive primer deposit in the bore. Instead, they leave a protective film, which guards against rusting, hence it is not necessary to clean the gun if it is to be fired on the next day. However, if you intend to put your gun away for any length of time, if you have changed the type of ammunition you are using, or if the gun has been through a sand storm or some other unusual weather condition, proceed as follows:

(1) Dip a flannel patch in water or light oil, center it with the tip of the cleaning rod over the breech (or the muzzle if necessary), push it straight through the bore and out the other end.

(2) Run two or three more cleaning patches through the bore, working each back and forth with the rod to swab the bore from one end to the other. Dip these patches in water or light oil as before.

(3) Wipe the cleaning rod with a clean dry patch and then swab again with five or six clean dry patches until the bore is thoroughly dried and cleaned.

(4) Dip a patch in gun oil and swab the bore with it. This will protect the bore for several days, but if you intend to store the gun for any length of time, wipe out the oil, swab the bore with a patch heavily coated with gun grease, wipe all moving parts with a dry rag, and then with an oily rag, and put the gun away.

(5) When you are ready to fire again, push a clean dry patch through the bore to remove oil and grease. If you dip a second patch in gasoline, it will help you to remove the grease, but follow this with more clean dry patches. If you leave oil in a gun, it will fire wildly at first and then settle down after the oil is gone. If you leave grease in a gun, it can cause the gun to rupture under certain conditions.

(6) Do not use too much oil on a gun because it will pick up sand and dust, which has the same effect as rubbing the action with emery paper if it reaches the moving parts. For the same reason, do not load a cartridge into a gun if it has been dropped on the ground before wiping it clean and dry.

(7) A thin coat of oil is the best rust preventive for all exposed metal parts, but do not do a halfway job of cleaning or oiling the bore if you intend to fire on the following day. Either leave the bore alone, or do a complete cleaning job as described above. The reason is that any attempted cleaning will remove the protective film left by the firing of modern noncorrosive ammunition.

(8) Unusual weather conditions justify a complete cleaning because they may cause the gun to sweat, thus inducing rusting.

# Chapter 20

## ACCESSORIES

### Sight-blackening Equipment

Successful shooters learn by experience that they can make better scores if they arrive at the range in plenty of time to get ready for firing and bring with them the proper equipment. If the range officers issue squadding tickets or other written assignments, get yours as soon as they are made out and find your firing point.

Examine your sight adjustment, and then blacken your sights. The sights are not the only parts to blacken. The barrel of your revolver or the slide of your automatic pistol must be black, and the rear end of your gun too. There must be no surface that will reflect light into your eyes.

The best all-around device for blackening sights is a carbide lamp. The usual lamp is of solid brass, polished and lacquered. It has a 2¾-inch chromium reflector and a flat hook that fits over the belt so that it can be used for camping as well as range firing. It has a sturdy burner assembly and is absolutely safe to use. As explained before, you should hold the portion of the gun to be blackened for a few seconds in the point of a small flame that is of such nature that a uniform coating of lampblack will be deposited on the metal.

If you forget your carbide lamp, use a candle, a small pine stick, shoe paste, a kerosene lamp, or a piece of camphor.

### Clothing

No special clothing is required for pistol shooting. It should be comfortable and inexpensive so that you will not worry about soiling or tearing it and can keep your mind on your shooting.

Your hat or cap should shade your eyes from the glare of the sun. Most shooters prefer a cap with a large visor. There is not much point in blackening your sights carefully and then wearing headgear that fails to shade your eyes.

Your shoes should be strong and comfortable. Avoid the extremes of low-cut oxfords and high boots. The type of shoe issued to the enlisted men of the Army and Marine Corps is the best all-around shoe for marksmanship, hiking, camping, or hunting.

## Shooting Glasses

Always wear carefully selected shooting glasses in all forms of shooting, whether it is pistol, rifle, skeet or trap shooting, or hunting. Glasses protect your eyes from the glare of the sun, dust, dirt, ricochet bullets, broken primers, powder gas, flying fragments from burst barrels and splinters from target frames.

Ordinary sun glasses, such as those usually sold in dime and drugstores, are not suitable. Buy glasses made by reputable manufacturers of optical equipment, such as The American Optical Company, Southbridge, Massachusetts; Bausch and Lomb Optical Company, Rochester, New York; and Belz Opticians, New York City.

Your shooting glasses should be of the type worn by military and naval aviators, similar to those shown in the accompanying illustration, made of optical glass, ground and polished, and of the same quality standards as regular spectacle lenses. Objects seen through the glasses should have the same comparative color relationship as when viewed with the naked eye. The lenses should have an extra wide angle, and the nose piece should be designed to give you a large amount of glass toward your nose. These features are desirable even if you have normal vision and do not wear spectacles. If you do wear spectacles to correct your vision, shooting glasses that do not have an extra wide angle and a nose piece giving you a large amount of glass toward your nose may cause you to look through the extreme outer edges of the lenses under some conditions. This causes marginal distortion and prismatic displacement, throwing off the accuracy of the glasses.

The frame should be equipped with a plastic perspiration bar

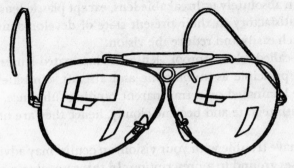

Fig. 1. The construction features of well-designed shooting glasses.

that rests on your forehead and keeps the lenses from steaming and getting soiled from the eyebrows and eyelashes. The bar holds the lenses sufficiently far away from the face to allow a circulation of air, thus preventing moisture from condensing on the lenses.

In general, your shooting glasses should have large lenses and light tints. The best all-around shade for a shooting lens is one that has a yellow-green formula. The yellow gives sharpness and definition in vision and accentuates the black and white. The green gives you the necessary protection against glare without reducing vision.

Many shooters wear glasses in conventional sun-glass tints of medium- and dark-green shades, which are much too dark for shooting and often handicap you more than help because they lack intensifying properties. If you want the maximum amount of intensification and if you are not unusually sensitive to the glare of the sun, wear a canary yellow lens that provides the highest amount of brilliance. In hunting, this lens acts as a filter and helps you to pick up game much more quickly when it blends in with the foliage.

The most satisfactory shooting glasses are annealed to give the lenses the additional strength required to stand up under blow-backs, ricochets, etc., but where the shooter desires the utmost in eye protection, case-hardened lenses are recommended. These are much harder than ordinary lenses and can be used with safety under hazardous conditions.

The case-hardening of lenses is a special tempering process that makes the lenses almost unbreakable. Actually, there is no such thing as an absolutely unbreakable lens, except plastic lenses, which are not satisfactory in their present state of development because they scratch easily and reduce the vision.

The so-called "shatterproof" lenses are laminated lenses made on the same principle as automobile and aircraft windshields. Two lenses are laminated on a transparent binding substance, but they tend to disintegrate and become cloudy, hence they are not recommended.

If you have trouble with your vision, an oculist may advise you to wear glasses ground to a prescription. In this case, obtain the necessary optical correction to your shooting glasses as well as your reading glasses. Always explain fully your working and recreational habits to an oculist so that he may take these factors into consideration in prescribing lenses. For example, you may find that the front sight of your pistol is hazy. The oculist can then equip your shooting glasses with a small segment of sufficient focal power so that the sight will appear clear and sharp, although there may be a slight haze on the target. It is impossible to grind a lens that will be equally sharp on both the sights and the target. It is more important to see the sights clearly than the bull's-eye.

If your left eye is your master eye, in firing with the right arm and hand and trying to aim with the right eye, you should partially close your left eye. If you try to keep both eyes fully open, the left eye will take the leadership in sighting and will cause you to cross-fire. This can be met by equipping your shooting glasses with a small opaque segment over the left lens. When you aim with your right arm, hand, and eye, the left eye automatically falls behind the opaque segment; you can keep both eyes fully open, and cross-firing is eliminated.

Do not make the mistake of thinking that the master eye is always the eye with the clearest, sharpest vision. Your master eye may be more deficient in vision than your other eye, and yet it is the dominant, controlling, supervising eye in lining up objects, whether or not you wear prescription glasses. Remember, in order to aim a firearm with both eyes open, or with one eye open and the other partially closed, the sights and bull's-eye are always brought into alignment with one eye only, and this is the master, dominant eye.

These special problems of shooting should be known to your oculist, hence it is an advantage to consult one who understands marksmanship if you want prescription lenses for shooting. If he is not a shooter himself, show him this book, and be sure he understands your own master-eye condition before he grinds your lenses.

We have discussed this subject in great detail because you have only one pair of eyes. Treat them with care, and you can continue to enjoy shooting until you are an old, old man.

## Optical Attachments or Orthoptic Devices

An optical attachment, sometimes called an orthoptic device and occasionally referred to as a peephole disk, is a small black disk having a tiny hole through which you look with your master eye to cut out objectionable side lights when your sights are blurred or fuzzy. The disk may be attached to one lens of your shooting glasses with either a small metal clamp or a rubber suction cup, according to its design. One type has an adjustable shutter to vary the size of the hole. Some shooters claim that this device improves their shooting, especially as they grow older, but most of the older experts do not use it.

## Pistol Cases or Shooting Kits

When your relay is called to the firing line, take your pistol case or shooting kit with you because you may need it unexpectedly. Pistol cases vary in design and construction. A good one affords protection against damage to one or more hand guns and provides regular spaces or compartments for stowing cleaning equipment, cartridges, and replacement parts. Some cases have an adjustable device for holding a spotting scope in position so that you can place your case on a post or stand and use the scope without removing it from the case.

The National Rifle Association permits the use of a shooting kit or pistol case at the firing point if it is of such size and construction that it does not interfere with adjacent shooters.

## Camp Stool

Take a camp stool wth you to the firing line. Sit down between the shots in slow fire and between the stages of rapid, sustained, and timed fire. When you sit down, relax completely, forget shooting momentarily, and you will resume firing with a physical and mental improvement that will usually mean at least a slight increase in your score.

## Chamois Skin

If you are nervous or if you are shooting on a hot day, take either a towel or a chamois skin with you to the firing line to dry your hands between shots in slow fire or between the stages of the faster rates of fire. If you use a chamois skin, soak it in water several hours in advance and then wring it out just before going to the range. Experienced shooters find that it absorbs moisture better than a towel.

## Resin

If you perspire during sustained, rapid, or timed fire, rub your hands with powdered resin to eliminate moisture. When not in use, keep it in a can or bottle having a tight cover so that it will not spill in your pistol case and get into the gun.

## Ear Stoppers

Some kind of ear stoppers are required by most shooters. Everyone agrees that they are a necessity during the din of rapid, sustained, and timed fire, but few appreciate the importance of using them during slow fire. During slow fire the longer intervals of time between shots makes the noise from adjacent guns more noticeable than it is during the high degree of concentration you must assume during the faster rates of fire. We recommend that you use little plugs of absorbent cotton, but if you prefer the improved appearance of commercial stoppers, use those made of pure soft rubber of the type adopted by the armed services. The use of commercial stoppers made of metal or empty cartridge cases is not recommended because of the risk of ear irritation and infection.

## Gloves

The National Rifle Association rules provide that gloves may be worn in pistol and revolver matches if they do not form an artifical support. Naturally, gloves are often needed in cold weather, but most shooters find that they interfere with ease and efficient shooting.

## Spotting Scopes

The National Rifle Association permits the use of a telescope to spot shots in all events, but no part of the telescope or telescope stand may touch any part of the shooter's clothing or person.

Before making specific recommendations, a few introductory remarks regarding the use of spotting scopes are necessary. Some shooters claim that it makes them nervous to look at their shot groups on the target through a spotting scope because it emphasizes their mistakes. Others spot only the first few shots. However, those who climb to the heights in hand-gun shooting learn by experience that failure to spot all of the slow-fire shots is foolish because this is the only way that you can be certain that you will not have a misplaced group caused by changes of your grip, standing position, the light, or some other unforeseeable condition. Your shot group may remain the same size throughout, but if it moves right or left or up or down, you may end with a very poor total score.

If you imagine that the use of a spotting scope makes you nervous in official competition, the remedy is to spot all of your shots in practice shooting until it becomes a fixed habit with you.

Another complaint about spotting scopes is that they may cause eyestrain if they are not properly constructed or adjusted. The remedy for this trouble is to avoid buying any scope until you can obtain one that is produced by a reputable American manufacturer especially for shooting purposes. Having obtained a good scope, spend some time in learning how to adjust it so that it will not cause eyestrain.

Unless you leave the spotting scope in the holding device of your pistol case, you will need a special stand. Regardless of the method adopted for holding the scope, it must stay firmly in position and yet allow adjustments to be made with one hand.

## Binoculars and Field Glasses

A binocular may be defined as a telescope adapted for the use of both eyes at once, that is, it really consists of two telescopes mounted side by side. This is the usual broad, common definition found in dictionaries, but technically it is not a binocular according to modern terminology unless it is made with prisms. A field glass is usually defined as a compact binocular telescope, but in modern usage it must be made without prisms. Of the two types, the binocular made with prisms is better, but most experts agree that both binoculars and field glasses are inferior to a good spotting scope for hand-gun shooting.

The objection to binoculars and field glasses is that if they are held steady enough for spotting shots on a target, the power must be so low that small bullet holes are difficult to find.

If you insist on using a field glass or a binocular, obtain one of American manufacture. If it is not bought new, have the glass examined by an expert and adjusted if necessary.

## Cartridge Block or Box

A cartridge block is merely a wooden block drilled to receive cartridges so that they will be instantly available in the correct number when you need them. A cartridge box is a cartridge block with a hinged cover drilled so that when it is closed the cartridges fit into both the block and the cover. In using either a block or a box during match firing, place the cartridges in the container in groups so that you will have the exact number you need for each stage of firing.

## Pistol Gunsmith Kit

A pistol gunsmith kit should contain tools and equipment for the repair and adjustment of hand guns in the field or at home. It is not essential for beginners but is recommended for experienced shooters who want to be independent. The items to be carried will vary according to the weapons to be repaired and the conditions under which you work. The kit itself may be either a canvas roll having pockets or a hardwood box, but it need not be either elaborate or large.

Although shooters normally carry cleaning equipment in their regular pistol cases, the gunsmith kit should contain cleaning rods, patches, oil, grease, etc. There should be a carbide lamp for blackening sights. Parts that may be broken, such as springs, firing pins, etc., should be part of the supplies.

Among the more strictly gunsmithing items to be carried are oil stones, tweezers, a hammer, screwdrivers, files, calipers, punches, a wood rasp, steel wool, emery cloth, a hand vise, a magnet, a jeweler's loupe, and rust-removing substances. A more complete discussion of this subject is found in the author's *Gun Care and Repair, a Manual of Gunsmithing.*

## Miscellaneous Supplies and Equipment

Ammunition, belts, holsters, targets, shot-hole scoring gauges, and other miscellaneous equipment and supplies are discussed in other chapters of this text.

# Chapter 21

# HUNTING WITH HAND GUNS

## *Advantages of Hand Guns Over Rifles*

There are three important reasons why pistols and revolvers are superior to rifles for hunting under certain conditions. First, they are much lighter in weight and hence less tiresome to carry long distances or over rugged country. Second, the hands are left free to carry other equipment. Third, the hand gun is in your holster at your side, ready for immediate use, and not left back in camp or leaning against a tree.

## *Advantages of Hand Guns Over Shotguns*

There are three reasons why hand guns are superior to shotguns for hunting deer in states where shotguns are permitted for the purpose. First, hand guns are more accurate than shotguns. The buckshot fired from a shotgun may be regarded as small slugs roughly equivalent to .22 caliber Long Rifle bullets, except that they are much less accurate at all hunting ranges, hence less effective. Second, hand guns are more humane. The buckshot thrown into a large circle at a distance of 40 yards or more will kill some deer but leave many wounded animals to die in agony. Third, hand guns are obviously lighter in weight and easier to carry.

Aside from the fact that hand guns are mechanically more accurate, there is a tendency for shotgun shooters merely to point in the general direction of the game, whereas hand-gun shooters instinctively make each shot an aimed shot, fired only after a quick but careful determination of distance, wind, and light.

## Methods of Range Estimation

The accurate estimation of the distance to the target is an important factor in all hand-gun hunting at all ranges and with all weapons. There are two methods of range estimation used in hunting—observation of fire and eye estimation. In warfare, the range is also determined by firing tracer bullets, which have burning composition in them to show the path of flight.

## Observation of Fire

Observation of fire is a method of range estimation sometimes used when the ground is dry and the strike of the bullets can be seen. The dust will appear slightly above the striking point of the bullet. As viewed by the shooter, the dust appears on the side toward which the wind is blowing. If the wind is blowing from right to left, dust will appear to the left of the point where the bullet hits. Having observed where your bullet hits, you can change your sight adjustment if you have time or change your aiming point.

## Eye Estimation

Eye estimation is the method of range estimation most generally used in hunting. This method requires training and experience. If you lack experience, your estimates will average about 15 per cent over or under the true range and may be even wilder. The way to gain experience is to practice eye estimation in advance of your hunting trip. You can train yourself if you follow the few simple suggestions given here.

Let us imagine that you decide to shoot squirrels or rabbits with your revolver. Get permission from the farmer who owns the land where you want to shoot in advance of the hunting season. Select good places of concealment, and measure the distance to various points where squirrels or rabbits are likely to enter or leave the corn field or other area under observation.

You can measure the various distances by pacing if you know the length of your step and count the paces to each important point. Do not guess. Measure a distance of 100 yards on flat ground, and see how many steps you take. Repeat your counting of paces and divide the total number into 3,600 inches to get your average pace. If you are not accurate, your estimates of ranges will be from 10 to 20 per cent wrong, over or under.

Having obtained a reasonably accurate measurement of distance to each of the critical points you can see from your observation post, learn to apply a short unit of distance so that you can estimate the range when the game is part way between you and one of the known-distance points. Ten yards is a good unit of distance for the .22 caliber revolver or semiautomatic pistol. Notice what the ground looks like 25, 50, 75, and 100 yards from your observation post.

Remember that the ground looks different at different seasons of the year. Try to come back to your chosen hunting ground a few days before the hunting season opens to check you eye estimation under the new conditions. On this visit you need not spend so much time and effort.

If you have a shooting partner, practice estimating ranges with him while you are going over different kinds of ground. Average your estimates, and you will increase your accuracy if you are both trained in the methods suggested here. The average of several estimates is always more accurate than one.

Another method of eye estimation of distance is to compare the apparent height of some object with the height of the front sight of your hand gun. Rail fences, standing cornstalks, or even the height of the game animal itself in relation to the height of the front sight can, with practice, be useful in estimating the distance to the target.

## Appearance of Objects

It may be very difficult to apply a unit of measurement in eye estimation because the ground between you and the target is hidden from sight. Under these conditions you can estimate range by the appearance of objects.

*Objects seem closer:* (1) when the object is in a bright light, (2) when the color of the object contrasts sharply with the color of the background, (3) when you are looking over water, snow, a wheat field, or any reasonably uniform surface, (4) when you are looking down from a height, (5) in the clear atmosphere of high altitudes, and (6) when you are looking over a depression most of which is hidden.

*Objects seem more distant:* (1) when you are looking over a depression most of which is visible, (2) when there is a fog or a poor light, (3) when only a small part of the object can be seen, and (4) when you are looking from low ground toward higher ground.

## Appearance of Game Animals

You can apply the various methods of range estimation more successfully if you have a good knowledge of the size, shape, and color of the animals you are hunting. These vary from one area to another and according to the season of the year.

One of the important considerations is length. A cotton tail rabbit may be 17 inches long while a jack rabbit in the same region may be 25 inches long. Knowing the average length of the particular kind of rabbit you are hunting, its apparent size at various distances is a good check on your other methods of range estimation.

## .22-Caliber Hand Guns

You can use a .22-caliber hand gun successfully in hunting squirrels, woodchucks at fairly short ranges, rabbits, and racoons in a tree. You can even hunt grouse with a .22, but you must shoot their heads off because they have a small vital area in their body which is hard to hit, causing many of them to escape wounded if you are not a good shot.

It is possible to kill coyotes, foxes, ground squirrels, deer, and even bears at a distance of a very few yards if they are not moving and if you hit them in a vital spot. Trappers frequently use hand guns for this purpose and many hunters have nothing more powerful than a .22-caliber hand gun for killing game wounded by a rifle shot. However, we repeat that the distance should be short, the game should not be moving, and you should be a good shot.

## .32 and .38 Special Hand Guns

The remarks pertaining to the .22-caliber hand guns apply to .32-caliber weapons. However, when a hunter or trapper wants a hand gun larger than a .22, he usually chooses a .38 Special revolver. This gives him an opportunity to use hand-loaded ammunition prepared for short, medium, or long ranges, and with this caliber he can kill woodchucks, coyotes, foxes and even deer at distances up to 100 yards, provided that he hits them while they are standing still, and in vital spots.

Deer are usually killed with a rifle at a range less than 150 yards, and certainly a great number are killed at less than 100 yards. If you want to increase your probability of killing one with a hand gun, stalk the deer or hide in a watering or feeding place and wait for it to come to you. This can be done but it requires more patience and knowledge of woodcraft than most hunters possess.

## The Old .44-40 Cartridge

The .44-40 centerfire cartridge was used in the Winchester Model 1873 Repeating rifle and also in the Colt Single-Action Army revolver known as the Frontier Model when chambered for this cartridge and made with a 7½-inch barrel. Fired in either the Winchester 1873 rifle or the Colt revolver, this cartridge brought down mountain lions, deer, bears, and about every kind of big game found in the United States in the last quarter of the past century. For example, soldiers, Indians, and other hunters killed buffalo while riding horseback beside them. There is ample historical justification for our claim that revolvers can be used successfully in hunting. Figure 1 shows Buffalo Bill and the Grand Duke Alexis of Russia hunting buffalo from horseback with revolvers in 1869.

## The .44 Smith and Wesson Special Cartridge

Wild boars are dangerous. When wounded, they often charge and cut a hunter with their razor-sharp tusks. A few years ago the author was hunting these animals with a friend who was an experienced shooter. We separated and he shot a boar at a range of about 100 yards with his rifle. Before he could fire again, the boar

Fig. 1. Buffalo Bill and the Grand Duke Alexis of Russia
hunting buffalo from horseback with revolvers in 1869.

charged and slashed his leg. He drew a Smith and Wesson .38/44
Outdoorsman revolver, aimed at the boar's ear, and killed him. The
cartridge was a .38 Smith and Wesson Special.

Although this is an example of the use of a revolver as an auxiliary weapon in hunting, it also shows what can be done at a short
range with a hand gun. Moose and elk charge a hunter frequently,
and a buck deer will charge often enough to make it a good practice
to carry a hand gun at your side.

## .45-Caliber Revolvers and Semiautomatic Pistols

The Colt automatic pistols, caliber .45, Models 1911 and 1911-
A-1, and the two caliber .45 Model 1917 revolvers made by Colt and
by Smith and Wesson are heavy but powerful sidearms to carry
as auxiliary weapons while hunting. When properly aimed they
are excellent hunting arms in themselves. They have been used
by the author to kill deer at ranges up to 50 yards.

## The Smith and Wesson .357 Magnum Revolver

The Smith and Wesson .357 Magnum revolver has a far greater
shocking power than any .38-, .44-, or .45-caliber hand gun ever

tested by competent shooters. Although we have explained the possibilities of hunting with less powerful hand guns, we strongly urge you to select this revolver if you want to hunt big game without a rifle or if you want an auxiliary weapon when you fail to kill game with your rifle.

Before the advent of the .357 Magnum, police squad cars sent out in large cities in answer to riot and burglary calls were equipped with one or more rifles. The .357 Magnum was developed to replace the long awkward rifle, but to do this it had to fire a 158-grain bullet, have a muzzle velocity of 1,450 feet per second, and a muzzle energy of 738 foot pounds. Actually, these characteristics are obtained in some loads, and with other cartridges using the same 158-grain bullet the muzzle velocity is 1,515 feet per second and the muzzle energy is 812 foot pounds.

The importance of this development may be seen by comparing the .357 Magnum with previous commercial hand-gun cartridges, which had a muzzle velocity of less than 1,300 feet per second, a muzzle energy of only 465 foot pounds, and a comparatively light bullet. Accuracy was not sacrificed because the new cartridge is in the same precision class with loads like the .38 Smith and Wesson Special Mid Range, which was a very reliable target cartridge. Furthermore, the .357 Magnum cartridge is accurate at ranges up to 600 yards, far beyond any distances attained with good scores with any previous load.

The word *magnum* means a two-quart bottle for wine or spirits, thus suggesting that the cartridge is of unusual size. Actually, the .357 Magnum cartridge has a bullet diameter the same as the .38 Smith and Wesson Special cartridge, hence the Magnum revolver can fire .38 Smith and Wesson Special Hi-Speed, .38 Smith and Wesson Special, .38 Smith and Wesson Special Super Police, .38 Smith and Wesson Mid Range, and .38 Colt Special cartridges.

In testing the .357 Magnum revolver and cartridge for police and sheriff purposes, it was found that the bullet would penetrate as many as three thicknesses of so-called "bulletproof" vests when these garments were swung freely on a rod. Figure 2 shows the Magnum revolver, a "bulletproof" vest, and a bullet passing through steel plates.

Fig. 2. The Smith and Wesson .357 Magnum revolver can pierce armor plate and "bulletproof" vests.

Before the .357 Magnum was introduced, the most powerful hand-gun cartridges used by police were the .38 Super Auto, and the .38/44 Smith and Wesson Special, illustrated in Figure 3, both of which failed to pass through duralumin plates, but the .357 Magnum bullet went right through such plates and still had some striking power left.

The penetration value of cartridges is usually given in terms of the number of 7/8-inch soft pine boards that will be passed through at a distance of 15 feet. It was found that with the new cartridge, the penetration value was only 11, little or no greater than that of the .38/44 Smith and Wesson Special. The reason was that velocity was great enough to produce true mushrooming of the solid lead bullet, showing that for the first time in commercial hand-gun ballistics history a maximum of efficiency and impact value had been reached.

The next problem was to test the shocking power, sometimes called the killing power, of the revolver and cartridge on flesh. Colonel Douglas B. Wesson, one of the members of the founding family, took a .357 Magnum with him on a hunting trip in Wyoming. He killed a moose at 100 yards and an elk at 135 yards but needed two shots to kill an antelope at a little over 200 yards.

Fig. 3. The .38/44 Smith and Wesson Revolver, brought out in 1930, was a favorite of the police in the pursuit of criminals escaping in automobiles but its bullets would not pierce duralumin plates sometimes used in armoring an automobile.

The publicity department of Smith and Wesson released this information, expecting to receive the congratulations of the hunting world on their successful development of a weapon and cartridge for big-game hunting. Instead, a torrent of criticism swept down on the heads of the owners. Some of the critics doubted the truthfulness of the reports, and others complained that it was not humane to shoot big game with a hand gun.

Colonel Wesson replied that the sporting element in hunting increases as the probability of hitting game decreases. In other words he believed that it required more knowledge of woodcraft, more patience and skill in stalking, and more accurate marksman-

Fig. 4. A hunter killing a bear at close quarters with the .357 Magnum.

ship to hunt with a hand gun than with a rifle. Reflections on the honesty of Wesson's reports were answered by publishing letters from hunters all over the world who had successfully killed big game with one shot from a .357 Magnum. Subsequent experiences related by nationally known sportsmen have confirmed all that was claimed for this powerful revolver.

Fig. 4 shows the .357 Magnum and a hunter shooting a large bear with it at close quarters. Fig. 5 is another drawing of the Magnum,

Fig. 5. A trophy display of animals killed with the .357 Magnum, including moose, leopard, and the great Alaskan Kodiak bear.

this time with a trophy display of animals killed with this revolver, including moose, leopard, and the great Alaskan Kodiak bear.

The author has seen hunters consistently kill deer with one shot at ranges up to 100 yards, but these were men who could make a score of 90 or more on an N.R.A. pistol target at 50 yards, and they placed their bullets in such vital spots as the neck, brain, or chest cavity. The author has killed cougars, sometimes called mountain lions, nearly eight feet long, at a distance of almost 100 yards, with one shot from the .357 Magnum and does not consider this a remarkable feat by any means. Practically any of the North American game, including moose, grizzly and Kodiak bears, and wild boars can be brought down with one shot from a .357 Magnum fired by a trained shooter.

Some idea of the power of the .357 Magnum can be had by comparing it with the older hunting weapons. For example, the Colt Frontier Model revolver with the 44-40 centerfire cartridge had 510 foot pounds of energy at 100 yards, far less than the Magnum's 800 foot pounds at that range, and yet it was used to kill buffaloes on the run. The .44-40 and the .38-55 cartridges were fired in rifles to kill deer successfully, and yet at 100 yards the former cartridge had only 510 foot pounds and the latter had 750 foot pounds of energy, both less than that of the Magnum at the same distance.

## Suggestions for Big-Game Hunting with Hand Guns

In spite of all that we have related regarding the use of hand guns in hunting, we strongly recommend that you attempt to hunt big game only with a .357 Magnum, using the smaller calibers for auxiliary weapons to kill game in an emergency. Even with a Magnum, the requirements are quite stiff. Here they are:

(1) Review such basic marksmanship principles as the correct grip, the proper standing position, aiming methods, trigger squeeze, breathing, calling your shots, and the rapid cocking of the revolver. The most important of these is the trigger squeeze. It must be smooth and fast with no tendency to jerk.

(2) Use only the black undercut Patridge-type post front sight, ⅛ inch wide, and the square-notch rear sight in both target shooting and hunting.

(3) Use a barrel as long as possible consistent with accuracy. The longest available factory-supplied barrel for the Magnum is 8¾ inches but you will probably find that a 6½-inch barrel is better.

(4) Be sure that the stock fits your hand. If necessary, have a good gunsmith fit special grips on the revolver.

(5) Practice on the N.R.A. 50-yard target at first with a six-o'clock hold at 50 yards. If you can average about 90, you should be able to kill deer with one shot at ranges up to 100 yards. When you acquire his skill, erect a round black disk, 6 inches in diameter, at 100 yards. Experiment with the center hold at this range, but determine for yourself the sight setting and hold, as well as the ammunition you need to keep your shots inside this target. If you can place all your bullets there and you practice consistently for about a month before going into the field, your probability of bringing back deer is good.

(6) Before the opening of the season, visit your hunting ground, practice range estimation, and learn all you can about the habits of the game you seek.

# Chapter 22

## COACHING AND FIRING LINE OPERATION

### The Coach-and-Pupil Method

When a group of beginners is being instructed by an expert, the coach-and-pupil method is an efficient form of training. The students are divided into pairs after receiving preliminary explanations of shooting fundamentals. Each man takes his turn as "coach," watches the actions and corrects the mistakes of his partner. He then performs the exercise himself as a "pupil." This allows each man to rest periodically without halting the progress of his training. It is especially helpful because teaching others a subject is one of the best ways of learning it.

In order to receive the greatest benefit from the coach-and-pupil method, each man must understand its purpose and his individual responsibility both as a coach and as a pupil. This method is used throughout all phases of marksmanship training.

The expert instructor is not relieved of responsibility in the coach-and-pupil method. He must keep himself informed of the progress of each individual and be sure that every student understands both the theory and application of each phase of marksmanship training. Furthermore, the instructor must be certain that each man has mastered each principle and its application before being instructed in the next phase.

### Coaching Not Intended for Record Firing

All instructions in coaching given in this chapter, except the coaching rules of the National Rifle Association, are intended for instruction practice and not for firing for record or in organized competitions.

## Correcting Mistakes Before They Become Habits

The instructor must observe and correct all mistakes before they become habits. If he waits until a shooter has repeated a mistake several times, it will require more time and effort to establish correct procedure than if the mistake is corrected early in the shooter's career.

For example, flinching is caused by jerking the trigger. The shooter who jerks the trigger and is not corrected at once continues this error until it becomes a fixed habit, which is often almost impossible to overcome.

## Coaching Slow Fire

During slow-fire practice, the coach stands on the left of the shooter in such a position as to be able to observe the latter's trigger finger, grip, shooting eye, and position. The coach must correct all mistakes as they occur. He fills the magazines for the firer, if a semiautomatic pistol is used, and hands them to him. At the beginning of practice firing, the magazines for semiautomatic pistols may be filled partly with regular ammunition and partly with dummy cartridges, but the shooter must not know how many dummies are in the magazine or the order in which they are loaded. This procedure can be applied to the revolver if the coach loads the revolver without being watched by the student.

Dummy cartridges are used to show the coach whether or not the student is squeezing the trigger correctly and, in the case of an improper trigger squeeze, to bring the mistake forcibly to the attention of the shooter. When a loaded cartridge is fired, the flinch is often hidden by the recoil of the pistol and the shooter does not realize that he flinched. When the hammer falls on a dummy that the shooter thinks is a regular cartridge, the sudden stiffening of the muscles and the thrusting forward of the hand to meet the expected shock that does not come are apparent to the shooter and to everyone near him. Mixing dummies with live rounds forces the shooter to make a special effort to squeeze the trigger correctly for all shots.

Dummy cartridges should be used in all stages of training. Many champions prepare for important matches by having a friend act as coach in loading a hand gun with a mixture of dummies and live cartridges to accomplish the same purpose.

## How the Coach Reviews Fundamentals

Under the supervision of a competent instructor, each coach explains and demonstrates the following to his pupil:

(1) Gripping the hand gun.

(2) The correct amount of force for gripping the hand gun. This is done by gripping the student's hand and saying, "This is too tight a grip" (gripping very tightly), "This is too loose a grip" (gripping very loosely), and "This is the correct amount of pressure" (gripping the student's hand with a firm but comfortable grip that should be used in shooting).

(3) The position of the body, feet, and shooting hand. The student should demonstrate this position to the satisfaction of the coach.

(4) Aiming.

(5) Aiming at the target with an empty gun, without squeezing the trigger, to show how long the shooter can hold the sights on or near the bull's-eye, thereby demonstrating the point at which the bullets will strike if the trigger is squeezed correctly. The coach has the pupil carry out this exercise and explains to him that it proves that any man can aim and hold well enough to obtain a good score.

(6) Squeezing the trigger.

(7) The coach requires the pupil to aim at the target with an empty gun and then press the trigger several times, as explained below under Target Squeeze Coaching, directing the pupil to call the shot each time the hammer falls, even though the gun is empty.

(8) The coach requires the pupil to aim at the target with a loaded gun and then press the trigger, as explained below under

Trigger Squeeze Coaching, ordering him to call the shot each time the gun is fired. Five shots should be fired in this manner.

(9) The coach requires the pupil to fire five shots, but this time the pupil squeezes the trigger himself to see if he can squeeze correctly and make as good a score as he made when the coach squeezed it for him in the two previous exercises.

## Trigger Squeeze Coaching

One of the best methods of showing a student how to squeeze the trigger correctly is to have him hold and aim the gun while the coach squeezes the trigger. This is done as follows:

(1) The coach places his hands in such a manner that he can apply pressure to the trigger finger of the pupil with his own left thumb on the end of the pupil's trigger finger without disturbing the pupil's grip or aim. The coach cautions the pupil that he must not assist or resist the coach's pressure but must concentrate on aiming and holding the gun.

(2) The coach must apply a slow, steady pressure to the trigger finger of the pupil and avoid interfering with the aim. From five to ten seconds is usually enough time for the coach to apply sufficient pressure on the pupil's trigger finger to fire the gun.

(3) While squeezing the pupil's trigger finger, the coach holds his head well to the rear to avoid having his left ear too close to the muzzle of the gun.

(4) If the shooter tends to apply the last part of the squeeze himself by giving the trigger a sudden pressure, the coach should have him place his trigger finger below the trigger guard, and the coach then applies the pressure directly to the trigger instead of through the finger of the pupil.

## Calling the Shot

The pupil should be required to call each shot in slow and timed fire, and in other rates of fire when practicable. If the shooter does not call the shot immediately after firing, the coach orders him to do this.

## The Use of Dummy Cartridges in Rates of Fire Other than Slow

A mixture of dummy and live cartridges can be used in rates of fire other than slow fire. When the hammer falls on a dummy cartridge, the shooter grasps the slide of the semiautomatic pistol with his left hand, pulls it fully back, and releases it. This ejects the dummy and loads another round. The time limit must be extended to make up for the time lost in ejecting the dummy cartridge, usually about two seconds. In firing the revolver, when the hammer falls on a dummy cartridge, the shooter cocks the gun and resumes the aiming position.

## Safety Precautions on the Range

(1) Never load your revolver or place a loaded magazine in a semiautomatic pistol until you are at your own firing point.

(2) Remove the magazine from a semiautomatic pistol and unload the pistol before leaving the firing point. Likewise, unload a revolver before leaving the firing point.

(3) Hold the loaded pistol at the position of raise pistol unless you are aiming at the target.

(4) When firing ceases temporarily, lock the gun and hold it at the position of raise pistol. Do not take any position except that of raise pistol without first removing the magazine of the semiautomatic pistol and unloading. In the case of the revolver, do not assume any position except raise pistol without first unloading.

(5) If one or more cartridges remain unfired at the end of a string at any rate of fire faster than slow fire, remove the magazine of the semiautomatic pistol and unload immediately. In the case of the revolver, unload immediately.

(6) The range must be kept thoroughly policed (clean and neat) at all times. The person in charge of firing must inspect to be sure that empty cartridge cases and unfired cartridges are separated from each other and from all trash. He must be sure that all empty cartridge cases and unfired rounds are turned in to the proper person (usually the range officer or the supply officer) immediately upon completing the day's firing.

## Coaching Rules of the N.R.A.

Coaching in individual matches is prohibited unless otherwise provided in the conditions of the competition. In team matches, the coach may help team members by calling the shots, checking time, checking scoring, ordering sight changes, etc., but he must so control his voice and actions as not to disturb other competitors, and he must not physically assist in loading guns or in making sight corrections.

Coaches must take such positions as will not interfere with competitors on other teams and must not serve as a windbreak for their own team in matches the conditions of which require that the firing points be opened so that the shooters may be exposed to prevailing winds.

## Firing-Line Operation Rules

The National Rifle Association of America publishes its official rules for the conduct of all pistol and revolver matches and tournaments in a booklet called *Pistol Rules,* which can be obtained for a few cents. You are advised to write to the N.R.A. at 1600 Rhode Island Avenue, N.W., Washington 6, D.C., for a copy of this publication and other pamphlets on marksmanship.

## Discipline on the Firing Line

The safety of competitors, range officials, and spectators makes it necessary for everyone to handle firearms carefully and exercise caution in moving around the range. Each person should discipline himself. The range officials are often too busy to act as policemen. If a person cannot discipline himself, it is the duty of the person nearest to him, regardless of his official position or lack of it, to bring to his attention violations of safety rules. If he persists in disregarding the rules prepared for his own safety and that of others, he should be reported to the officials, who should immediately eject him from the range.

## Commands Given on the Firing Line

The commands given on the firing line by the range officer must be spoken in a military manner in order that they may be understood and obeyed instantly by everyone. In the following instructions, based on N.R.A. rules, the command is printed in italics in order that you may understand that it is given by the range officer in a firm, loud voice.

"*Load.*" Load exactly 5 cartridges into your revolver cylinder or pistol magazine and hold the revolver or the magazine so that it can be inspected by the range officer if he so desires.

"*Lock.*" The range officer gives this command after he has inspected cylinders of revolvers or magazines of semiautomatic pistols. You must close the cylinder of your revolver, hammer down on an empty chamber, or in the case of the semiautomatic pistol you must insert the magazine, close the slide, and engage the safety lock. You then assume the raise-pistol position.

"*Ready on the right*" (or *left*). This means that you are to announce at once if you are not ready to fire. If you are not, shout, "Not ready on target Number ———." The range officer will come over to see why you are not ready and either help you to correct the trouble or, in case your gun or equipment is broken, order you to leave the firing line so that you will not delay progress. If no shooter has called "not ready," all guns may be cocked or safety locks disengaged.

"*Ready on the firing line.*" You and all of your fellow shooters should be ready to fire. This command also means that targets will be exposed or the signal to commence firing will be given within three seconds. You may point your gun toward the target as soon as this command has been given.

"*Commence firing.*" Start firing. If the firing is timed, the time is counted from this command. Instead of a verbal command, a short, sharp blast on a whistle may be given, or the targets may be brought into view.

"*Cease firing.*" Stop firing at once and open the action of your gun. Even if you are just about to fire a good shot, hold your fire and open the action of your gun. If you do not obey this command, you may injure or kill someone who has wandered between the firing line and the targets or even behind the targets. The cylinder of a revolver must be opened. The slide on a semiautomatic pistol must be locked back. All guns must be placed on the shooting stands beside the firing points and not touched until the range officer gives another command. He may give the cease-firing command verbally, by blowing a short, sharp blast on a whistle, by extinguishing range lights, or by having the targets moved out of view.

*"Police firing points."* Pick up your fired cartridge cases, empty cartridge cartons, cigarette butts, and any trash on the ground. Do not argue with the man at the next firing point about who dropped what. Leave the firing line neat and clean. Do a little more than your share of the work.

*"As you were."* This command means to disregard the last command given by the range officer. For example, if he gave the command "ready on the firing line" and then found that some shooter was not ready, he could give the command "as you were," and this would require you to engage the safety lock of your gun just as though the command "ready on the firing line" had not been given.

*"Carry on."* This command means that you are to go on with whatever you were doing before you were interrupted.

## Qualifications and Duties of a Range Officer

The range officer is in charge of the firing line and responsible for the safety and discipline of all range personnel, shooters, and spectators in his area. He must be firm but courteous, alert to observe all that takes place in his sector, impartial in the control of shooters, intelligent, industrious, and diplomatic. He must be familiar with the rules and program of the match where he is officiating and know the rules of the National Rifle Association thoroughly. He must carry out the orders of his superiors and co-operate with other range officials. In a large organization, there may be a chief range officer and several assistant range officers, one for each of the several ranges at which shooting takes place.

## Other Match and Tournament Officials

In addition to the range officer, there may be other officials, especially if the match or tournament is conducted in accordance with the N.R.A. rules for registered events. The executive officer is in charge of an entire tournament. An official referee enforces rules and makes decisions in cases of protests and challenges. A chief target officer, aided by assistant target officers, has charge of targets and frames. A statistical officer is in charge of all records except the actual recording of scores when this is done on the range, and he may be aided by assistant statistical officers.

## Scoring Targets

There are many details of scoring targets that are covered by the N.R.A. pistol rules, but the one that is probably the most important to remember is that if the leaded edge of a shot hole comes in contact with the outside of the bull's-eye or scoring rings of a target, it is given the higher value. For example, in Figure 1 the hole touches the bull's-eye and is counted as a 10, while the hole in Figure 2 does not touch the bull'e-eye but is in the 9 ring and hence counts as 9.

Fig. 1. The shot is scored as a ten. (*Courtesy National Rifle Association*)

Fig. 2. The shot is scored as a nine. (*Courtesy National Rifle Association*)

# Chapter 23

## THE TRUTH ABOUT FIRE-ARMS REGISTRATION LAWS

### *Antigun Arguments*

From time to time, members of the various state legislatures, members of the Congress of the United States, county supervisors, and city councilmen introduce bills that provide for the compulsory registration of firearms. Such bills vary in details but they all require the purchasers and owners of firearms to register their weapons with the police, the sheriff or some other law-enforcement agency.

The reasons advanced for such proposed laws are usually as follows: (1) registration of weapons reduces crime by making it more difficult for undesirable persons to obtain weapons, (2) solving crimes would be easier because the weapons used in the commission of crime could be traced through the registration records, (3) it would be possible to arrest all persons found possessing unregistered weapons, thereby making it easier for the police to apprehend criminals wanted on more serious charges, (4) gun registration keeps guns out of the hands of children, mental defectives, habitual drunkards, drug addicts, and other persons who should not have firearms, and (5) stolen guns can be returned to the owners more easily.

Having offered these arguments for firearm registration, those favoring such legislation then present a clincher. They ask very innocently, "Since you do not object to registering your automobile, why do you object to registering your guns?"

## Antigun Laws Do Not Keep the Criminal From Obtaining Guns

Laws compelling gun owners to register their weapons make it more difficult for honest citizens to obtain firearms for recreation and personal defense. Such laws do not add materially to the difficulties encountered by a criminal who wants a gun. Most of the guns carried by criminals, especially in the commission of major crimes, are not bought from sporting-goods stores. They are stolen arms, just as the automobiles used in crimes are usually stolen cars.

In one six-year period, there were 493 robberies of United States armories. In one five-year period, 2,047 guns and 273,326 rounds of ammunition were stolen from United States armories. In one shipment on an Army pier in Brooklyn, 83 revolvers were stolen from under the noses of United States guards. These are just a few official figures released by the Federal Bureau of Investigation and the United States Department of Justice. During the same period, countless firearms were stolen from state, county, and municipal organizations, and hundreds were stolen from hardware and sporting-goods stores. When it is so easy to steal guns, criminals need not worry about firearm-registration laws.

## Antigun Laws Do Not Aid in the Solution of Crimes

When stolen guns are used by criminals, even if the law-enforcement authorities get possession of such weapons, gun registration records merely lead back to some governmental agency, a hardware store, a sporting-goods dealer, or an innocent citizen.

If you leave town on a vacation, thieves may steal your firearms, use them in the commission of a murder or robbery, and then when you return home, the police will be waiting for you with a demand that you provide an alibi to prove that you were not the murderer or the robber. Under firearm-registration laws, the innocent man is on the defensive.

## Criminals Can Be Arrested
## Without Antigun Laws

Under the United States Constitution, law-enforcement officers have no right to stop people on the street and search them for weapons. Likewise, a home cannot be searched legally without a warrant. If a policeman has a legal reason to search a person or a home, he has enough evidence to arrest a person on a more serious charge than that of possessing unregistered firearms.

The penalities for such felonies as murder, burglary, robbery, and similar offenses are far greater than any penalties that can be imposed under a firearm-registration act. If the police make an intelligent and industrious effort to enforce the existing laws, they do not need antigun laws. Therefore, firearm-registration laws do not aid in the apprehension of criminals.

## Registration Laws Cannot Keep Guns
## Out of the Hands of Undesirables

Most states already have laws prohibiting the sale or transfer of firearms to minors, mental incompetents, drug addicts, habitual drunkards, and others who are obviously unfit for the possession of weapons. The same laws prohibit the possession of guns by such persons. Firearm-registration laws will do no more.

## Registration Laws Are of Little Value
## in Returning Guns to Owners

Law-enforcement officers usually return stolen guns to the rightful owners under existing laws. Firearm-registration laws would add little or nothing to the effectiveness of the present procedure.

## Auto Registration versus Gun Registration

The registration of an automobile is automatic. When a license is granted, no one questions a person's right to own an automobile. If the tax is paid, the license tag is issued without question. Of course, most states require the driver to pass some sort of a test before he can drive a car, but he can own an automobile even if he is deaf, dumb, and blind!

The essential feature of firearm registration is the power of law-enforcement authorities to say *who* may own a gun. The difference between automobile and firearm registration is obvious and vital under our constitutional form of government.

There is another difference between automobile and firearm registration. A man's ability to defend his wife, children, and home does not depend upon the ownership of an automobile. The right of the people of the United States to keep and bear arms is guaranteed under the Constitution and should not be taken from reputable citizens. The registration of an automobile and the registration of a gun are not in the same class.

## Firearm-Registration Laws
## Do Not Reduce Crime

A new administration comes into power in a city and appoints a new chief of police. He announces that he will immediately reduce crime if the city council will pass an ordinance forbidding anyone to possess a firearm, even in his own home. When the council fails to pass the proposed ordinance, the police chief pretends that he has an excuse for not apprehending criminals. This is just a smoke screen. Firearm-registration laws have never reduced crime on a national, state, or municipal basis.

## Only Honest Citizens Comply
## with Registration Laws

The only objective of firearm-registration laws is to make it possible for the political authorities, acting through the law-enforcement agencies they control, to seize weapons when, in their opinion, such seizure is politically desirable. Those advocating firearms registration deny this. They say, "All that we want to know is *who* has guns and what kind of guns they have." Under cross-examination, the proponents of antigun legislation will admit that they do not expect criminals to come forward and register their guns.

Since no criminal in his right mind will register his guns, the registration lists contain the names and addresses only of honest, innocent citizens who own guns only for recreation and for guarding their families and homes. Under these conditions, a gun-registration list is of no value to sincere law-enforcement authorities. It can be used for only two purposes: (1) as an excuse for taxation, which can become so burdensome that innocent citizens will get rid of their guns, or (2) as a means of disarming honest citizens. If the second purpose is attained, all guns are then in the hands of the criminals and the politically controlled police.

## Homer Had a Dream

When Homer Cummings was United States Attorney General, he was the leading advocate of firearm-registration laws in the United States. Homer was no piker. He was an all-or-nothing man. In a speech before the International Association of Chiefs of Police, at Baltimore, Maryland, October 5, 1937, he said, "The criminal's arsenal is today made up not only of pistols and revolvers but of ordinary shotguns and rifles. I am convinced of this—any practical measure for control of firearms must *at least* contain provision for the registration of all firearms."

Homer added, "A review of the laws of the principal countries of the world reveals that America is far behind in her solution of the problem. Canada, Great Britain, France, Italy, Germany, Sweden, Belgium and the Netherlands are typical of the countries which, in recent years, enacted comprehensive firearms laws, each requiring extensive records of manufacture, sale, and individual registration. I do not suggest that registration will disarm the criminal, but I do say it is the first step in the control of the firearms traffic."

Since registration would not disarm the criminal, what purpose did the United States Attorney General have in mind?

In addition to the countries listed by Homer as requiring firearms registration, he could have truthfully included Norway, Denmark, Austria, Rumania, Spain, Japan, and India.

## The Fate of Countries Having Firearms Registration Laws

When Cummings was making his speech, Hitler had been in power in Germany four years and had reoccupied the Ruhr twenty months. At the same time, Franco had started his campaign to establish a Fascist government in Spain, aided by Hitler and Mussolini. Meanwhile, Mussolini had controlled Italy for fifteen years, using a firearms-registration law to disarm all who opposed him, arming only his Fascist gangsters. All of these countries—Germany, Spain, and Italy—had firearms-registration laws at the time Cummings made his speech advocating depriving American citizens of the right to own firearms.

## How Firearms-Registration Laws Helped Hitler

Within six months of the Cummings speech, Hitler had invaded Austria, helped by Austrian firearm-registration lists, which enabled the Gestapo and the Austrian fifth-column traitors to know which homes to violate and which men to throw into jail.

Within two years after the Cummings speech, the Gestapo was in Poland and within thirty months Norway and Denmark were under the German heel. In each country, the firearm-registration list marked those who were the first to be arrested. Then came France, Belgium, and the Netherlands. Always the story was the same—a whole people was disarmed by its own police and politicians with convenient lists of those few persons permitted to retain arms on file at the City Hall. All of the countries listed by Cummings had firearm-registration laws, just as he said they did when he spoke in 1937, and yet by 1940 they were conquered nations.

## The English Firearm-Registration Act

The National Firearms Act went into effect in England in 1921. This was the model law often cited as desirable for the United States. By 1939, the British firearms-manufacturing industry was almost entirely out of existence. The number of gun owners had decreased so greatly that when the German armies faced England across the Channel, an appeal was made to the United States for help. Americans drew on their war reserve to furnish the British Army with rifles. A campaign, sanctioned by the United States government, was conducted to obtain the donation of shotguns, rifles, revolvers, pistols—anything that would fire a cartridge—for arming the British police and civilians. England had a firearm-registration law when Cummings made his speech, but less than three years later the lawless Yankees had to replace the guns taken from the British by their own government.

## Summary

A firearm-registration law does not disarm the criminal. Proponents of such legislation who are honest admit that this is true. Antigun laws discourage the ownership of firearms by honest citizens through the imposition of extra taxes, inconveniences, and trips to police stations, which the average person wishes to avoid. Reputable firearms manufacturers turn to other products and are not able to produce quickly firearms in quantity when they are needed in times of national emergency.

Regardless of the good intentions of some people who favor registration, such laws play into the hands of unscrupulous seekers for political power, bootlegging of arms springs into existence, reputable citizens are disarmed, and criminals are better able to prey on the people. Finally, no dictatorship, whether operating under the name of communism, socialism, fascism, nazism, or welfare statism, has ever been imposed on a nation of free men who have not been first required to register their privately owned firearms.

# Bibliography

Albaugh, William A., III, and Edward N. Simmons, *Confederate Arms*. Harrisburg, Penna.: The Stackpole Co., 1957.

Baker, Ezekiel, *Remarks on Rifle Guns,* also titled *Baker's Remarks on the Rifle*. London: Joseph Mallett, 1835.

Bannerman, David B., *Military Goods Catalogue*. New York: Francis Bannerman Sons, 1955, *et seq.*

Bartholomew, Ed, *The Biographical Album of Western Gunfighters*. Houston: The Frontier Press, 1958.

Bosworth, N., *A Treatise on the Rifle, Musket, Pistol and Fowling Piece*. New York: J. S. Redfield, 1846.

Brown, F. R. (Bob), *Encyclopedia of Modern Firearms*: Parts & Assembly (Vol. 1). Montezuma, Iowa: F. R. (Bob) Brownell, 1959.

Burrard, Gerald, *The Modern Shotgun* (2 vols.). New York: Charles Scribner's Sons, 1931.

Chapel, Charles Edward, *The Boy's Book of Rifles*. New York: Coward-McCann, Inc., 1948, Revised Edition, 1960.

———, *Field, Skeet, and Trap Shooting*. New York: Coward-McCann, Inc., 1949.

———, *Forensic Ballistics*. Chicago: Institute of Applied Science, 1933.

———, *Gun Care and Repair: A Manual of Gunsmithing*. New York: Coward-McCann, Inc., 1943.

———, *Gun Collecting*. New York: Coward-McCann, Inc., Revised Edition, 1960.

———, *The Gun Collector's Handbook of Values*. New York: Coward-McCann, Inc., Revised Edition, 1960.

———, *Simplified Rifle Shooting*. New York: Coward-McCann, Inc., 1950.

———, *Guns of the Old West*. New York: Coward-McCann, Inc., 1960.

———, *Simplified Pistol and Revolver Shooting*. New York: Coward-McCann, Inc., 1950.

Clephan, Robert Coltman, *An Outline of the History and Development of Hand Firearms, Etc.* London: The Walter Scott Publishing Co., 1906.

Cline, Walter M., *The Muzzle-Loading Rifle, Then and Now.* Huntington, West Virginia: Standard Printing and Publishing Co., 1942.

Connecticut Historical Society, *Samuel Colt's Own Record of Transactions with Captain Walker and Eli Whitney, Jr., in 1847.* Hartford, Conn.: The Connecticut Historical Society, 1949.

Damon, G. E., *Gun Fun with Safety.* Huntington, West Virginia: Standard Publications, Inc., 1947.

Deane, *Deane's Manual of the History and Science of Fire-Arms.* London: Longman, Brown, Green, Longman's & Roberts, 1858.

Dillin, John G. W., *The Kentucky Rifle.* Wilmington, Delaware: George N. Hyatt, 1959.

Dougall, James Dalziel, *Shooting: Its Appliances, Practice, and Purpose.* London: Sampson Low, Marston, Searle & Rivington, 1881.

Edwards, William B., *The Story of Colt's Revolver.* Harrisburg, Penna.: The Stackpole Co., 1957.

Freidel, Frank, *The Splendid Little War.* Boston: Little, Brown & Co. 1958.

Fuller, Claud E., *The Breech-Loader in the Service.* Topeka, Kansas: F. Theodore Dexter, 1933.

———, *The Rifled Musket.* Harrisburg, Penna.: The Stackpole Co., 1958.

———, *Springfield Muzzle-Loading Shoulder Arms.* New York: Francis Bannerman Sons, 1930.

———, *The Whitney Firearms.* Huntington, West Virginia: Standard Publications, Inc., 1946.

———, and Richard D. Steuart, *Firearms of the Confederacy.* Huntington, West Virginia: Standard Publications, Inc., 1944.

Gardner, Robert E., *American Arms and Arms Makers.* Columbus, Ohio: The F. J. Heer Printing Co., 1938.

George, J. N., *English Guns and Rifles.* Plantersville, S.C.: Small-Arms Technical Publishing Co., 1947.

George, J. N., *English Pistols and Revolvers.* Onslow County, N.C.: Small-Arms Technical Publishing Co., 1938.

Gluckman, Arcadi, *Catalogue of United States Martial Pistols.* Buffalo: Otto Ulbrich Co., 1939.

———, *United States Martial Pistols and Revolvers.* Buffalo: Otto Ulbrich Co., 1939.

————, *United States Muskets, Rifles and Carbines.* Buffalo: Otto Ulbrich Co., Inc., 1948.

————, and L. D. Satterlee, *American Gun Makers.* Harrisburg, Penna.: The Stackpole Co., 1953.

Grant, James, *More Single-Shot Rifles.* New York: William Morrow and Co., 1959.

————, *Single-Shot Rifles.* New York: William Morrow & Co., 1947.

Gunther, Jack Disbrow, and Charles O. Gunther, *The Identification of Firearms.* New York: John Wiley & Sons, Inc., 1935.

Hardee, W. J., *Rifle and Light Infantry Tactics* (2 or more vols.). Philadelphia: Lippincott, Grambo & Co., 1855.

Hatch, Alden, *Remington Arms in American History.* New York: Rinehart & Co., Inc.

Hatcher, Julian S., *Hatcher's Notebook.* Harrisburg, Penna.: Military Service Publishing Co., 1947.

————, *Textbook of Firearms Investigation, Identification and Evidence.* Marines, Onslow County, N.C.: Small-Arms Technical Publishing Co., 1935.

Haven, Charles T., and Frank A. Belden, *A History of the Colt Revolver.* New York: William Morrow & Co., 1940.

Held, Robert, *The Age of Firearms.* New York: Harper & Brothers, 1957.

Hicks, James E., *Notes on United States Ordnance,* Vol. I: *Small Arms,* 1940. *Notes on United States Ordnance,* Vol. II: *Ordnance Correspondence,* 1940. *Notes on German Ordnance,* 1937. *Notes on French Ordnance,* 1937. *Notes on French Ordnance* (Translation of *Memoires d'Artillerie*), 1939. *U.S. Firearms* (Revision of Vol. I, above), 1946. [The books by James E. Hicks were published by him at Mt. Vernon, N.Y.]

Hunter, J. Marvin, and Noah H. Rose, *The Album of Gun-Fighters.* San Antonio, Texas: Published by the Authors.

Johnson, Melvin M., Jr., and Charles T. Haven, *Automatic Weapons of the World.* New York: William Morrow & Co., 1945.

Kalman, James M., and C. Meade Patterson, *Pictorial History of U.S. Single-Shot Martial Pistols.* New York: Charles Scribner's Sons, 1957.

Karr, Charles Lee, Jr., and Carroll Robbins, *Remington Handguns.* Harrisburg, Penna.: The Stackpole Co., 1951.

Leffingwell, William Bruce, *The Art of Wing Shooting.* Chicago: Rand, McNally & Co., 1894.

Lenz, Ellis Christian, *Muzzle Flashers*. Huntington, West Virginia: Standard Publications, Inc., 1944.

——, *Rifleman's Progress*. Huntington, West Virginia: Standard Publications, Inc. 1946.

Logan, Herschel C., *Cartridges—A Pictorial Digest of Small Arms Ammunition*. Huntington, West Virginia: Standard Publications, Inc., 1948.

——, *Hand Cannon to Automatic*. Huntington, West Virginia: Standard Publications, Inc., 1944.

McClellan, George B., *Manual of Bayonet Exercises, Prepared for the Use of the United States Army*. Philadelphia: J. B. Lippincott & Co., 1852.

McConnell, Duncan, *Grandpappy's Pistol*. New York: Coward-McCann, Inc., 1956.

McGivern, Ed, *Ed McGivern's Book on Fast and Fancy Revolver Shooting and Police Training*. Springfield, Mass.: King Richardson Co., 1938.

McHenry, Roy C., and Walter F. Roper, *Smith & Wesson Hand Guns*. Harrisburg, Penna.: The Stackpole Co., 1958.

Mayer, Dr. Joseph R., *Five Centuries of Gunsmiths, Swordsmiths and Armourers, 1400–1900*. Columbus, Ohio: Walter F. Heer, 1948.

Metschl, John, *The Rudolph J. Nunnemacher Collection of Projectile Arms*. Milwaukee: The Milwaukee Public Museum, 1928.

Nutter, Waldo E., *Manhattan Firearms*. Harrisburg, Penna.: The Stackpole Co., 1958.

Parsons, John E., *Henry Deringer's Pocket Pistol*. New York: William Morrow & Co., 1952.

——, *The Peacemaker and Its Rivals*. New York: William Morrow & Co., 1950.

——, *Smith & Wesson Revolvers: The Pioneer Single-Action Models*. New York: William Morrow & Co., 1957.

——, and John S. DuMont, *Firearms in the Custer Battle*. Harrisburg, Penna.: The Stackpole Co., 1954.

Pollard, H. B. C., *A History of Firearms*. London: Geoffrey Bles, 1931. Boston: Houghton Mifflin Co., 1931.

Rohan, Jack, *Yankee Arms Maker*. New York: Harper & Brothers, 1948.

Rosebush, Waldo E., *Frontier Steel, the Men and Their Weapons*, Appleton, Wisconsin: C. C. Nelson Publishing Co., 1958.

Russell, Carl P., *Guns of the Early Frontiers*. Berkeley, California: University of California Press, 1957.

Rywell, Martin, *Samuel Colt, A Man and an Epoch.* Harriman, Tenn.: Pioneer Press, 1952.

Sandoz, Mari, *The Buffalo Hunters.* New York: Hastings House Publishers, 1954.

Satterlee, L. D., *A Catalog of Firearms for the Collector.* Detroit: Published by the author, 1939.

Sawyer, Charles Winthrop, "The Firearms In American History Series." *Firearms in American History, 1600–1800,* 1910. Out of print. *Firearms in American History, Vol. II: The Revolver, 1800–1911,* 1911. Out of print. NOTE: The second printing of this book was a limited, numbered edition of 1,000 copies, published in 1939 by Charles Edward Chapel, and clearly marked as a new printing, but it is also out of print. *Firearms in American History, Vol. III: Our Rifles,* 1920. Out of print. NOTE: The second printing of this book was a trade edition published in 1941 by Williams Book Store, Boston, Mass. *United States Single-Shot Martial Pistols,* 1913 (paper-bound only). Out of print.

NOTE: The only book in the above series or four which carried the so-called volume number on the cover was the one on the revolver, marked "Volume II," although it was a distinctly separate book from the others. Also, notice that the book on single-shot pistols was published between the date of the so-called Volume II and the so-called Volume III. The first editions are extremely rare, and the reprint of Volume II is already a collector's item.

Scott, Winfield, *Abstract of Infantry Tactics.* Boston: Hilliard, Gray, Little & Wilkins, 1830.

——, *Infantry Tactics in Three Volumes.* New York: Harper & Brothers, 1858.

Serven, James E., *Colt Firearms.* Santa Anna, California: James E. Serven, 1954.

Sharpe, Philip B., *The Rifle in America.* New York: Funk & Wagnalls Co., 1938.

Sherlock, Herbert Arment, *Black Powder Snapshots.* Huntington, West Virginia: Standard Publications, Inc., 1946.

Shields, Joseph W., *From Flintlock to M-1.* New York: Coward-McCann, Inc., 1954.

Smith, Lawrence B., *Shotgun Psychology.* New York: Charles Scribner's Sons, 1938.

Smith & Wesson, Inc., *Burning Powder.* Springfield, Mass.: Smith & Wesson, Inc., 1921, *et seq.*

Stevens, Captain C. A., *Berdan's United States Sharpshooters in the Army of the Potomac, 1861–65*. St. Paul, Minnesota: Price-McGill Co., 1892.

Ulrich, Arthur L., *A Century of Achievement, 1836–1936: Colt's 100th Anniversary Fire-arms Manual*. Hartford, Conn.: Colt's Patent Fire Arms Manufacturing Co., 1936.

Van Rensselaer, Stephen, *An Histology of American Gunsmiths, Arms Manufacturers, and Patentees with Detailed Description of Their Arms*. Morristown, N.J.: Mrs. Stephen Van Rensselaer, 1947.

Williamson, Harold F., *Winchester, the Gun That Won the West*. Washington, D.C.: Combat Force Press, 1952.

Winant, Lewis, *Early Percussion Firearms*. New York: William Morrow & Co., 1959.

———, *Firearms Curiosa*. New York: Greenberg: Publisher, 1955.

———, *Pepperbox Firearms*. New York: Greenberg: Publisher, 1952.

# Index